AMERICA'S WAR ON TERROR

For Katherine, Amber and Claudia

America's War on Terror

Edited by
PATRICK HAYDEN
TOM LANSFORD
ROBERT P. WATSON

ASHGATE

Published by
Ashgate Publishing Limited
Gower House
Croft Road
Aldershot
Hants GU11 3HR
England

Ashgate Publishing Company
Suite 420
101 Cherry Street
Burlington, VT 05401-4405
USA

Ashgate website: http://www.ashgate.com

British Library Cataloguing in Publication Data
America's war on terror
    1.Bush, George W. (George Walker), 1946- 2.War on
    terrorism, 2001- 3.United States - Foreign relations -
    2001-
    I.Hayden, Patrick, 1965- II.Lansford, Tom III.Watson,
    Robert P., 1962-
    327.7'3

Library of Congress Control Number: 2003106033

ISBN 0 7546 3797 2 (Hbk)
ISBN 0 7546 3799 9 (Pbk)

Printed and bound in Great Britain by MPG Books Ltd, Bodmin, Cornwall.

Contents

CONCLUSION: REFRAMING THE WAR ON TERROR

APPENDICES

List of Contributors

Neal Allen is a doctoral student in Political Science at the University of Texas at Austin, and adjunct instructor of Political Science at Southwestern University in Georgetown, Texas. His research interests include the American Supreme Court, the presidency, and American political development.

Kristin Andrews is Assistant Professor of Philosophy at York University in Toronto. She specializes in the philosophy of psychology and has research interests in moral psychology and comparative cognition. Her most recent publication is 'Knowing Mental States: The Asymmetry of Psychological Prediction and Explanation', in *Consciousness: New Philosophical Essays*, Quentin Smith and Aleksander Jokić (eds) (Oxford University Press, 2002). She received her PhD in Philosophy from the University of Minnesota in 2000.

Jack Covarrubias is a graduate student in Political Science at the University of Southern Mississippi.

John Davis teaches at Howard University. His articles include 'The Evolution of American Grand Strategy and the War on Terrorism: Clinton-Bush Perspectives', 'The Evolution of the Doctrine of Preemption', and 'The History of The War on Terrorism'. Davis also has a forthcoming book, *The Howard Project: Black Leadership in the Post-Civil Rights Era*. Davis was a researcher with the National Defense University at Fort McNair in Washington, DC.

Michael G. Dziubinski is a retired military officer with expertise in nuclear command and control, national intelligence, information operations and joint operations. He is currently researching future joint warfighting and is a graduate student at Old Dominion University.

Mark Evans is Lecturer in Politics at the University of Wales Swansea. He is the editor of *The Edinburgh Companion to Contemporary Liberalism* (Edinburgh University Press, 2001), the author of *Liberal Justifications* (forthcoming) and of numerous articles in scholarly publications on problems in liberal political theory. He is Associate Editor of the *International Journal of Politics and Ethics* and is currently working on studies of just war theory and the role of personal ethical ideals in domestic liberal-democratic politics.

Patrick Hayden is Lecturer in Political Theory at Victoria University of Wellington, New Zealand. His publications include *The Philosophy of Human Rights* (Paragon House, 2001) and *John Rawls: Towards a Just World Order* (University of Wales Press, 2002). He is also Editor of the *International Journal of Politics and Ethics* and is currently working on issues of global justice and justice in democratic transitions.

Tom Lansford is Assistant Professor of Political Science at the University of Southern Mississippi-Gulf Coast and a Fellow of the Frank Maria Center for International Politics and Ethics. He is a member of the governing board of the National Social Science Association, the editorial board of the journal *White House Studies* and is the book review editor for the *International Journal of Politics and Ethics*. He has published articles in journals such as *Defense Analysis, The Journal of Conflict Studies, European Security, International Studies, Security Dialogue* and *Strategic Studies*. Lansford is the author of a number of books including his most recent, *All for One: NATO, Terrorism and the United States* (Ashgate, 2002).

Jack Lechelt is a graduate student in the University of South Carolina's Government and International Studies Department. He has numerous scholarly publications. His research interests include the presidency, vice-presidency, and foreign policy.

Robert J. Pauly, Jr is an Adjunct Professor of History and Political Science at Norwich University and Midlands Technical College in Columbia, South Carolina. His research pursuits include US foreign policy, American-European relations, American-Middle Eastern relations and European and Middle Eastern politics and security. He is presently developing a book titled, *US Foreign Policy and the Persian Gulf: Safeguarding American Interests through Selective Multilateralism*, for Ashgate Publishing.

Vaughn P. Shannon is a Visiting Assistant Professor of Political Science at Miami University in Oxford, Ohio. He has published in top journals, such as *International Studies Quarterly* (2000) and *International Organization* (2001). Shannon's major international relations works concentrate on foreign policy, international security and comparative politics focused on the Middle East. He has published on the Middle East before, writing about the Gulf War in *Magill's Guide to Military History* (2001).

Robert P. Watson is Associate Professor of Political Science at Florida Atlantic University and Editor of the journal *White House Studies*. He is the author, editor, or co-editor of 15 books and has published over 100 scholarly articles and essays. Watson has been interviewed by CNN, MSNBC, *USA Today* and numerous other media outlets, has appeared on C-SPAN's *Book TV*, was a guest for CNN.com's coverage of the 2001 presidential inauguration, and directed the first-ever 'Report to the First Lady', which was presented to the White House in 2001. He has lectured as a visiting scholar and fellow at several universities and presidential libraries and historic sites.

Steve A. Yetiv is Associate Professor of Political Science at Old Dominion University. His forthcoming book is *Explaining Foreign Policy Behavior* (Johns Hopkins University Press, 2004).

Preface

A History of Terror

On the morning of 11 September 2001, four US commercial aircraft were hijacked and used as weapons of mass destruction by 19 terrorists of the radical Islamist terror network al-Qaeda. (Al-Qaeda is spelled various ways around the world, but the present form will be used in this text.) After seizing control of the planes, terrorists crashed two into the twin towers of the World Trade Center in New York City, while another was flown into the Pentagon in the US capital city. After learning of the fate of the other aircraft from loved ones by cell phone, passengers of the fourth plane struggled for control of the aircraft and succeeded in diverting it from its intended target. The plane crashed into the ground in western Pennsylvania, killing all aboard but not a single individual beyond those on the flight. These tragic events produced a death toll reaching into the thousands and marked the start of America's War on Terror.

As horrific as the events of 11 September were, the sad reality is that they were merely the latest in a long history of terrorism (see Appendix for a list of worldwide terrorist acts since 1990). Even though the 9/11 tragedy prompted America's War on Terror and were the first acts of foreign aggression of considerable magnitude on US soil since the War of 1812, numerous terror incidents have been directed against US targets and citizens. In April of 1983, for example, the US Embassy in Beirut, Lebanon was bombed, killing 63. Later that same year, in October the US Marine Corps barracks in Beirut were attacked, killing 299. Some years later, another US military complex, this time in Reyadh, Saudi Arabia, was bombed and 19 were killed. Other US embassies in Nairobi, Kenya and Dar es Salaam, Tanzania were bombed in August of 1998, resulting in 223 deaths. Almost one year before the 9/11 attack, 17 were killed when the *USS Cole* was bombed while in port in Aden, Yemen in October of 2000.

One of the most infamous incidents of terrorism before the 9/11 tragedy occurred during the 1972 Munich Olympics when Palestinian terrorists infiltrated the Olympic compound and killed Israeli athletes. Both incidents struck bloody and symbolic blows against not only their foes, but also the international community of nations, using violence, publicity and the lives of innocent people to achieve their objectives.

The start of modern international terrorism is widely seen as occurring on 22 July 1968, when three terrorists of the Popular Front for the Liberation of Palestine (PFLP) hijacked an El Al airliner en route from Rome to Tel Aviv. The plane was carrying 38 passengers plus 10 crew members and was commandeered to Algiers by the terrorists. Unlike the trend it started and so many recent terrorist events, this hijacking did not end in tragedy, as negotiators eventually were able to obtain the release of the passengers and crew. The hijacking did, however, usher in a new approach and a new element to international terrorism, especially by Islamic extremists; that being, dramatic mass attacks designed to generate publicity (and covered intensely by the international media) and employing instruments of modernity (aircraft).

Types of Terrorists and Terrorism

Increasingly, terrorists since the El Al hijacking in 1968 have been motivated by one of two general – and at times a hybrid of both – factors: religious extremism and ethnic nationalism. The perpetrators of the hijacking in 1968, as is the case of those attacking the United States on 9/11 and the other incidents mentioned above were Islamic extremists of Arabic or Middle Eastern identity. As shall be discussed below, there are many forms of terrorism and equally as many types of terrorists. Yet, arguably, Islamic extremists have posed the gravest danger to the United States and much of the West, and have committed many of the high profile, more deadly attacks against American and European citizens and interests.

What makes such terrorists especially dangerous (and effective) and that which is worth noting in an effort to both study and combat them are the following: 1) Islamic extremists have many supporters worldwide and a global reach to their terror network; 2) they are marked by the fanaticism of their members with a willingness to go to great lengths – including suicide – to achieve their objectives; 3) they generally exhibit little or no allegiance to nations or any organization beyond their terror network; 4) they ignore international agreements, civil law and even the most rudimentary codes of humanity and civility, along with basic notions of innocent civilians and 'just causes' of war; 5) they act in ways opposed to modern notions of rationality; 6) they are sub-state actors; and 7) they resort to violence without efforts to engage in peaceful resolution of grievances.

Many of this brand of terrorist are raised in a culture of violence, oppression and despair, one whereby suicide terrorists are seen as glorious martyrs by even family members. The terrorists themselves are younger and younger and increasingly aggressive, using explosives such as grenades and pipe bombs. Many Muslim terrorists are Mujahideen and declare Jihad – or a 'holy war' – against their enemies (frequently the United States and the West). Terror training camps are appearing with increased frequency, while terrorists are more skillful in weaponry, false documentation, and explosives. Osama bin Laden, with his vast wealth and organizational prowess, offers a good example of the changing dynamic of terrorism. The world is faced with a new variety of suicide bombers and terrorists seeking and using weapons of mass destruction. More sophisticated methods and targets – high profile, crowded public places, government offices – designed to inflict maximum terror to innocent civilians, are replacing random, isolated and low-tech attacks. Nerve agents were used by the Aum Shinri Kyo cult in Japan in 1995, while al-Qaeda resorted to commercial airliners in the 2001 attacks on the United States.

Even within the profile of radical Islamic terrorism, it is inaccurate to describe the phenomenon as monolithic. For instance, Sunni terrorists are more likely to be individual, militant Islamicists acting apart from the state, whil Shia terrorists are at times more collective in their actions and have supported regimes such as the Iranian government. Indeed, states do sponsor terrorism, with governments in Libya, Sudan, Syria, Iran, Iraq and elsewhere having connections (fundraising, offering safe haven, and so forth) to terrorists.

In addition to religious extremism, ethnic nationalism often factors into modern international terrorism. The world has witnessed the devastating effects of an array of nationalist and ethnic disputes, including long-running hostilities by the Palestinians,

Basques, Kurds, Timorese, and the IRA in Northern Ireland. Such groups fight for separatism, the right of self-governance or sheer hatred. Ideology is at times a rationale used by such movements. This occurs in both left-wing and right-wing movements. Often it is mixed with ethnic hatred and religious extremism as in the case of the Shining Path (Peruvian Sendero Luminoso) guerrillas and Turkish Revolutionary People's Liberation Front on the left, or the Ku Klux Klan and Christian Identity movements on the right in the United States.

Defining Terrorism

Terrorism is worldwide and knows no borders. In the modern era of international terror starting with the El Al hijacking of 1968, terrorism has frequently involved airline hijackings and bombings. For instance, terrorists were responsible for an Air India wreck in June of 1985 over the Irish Sea that killed 329, a Pan Am flight that crashed over Lockerbie, Scotland in December 1988 killing 270, the UTA flight over Chad in September of 1989 which resulted in 170 deaths, and many others.

Indeed, many international terrorists have attempted commercial airline hijackings. But, the 9/11 tragedy might have marked yet another historic turning point just as did the El Al hijacking by Palestinian terrorists. Both involved an aircraft and a radical Islamic group seeking to make a statement and inflict terror. Yet this time the aircraft was used not just as the means for drawing attention but as a weapon. As such, 9/11 might be seen as the perversely inevitable outgrowth of the suicide bombing trend. After all, young, male (and now a few female) Islamic radicals have been launching suicide attacks on Israel with alarming frequency. The aircraft remains as a powerful symbol of modernity, source of publicity, and mechanism not bound by geography (like terrorism itself). As was mentioned in the opening paragraphs, international terrorism is undergoing a metamorphosis, even though some of the old practices and causes remain.

There are many types and forms of terror, from camouflaged guerrilla combatants in the jungles of Colombia and Peru, to the IRA in the streets of Northern Ireland, to right-wing militia groups in the United States. As the United States learned so tragically in April of 1995, terrorism can be 'home grown': Timothy McVeigh, a military veteran who was also an adherent of the ultra right-wing militia movement, detonated a bomb in front of the Alfred P. Murrah Federal Building in Oklahoma City that killed 168, while a hermit with a PhD known as the 'Unabomber' terrorized the country by mailing explosive devices to his victims. It should also be said that the ugly history of slavery and the actions of white supremacists in the years after abolition leading up to the Civil Rights Movement in the American Deep South mark a long history of acts that meet the definition of terrorism.

There is no universally accepted definition of terrorism, in part because there are so many varieties of terror incidents. Moreover, one person's terrorist might be another's freedom fighter.

Accordingly, diplomats and governments often disagree about which incidents fit the definition and what definition to use to describe terrorism. But we believe there are some basic tenets of terrorism that are key to defining it. Key to any definition are concepts such as civilians being targeted by violence during times of peace or when the party attacked is not at war. Yet, terrorism can occur during times of war if it targets civilians or noncombatants. This definitional threshold can be extended to include military personnel if they are not on duty or are unarmed, or if attacks on military facilities or personnel are performed when the nation is not at war or engaged in hostilities.

US federal statute [22 USC. 2656f(d)] defines terrorism as follows: 'The term "terrorism" means premeditated, politically motivated violence perpetrated against non-combatant targets by sub-national groups or clandestine agents, usually intended to influence an audience.' It further defines international terrorism as: '... terrorism involving citizens or the territory of more than one country.' The United States also classifies a terrorist group as: '... any group practicing, or that has significant subgroups that practice, international terrorism.' The US Immigration and Nationality Act [Section 212 (a)(3)(B)] offers a definition of terrorist activity that includes examples of terror:

1 the hijacking or sabotage of any conveyance (including aircraft, vessel, or vehicle);
2 the seizing or detaining, and threatening to kill, injure, or continue to detain, another individual in order to compel a third person (including a governmental organization) to do or abstain from doing any act as an explicit or implicit condition for the release of the individual seized or detained;
3 a violent attack upon an internationally protected person of the United States;
4 an assassination;
5 the use of any: biological agent, chemical agent, or nuclear weapon or device; explosive or firearm (other than for mere personal monetary gain), with intent to endanger, directly or indirectly, the safety of one or more individuals or to cause substantial damage to property;
6 a threat, attempt, or conspiracy to do any of the foregoing: the term 'engage in terrorist activity' means to commit, in an individual capacity or as a member of an organization, an act of terrorist activity or an act which the actor knows, or reasonably should know, affords material support to any individual, organization, or government in conducting a terrorist activity at any time, including any of the following acts:
   a the preparation or planning of a terrorist activity;
   b the gathering of information on potential targets for terrorist activity;
   c the providing of any type of material support, including a safe house, transportation, communications, funds, false documentation or identification, weapons, explosives, or training, to any individual the actor knows or has reason to believe has committed or plans to commit a terrorist activity;
   d the soliciting of funds or other things of value for terrorist activity or for any terrorist organization;
   e the solicitation of any individual for membership in a terrorist organization, terrorist government, or to engage in a terrorist activity.

The US Department of State develops a list of international terrorist groups. The 'Foreign Terrorist Organizations' list is updated and revised periodically and terrorist group designations must be reclassified in subsequent reports, typically completed every two years. The first such list appeared in October of 1997 during the presidency of Bill Clinton and was completed by Secretary of State Madeleine Albright. In it Albright identified 30 groups. In 1999, Secretary Albright recertified 27 groups, removed three from the list, and added a new group (which happened to be al-Qaeda). Another group was added in 2000. The administration of George W. Bush continued the list, with Secretary of State Colin Powell recertifying 26 of the groups in Albright's list in his 2001 report. Several additional groups were added over the course of 2001 and 2002.

The significance of such a designation is that it becomes illegal for a person in the United States to provide funding or support for a group or member of any group designated as a 'Foreign Terrorist Organization'. Members of these groups can be denied travel visas and can be excluded from entering the United States, and the list also raises awareness internationally of such groups, with the goal of isolating any support for the group in the international community. Three simple criteria are used in developing the list (see Appendix for the official list):

1 the organization must be foreign;
2 the organization must engage in terrorist activity as defined by (US) federal code [Section 212(a)(3)(B) of the Immigration and Naturalization Act];
3 the organization's activities must threaten the security of US nationals or national security.

Components of America's War on Terror

Terrorism is a multifaceted problem and, accordingly, requires an aggressive, multifaceted, and long-term solution. Because of its nature, any war against terror requires collaboration among governments worldwide, as well as collaboration among governmental units domestically. This is the case with America's War on Terror, although many suggest the campaign has lacked adequate efforts to enlist the international community, and it remains to be seen just how much intergovernmental cooperation results within the US federal bureaucracy. Some intelligence and security agencies opposed consolidation within the new Department of Homeland Security, while many states complained of being shortchanged by the Bush Administration in terms of financial aid to the states to implement homeland security measures and the information flow from Washington to the states.

There are many sides to the American War on Terror, as it is being fought on the military, diplomatic, financial, homeland security and other fronts. The military attacks that routed the Taliban regime from power in Afghanistan in late 2001 and the war against Iraq in 2003 are only the most visible and newsworthy facets of the war against terror. For instance, the effort involves the following actions (which constitute only a small but representative part of the war effort):

• President Bush signed the Anti-Terrorism Act on 26 October 2001, expanding the powers of and tools available to the nation's intelligence and law enforcement communities;

- the US Department of State, under the direction of the Secretary of State in consultation with the Attorney General and Secretary of Treasury, periodically develops a 'Foreign Terrorist List';
- diplomatically, the United States works with other countries and international organizations to combat international terror. For instance, the United States sent a delegation to the Inter-American Committee Against Terrorism (part of the Organization of American States), which met in San Salvador in March of 2003, where efforts were made to improve technological measures to prevent terrorism. The United States also participated in the Conference on Combating Money Laundering and Terrorist Financing, which was held in Bali, Indonesia in December 2002 and was sponsored by Australia and Indonesia;
- Presidential Executive Order 13224, signed on 23 September 2001, blocked the ability of people who commit terrorist acts or aid or support terrorist activities from conducting various financial and property transactions in the United States;
- the US Department of State submits an annual report titled 'Patterns of Global Terrorism' to Congress on the activities of terrorists and membership of terrorist organizations;
- federal agencies promote awareness of terrorism and offer training programs for other countries. For example, the United States participated in a 'Tri-border' terrorism conference in Argentina in December of 2002 focusing on cooperation among neighbors Argentina, Brazil, and Paraguay that examined terrorist fundraising efforts and financial intelligence sharing;
- the Office of the Coordinator of Counter-terrorism has a Foreign Emergency Support Team, charged with helping to quickly respond to terrorist attacks and preparing officials to deal with terrorists and terrorism;
- Counter-terrorism Policy Workshops are convened for the purpose of bringing together US officials and their counterparts in other countries to discuss policy responses and cooperation in combating terrorism. For instance, on 21 January 2003 a two-day Counter-terrorism Finance Workshop was hosted by Singapore and the United States and held in Singapore for senior officials from over 20 countries in the Association of Southeast Asian Nations (ASEAN) and the Pacific Islands Forum (PIF).

The US Congress has enacted numerous measures since the War on Terror began. Immediately after the 9/11 attacks, President Bush enjoyed considerable support among the American public and in Congress. In the immediate period following the 9/11 attacks, Congress moved quickly to provide the President with support for the war. Although Bush's approval rating dropped gradually after the conclusion of the campaign to eliminate the Taliban in Afghanistan, at the outset of fighting in Iraq in 2003 the Congress again rallied around the flag and offered the President (and the American troops) support for discharging the war. In addition to regular intelligence and national security authorizations – and considerable amounts of money for supplemental and emergency appropriations in the wake of 9/11 and after the war in Iraq commenced – the Congress has played an active role in the effort. Countless symbolic measures – honoring those who lost their lives, marking the anniversary of the 9/11 attack, awarding medals for New York City fire and police officers, providing a tribute to New York City – were passed and a host of bills enacted. This includes the following (which constitute only a small but representative part of the war effort):

- Victims of Terrorism Relief Act of 2001 (HR 2884; PL 107-134);
- Bioterrorism Response Act of 2001 (HR 3448; PL 107-188);
- Enhanced Border Security Act of 2002 (HR 3525; PL 107-173);
- Aviation and Transportation Security Act of 2001 (S 1447; PL 107-71);
- Authorizing Use of Force Joint Resolution of 2001 (S.J. Res 23; PL 107-40).

The Book

America's War on Terror is designed to serve several goals and several audiences. It is never an easy undertaking to produce a book suitable for a wide readership, but this focus was never far from the editors' or contributors' minds. The book was designed to provide scholars, students and the general public with a highly readable yet scholarly overview of the War on Terror. The book is suitable for the undergraduate classroom and general readers, as it introduces readers to a host of theoretical and conceptual underpinnings of terrorism and the American response to the terrorist attacks of 9/11. Every effort was made to produce a balanced and fair account of the war, and one that incorporates a variety of perspectives, from supporters of President Bush and the war to critics of both. Informed citizens and experts on international relations and national security should also find it to be of interest, as the contents are both timely and probing. So too was an international audience kept in mind throughout the effort to produce the book.

It is also quite a challenge produce a book at the relative outset of such a war, especially one without any direct precedent. This war is unlike any other and, in our effort to produce an initial, timely assessment of the reasons for and consequences of a war against terrorism, we did not attempt to address only specific facets of the war. Rather, the focus of the book encompasses the concepts, background, and emerging views of terrorism and the American response to terrorism.

This effort would not have been possible if not for the enthusiasm of the contributing authors. The contributors represent a wide array of perspectives in their writings, which we feel is a real strength of the book, and come from equally diverse scholarly backgrounds. We also acknowledge the staff of professionals at Ashgate and thank them for their support of our project and for their quality work on this book. Finally, we would like to thank Lou Fisher for his generous encouragement of this work.

It is difficult to know how the international war against terrorism will progress. It is certain only that the war will experience both success and failure, that serious challenges will remain, new threats will arise, and casualties will occur. It is our hope that this book will help readers understand some of the fundamental forces shaping international terrorism and American efforts to combat it. It is our sincere hope too that, as much as it is possible, a peaceful and timely resolution to some of the most pressing threats of international terror will result.

Patrick Hayden
Tom Lansford
Robert P. Watson

Foreword

Louis Fisher
Congressional Research Service

The terrorist attacks of 9/11 forced a major redistribution of political power within the United States, shifting unprecedented authority to the presidency, the military, and the law enforcement community. In taking military action first against the Taliban in Afghanistan and later against Saddam Hussein in Iraq, the United States signaled its intention to act with or without allies, with or without the UN Security Council, and with or without public support. In both wars, President Bush received statutory authority from Congress. In some cases, as with his military order of 13 November 2001, which authorized the creation of military tribunals, he acted alone. Throughout the first two years of emergency authority, there were few checks from Congress or the judiciary. The scope of presidential power seemed to be curbed primarily by executive self-restraint in the face of criticism from the public, the press, and organizations.

US military action against Afghanistan attracted broad support throughout the world, with nations in all regions recognizing that the United States had a right to destroy al-Qaeda's training bases and its capacity to plan and execute future attacks. President Bush received the assistance of many countries in stripping al-Qaeda of its financial and organizational assets. However, when the Bush administration requested action against Iraq, international support took the form only of a Security Council resolution to send inspectors back to Iraq. The Security Council refused to back a second resolution to authorize military action. China, Russia, France, Germany, Turkey, and other countries withheld support.

Thus far, the Bush administration has demonstrated a greater capacity for military victory than for securing the peace and stabilizing a defeated nation. In Afghanistan, the United States was particularly on notice that it should not duplicate its earlier mistake of intervening only to help check Soviet designs and then vacating the territory, creating a vacuum that invited control by the Taliban and the al-Qaeda terrorist network. Yet following the military triumph in November 2001, the promise of international reconstruction efforts in Afghanistan has seen little follow-through. The result is resentment among Afghanis, who conclude that once again a commitment by an outside power remains unfulfilled. Without an effective reconstruction program, the existing Karzai government is threatened by competing warlords and the possible resurgence of strength among the Taliban and al-Qaeda.

In Iraq, the US military took special care to avoid the destruction of bridges and other parts of the infrastructure. The goal was to preserve as much as possible of the Iraqi economy to permit it to return quickly to a productive, stable, and independent society. Nevertheless, following the military victory in the spring of 2003, the United States seemed wholly unprepared to stop the widespread looting that devastated much of Iraq's capacity to sustain itself. Having begun a war for the purpose of destroying the existing legal and police order, the Bush administration had an obligation to send in sufficient troops to secure government buildings, museums, hospitals, fire stations, schools, neighborhoods, power plants, and oil fields. That was not done. Spare parts, vehicles, furniture, computers, and other equipment were stolen. Seven nuclear sites in Iraq were not only looted but resulted in the spread of materials that could be used to build a nuclear or radiological bomb, and the release of scientific files that could easily speed development by terrorists of weapons of mass destruction.

There has been much commentary about President Bush's doctrine of 'preemptive' wars, which was highlighted during his speech at West Point on 1 June 2002, and in the administration's report on *National Security Strategy*, released in September 2002. A preemptive use of military force is generally considered to be the use of military action against another nation in response to an imminent military threat, such as enemy forces massing on one's border. Because of 9/11, President Bush made it clear that the United States was not prepared to absorb another attack, but would, instead, act first under the doctrine of self-defense. History, he said in *National Security Strategy*, 'will judge harshly those who saw this coming danger but failed to act. In the new world we have entered, the only path of peace and security is the path of action'.

Although the United States has often spoken about preemptive wars, it was a theoretical concept never used until military action against Iraq in 2003. During the Cuban Missile Crisis of 1962, the Kennedy administration considered the preemptive use of military force to destroy Soviet missiles introduced into Cuba, but the issue was resolved diplomatically. The war against Iraq in 2003 thus ushers in a new doctrine, not as concept but as reality. Iraq had not attacked the United States, nor did it represent an imminent threat.

In *National Security Strategy*, President Bush warned against enemies seeking weapons of mass destruction, pledging to act against 'emerging threats before they are fully formed'. The Bush administration was therefore prepared to go well beyond self-defense or preemptive war, where the triggering event is a threat that is imminent, direct, and offers no alternative but the use of force. Instead of an imminent threat it is now an emerging threat, which some analysts call not preemptive war but 'preventive war'. In the *Legal Times* for 7 April 2003, Miriam Sapiro said that the war against Iraq was 'not designed to pre-empt a specific, imminent threat, but to prevent Saddam Hussein from threatening the United States in the future'.

Whether the concept is preemptive or preventive war, the world would be at great risk if nations believe they are at liberty to use military force against emerging threats. In his West Point address on 1 June 2002, President Bush cautioned against broad justifications for military force, stating that he would 'not use force in all cases to preempt emerging threats, nor should nations use preemption as a pretext for aggression'. Still, he warned that in a world where enemies seek destructive technologies, 'the United States cannot remain idle while dangers gather'.

If the United States possesses a legal and moral right to act first in the face of gathering dangers, what of India, Pakistan, and other countries that decide that their national interest is improved by acting first, particularly by using nuclear weapons? The Bush administration instructs them to eschew military force and rely instead on diplomacy to defuse military confrontations. In the past, preemptive wars were guided by universal principles that applied to all nations. It appears that the new doctrine of preventive war allows military action only by the United States.

The essays in this book examine terrorism and analyze the policies adopted by the United States to deal with unconventional war. The unrivaled US military capacity is not in doubt. More in question is the ability of the United States to understand the threats, deal constructively with them, and forge a broad international consensus. These essays are an important step in moving us in that direction.

PART I
ORIGINS OF THE WAR ON TERROR:
DEBATES AND ISSUES

Chapter 1

Osama bin Laden, Radical Islam and the United States

Tom Lansford and Jack Covarrubias

Introduction

On 25 December 1979, 100,000 Soviet troops crossed the border into Afghanistan and began an occupation of the country that would initiate 20 years of internal conflict and would profoundly affect the growing militancy of radical Islamic groups throughout the world. The Soviet invasion and occupation would set the stage for the rise of the Taliban in Afghanistan and the concurrent rise of the al-Qaeda terrorist network of Osama bin Laden. During the occupation, the United States provided a variety of overt and tacit assistance to the anti-Soviet rebels, or mujahideen. Once the Soviets withdrew, US strategic interest in Afghanistan ended and the vacuum created by the disengagement of both superpowers created the conditions which produced the Taliban and al-Qaeda.

This essay examines the evolution of radical, militant Islamic groups in the context of US policies toward Afghanistan during the Soviet occupation and the period of Taliban rule. The work details the rise of Osama bin Laden and the al-Qaeda network. It further explores the broader patterns of Islamic fundamentalism within the region and the subsequent proliferation of anti-US and anti-Western sentiment. Specifically, the essay seeks to answer a variety of questions related to US foreign policy during the period from 1979 to the present day: 1) did US actions and programs exacerbate the radicalization of Islamic fundamentalist groups in South Asia; 2) what events led the mujahideen to turn against their former benefactors; 3) were there steps that successive US administrations could and should have taken to contain the growth of the Taliban and al-Qaeda; and 4) what polices can the US and Western powers now adopt to contain or ameliorate conflict within the region and to constrain the spread of radical Islam?

The Soviet Invasion and Occupation

In 1973, Mohammad Daoud Khan overthrew his cousin King Zahir Shah and established a republic in Afghanistan. Over the next few years, Daoud's increasingly repressive regime lost what little support it had among the Afghan people while Moscow increasingly signaled a willingness to back a revolt by Afghan communists. By 1977, the leadership of the Afghan Communist Party, the People's Democratic Party of Afghanistan (PDPA), began to develop concrete plans to overthrow Daoud and was actively recruiting among the Afghan military; many of whom had been trained in the

Soviet Union. Within a year, the PDPA had expanded their support within the Army by 100 per cent.[1] On 26 April 1978, Daoud ordered the arrest of top PDPA leaders which led the communists to launch a coup.

The next day, Afghan Army units loyal to the communists attacked the presidential palace where Daoud and his family were killed. PDPA leader, Nur Mohammad Taraki, became president and Hafizullah Amin became Deputy Prime Minister. The PDPA coup was not a broad-based uprising, only about 600 troops took part in the main attack, and the new regime did not enjoy popular support. As the regime tried to consolidate its power, it engaged in ever-increasingly repressive measures, including wide-spread executions. By 1979, there were widespread revolts throughout the countryside which culminated in a major uprising in Herat in March of that year which left 5,000 dead, including 100 Soviet advisers and their families. On 14 September 1979, Amin overthrew Taraki as political chaos spread throughout Afghanistan. The increasing instability prompted Moscow to begin considerations about military intervention. Raymond Garthoff asserts that by the eve of the invasion:

> The real Soviet fear was that Amin was neither reliable as a partner nor subject to Soviet guidance, and at the same time was ineffective in controlling the growing resistance. In desperation Amin might turn to the United States as Egyptian President Sadat and Somali General Siad had done. Alternatively, he would likely be swept away by a populist Islamic national movement. In either case the Soviet Union would lose all its cumulative investment in Afghanistan.[2]

In response, the Kremlin ordered Soviet troops in Afghanistan put on alert and increased deployments along the border. On 24 December, the invasion decision was made.[3] The following day Soviet troops crossed into Afghanistan. Resistance was light and the invasion force suffered only 20–30 killed and approximately 300 wounded. Amin was killed on 27 December when Soviet forces stormed the presidential palace and by the beginning of the New Year, the Soviets had control of all major Afghan cities.

The US Reaction

In the initial aftermath of the coup which deposed Daoud, the administration of Jimmy Carter endeavored to retain ties with the Taraki government. The Administration was not even sure if the new regime was Communist.[4] Even once the true nature of the regime became apparent, US programs were continued and Zbigniew Brzezinski, Carter's National Security Advisor, even asserted that the Administration should strive to develop a 'restrained' policy toward Taraki to keep the Afghans from growing closer to the Soviet Union.[5] US policy changed following the death of its ambassador, Adolph Dubbs, who was killed during a rescue attempt after he had been kidnapped in February 1979. The Afghans refused to cooperate with the US investigation of the ambassador's death. Carter then began to curtail US aid and authorized the CIA to use $500,000 to aid anti-government factions in Afghanistan.[6]

By December 1979, there was increasing intelligence that the Soviets were preparing for an invasion of Afghanistan, however as was noted at the time, 'private warnings to presidential aides last month that the neutralist regime in Afghanistan was "ripe like a red apple" for a pro-Soviet communist takeover met official silence here, a non-response highlighting the administration's dangerous inertia in meeting the current Soviet worldwide offensive'.[7] Nonetheless, as the historian John Lewis Gaddis points-out, Carter had the 'misfortune to come to power at a time when the Soviet Union was launching a new series of challenges to the global balance of power' but the United States faced a 'general decline in super-power authority' and the 'effects of the post-Vietnam conviction' about the 'use of force'.[8] Carter had already faced the fall of pro-American regimes in Iran and Nicaragua and was constrained by domestic issues such as the struggling US economy.

Aid for the Mujahideen

The Soviet invasion united the hawks and doves within the Administration and Carter was personally angry with Moscow. The Soviet invasion marked a sea change in US policy toward the Soviet Union. At the heart of the new American attitude was the Carter Doctrine, which was promulgated in the State of the Union Address on 23 January 1980. Carter stated that: 'An attempt by any outside force to gain control of the Persian Gulf region will be regarded as an assault on the vital interests of the United States of America, and such an assault will be repelled by any means necessary, including military force.'[9] The President further declared that 'verbal condemnation is not enough. The Soviet Union must pay for its aggression'.[10] Carter would impose economic sanctions on the Soviets, boycott the 1980 Moscow Olympics and authorize covert military assistance for the mujahideen, including arms transfers.[11]

The election of Ronald Reagan in 1980 accelerated US aid for the mujahideen, especially in the aftermath of the announcement of the Reagan Doctrine which promised US military support for 'those risking their lives on every continent from Afghanistan to Nicaragua to defy Soviet-supported aggression'.[12] In order to operationalize the Reagan Doctrine in Afghanistan, in March 1985, the President signed National Security Decision Directive (NSDD) 166. This Directive authorized the CIA to help the mujahideen with 'all means available'.[13] US military assistance to the mujahideen rose from $122 million in 1984 to $250 million in 1985, and from $470 million in 1986 to $630 million by 1987.[14] The CIA provided the rebels with a range of military equipment, including Stinger missiles beginning in May 1986,[15] and intelligence support such as satellite images and communications intercepts. The United States also worked with its allies, including Saudi Arabia and other Gulf states to coordinate other financial aid. By the mid-1980s, non-US aid reached about $25 million per month or $300 million per year.

Still, by 1985, the groundwar had reached a stalemate. The Soviets had about 100,000 troops deployed while the mujahideen fielded about 250,000. Military parity was achieved by the Soviets because of their aerial superiority.[16] However, the introduction of the Stinger missile dramatically changed the air war. Stingers were credited with destroying 279 Soviet aircraft from 1986 to 1989.[17] In addition, Afghan air force losses doubled from 1986 to 1989 with 17 planes and 12 helicopters shot down in 1986, 33 planes and 21 helicopters downed in 1987, and 44 planes and 24 helicopters destroyed in 1988.[18] The missiles forced the Soviets to change their tactics and utilize high-level bombing and eliminate some aerial missions. This, in turn, gave the mujahideen greater operational freedom and resulted in increased operations.[19]

The Soviet Withdrawal

The introduction of the Stinger and growing casualties led Soviet leader Mikhail Gorbachev to begin negotiations with the United States over withdrawal. These talks culminated in the April 1988 Geneva Accords which called for a Soviet withdrawal in February 1989 and an end to military aid by both superpowers. On 15 February 1989, the last Soviet troops withdrew from Afghanistan and the period of superpower rivalry in the country came to an abrupt end. The Soviets officially lost 13,310 dead, 35,478 wounded and 310 missing during their eight-year occupation, a figure roughly proportional to American losses in Vietnam in terms of the number of troops deployed.[20] Meanwhile, the amount of US military aid during the period of the Soviet occupation was five times the dollar amount of total US assistance from 1947 to 1979.[21]

The United States and the Soviet Union continued to provide arms and supplies to their respective factions even after the withdrawal as a means to prevent the opposing sides from gaining ascendancy in Afghanistan.[22] This exacerbated the country's civil war and extended the fighting. In testimony before the US Congress, Deputy Assistant Secretary of State, Robert A. Peck described US policy in the following terms when asked why the United States did not stop unilateral arms shipments:

> The obligation which the United States would take as a 'guarantor' would relate exclusively to our own policies. We would bear no responsibility for the actions of others, or for the successful implementation of the agreement as a whole. We and the Soviet Union would agree to the same basic commitment regarding noninterference and nonintervention. We would be prepared, if completely satisfied with the agreement, to prohibit US military assistance to the Afghan resistance. We would expect the Soviet Union to show reciprocal restraint under the Geneva accords in stopping its military support for the Kabul regime.[23]

The end of the Cold War expedited efforts to end external arms transfers, however, and by December 1990, the superpowers reached a tentative agreement to end their involvement in the conflict. The Gulf War further added impetus to the need to end arms shipments as militant Islamic groups supported Saddam Hussein to the dismay of the Saudis and Pakistanis. A final agreement between the United States, Russia, Pakistan and Saudi Arabia was reached in December 1991.[24] None of the major Afghan groups, including the pro-Soviet regime in Kabul, participated in the discussions. That their main supporters, including the United States and Saudi Arabia would cut-off their arms and supplies without significant consultations would infuriate many mujahideen leaders and increase tensions with the West while it also reinforced the notions about the corruptness and shallowness of the Saudi regime.

While most observers expected the pro-Soviet regime to immediately collapse after the withdrawal, infighting among the mujahideen groups allowed the regime to remain in place until 1992, when rebel forces captured Kabul. However, civil war and political fragmentation continued until 1996 when a relatively new group, the Taliban, was able to fill the political vacuum and ultimately gain control of approximately 90 per cent of the country. The ethnic and religious differences of the mujahideen, which caused the lengthy post-Soviet civil war, reflected the tensions and political infighting of both Afghan history and the more contemporary problems that emerged during the Soviet occupation.

The Mujahideen

In 1979, Afghanistan remained a conservative Islamic country. The PDPA was determined to reform the country by minimizing the power of Islam. It introduced a variety of new programs to secularize the legal and educational systems and the new leaders even publicly disparaged Islam. For instance, the new president, Taraki, declared in an interview that 'we want to clean Islam in Afghanistan of the ballast and dirt of bad traditions, superstition and erroneous belief'.[25] These efforts turned the overwhelming majority of Afghanistan against the regime. As R. Lincoln Keiser points out, 'the introduction of communist ideology and the debunking of Muslim beliefs in the schools ... not only aroused the emotions of the tribes against the Taraki/Amin regime, but also destroyed the foundation of the central government's legitimacy'.[26] The PDPA's policies 'violated practically every Afghan cultural norm, and strayed far beyond the allowable bounds of deviance in the social, economic, and political institutions. It appears that they systematically planned to alienate every segment of the Afghan people'.[27]

All of the main opposition groups that developed in response to the Communist government were Islamic in nature. Prior to the Soviet invasion there were already six Islamic insurgency groups working to overthrow the Taraki regime. Following the invasion, that number rose to 22 major groups based in Pakistan with an additional 10 in Iran.[28] The majority of the mujahideen tended to divide themselves along traditional ethnic divisions. Afghanistan's largest ethnic group is the Pashtuns who comprise about 51 per cent of the population and who have dominated Afghan politics throughout the state's modern history. The Tajiks are the second largest groups and make-up about 25 per cent of the people. The Hazara form 10 per cent of the population, the Uzbeks, 8 per cent, while the Turkmen, Balochs and Aimaks comprise a combined total of 11 per cent of the population.[29]

The main fundamentalist mujahideen groups came together in a broad coalition known as the Islamic Alliance. The Alliance advocated the establishment of an Islamic republic along the lines of Iran and had substantial external support from states such as Iran, Saudi Arabia and Pakistan.[30] Within the coalition, there emerged an ethnic division that would lead to later conflict after the Soviet withdrawal. The Islamic Society was made-up of mainly ethnic Tajiks and Uzbeks. The Society's political leader was Dr Burhanuddin Rabbani and its military commander was Ahmad Shah Massoud. In 1992, Rabbani would become the first post-Soviet president of Afghanistan. The Society's major rival, the (mainly Pashtun) Islamic Party, was led by Gulbuddin Hikmatyar who would ultimately challenge Rabbani's rule and help sow the seeds for the rise of the Taliban.

Local mujahideen commanders often had little loyalty to the Afghan political leadership in Pakistan or to their nominal superiors. Barnett R. Rubin wrote that 'the affiliation of commanders to parties is determined by a combination of patronage, traditional networks, reaction to local rivalries (a commander will join a different party from that of his traditional rival) and ideology'.[31] In 1982, Amaury de Riencourt, a noted French scholar of the region, observed that the mujahideen 'seem to be more interested in fighting for the complete autonomy of their areas than in any common struggle against the Russian invaders – a vivid illustration of the fact that, up to now, Afghanistan never was a homogeneous nation-state'.[32] One result was that the different ethnic mujahideen often fought each other as much as they fought the Soviets. Successive efforts by both the United States and Pakistan to establish a broad-based political coalition to serve as a true government-in-exile never truly succeeded.

The Arabs and Fundamentalist Islam

Internal conflicts among the mujahideen were exacerbated by the presence of non-Afghan, Arab volunteers. From 1982 through 1992, approximately 35,000 Muslims (including 25,000 Arabs) fought as mujahideen against the Soviets.[33] Often 'the Arabs that did travel to Afghanistan from Peshawar were generally considered nuisances by mujahideen commanders, some of whom viewed them only slightly less bothersome than the Soviets'.[34] These foreign-born mujahideen usually did not appreciate or accept the goals of the local commanders. They were also mainly Shia while the overwhelming majority of Afghans were Sunni (among the Afghan people, only the Hazaras were predominately Shia). Before they were deployed, many of the Arabs spent time in Pakistani religious schools, or madrassas, which reinforced their fundamentalist beliefs.

These Arabs reflected the growing radicalization of Islam among certain groups. This religious militancy has been termed 'Islamic fundamentalism', 'radical Islam' or simply 'militant Islam'. All of these terms describe a transnational trend of the late twentieth century marked by an increasing opposition to what Samuel Huntington described as 'Western ideas of individualism, liberalism, constitutionalism, human rights, equality, liberty, the rule of law [and] democracy'.[35] This opposition is based on the fact that as a theology Islam 'created a religion and a state at the same time'.[36] Consequently, as Hilal Khashan notes:

> according to the fundamentalists, it is completely unacceptable for Muslims to be ruled by any system of government unless it is based on *Shari'a* [italics in original]. Western-inspired secular laws, now applies in most Islamic states contradict Islamic tenets, and most fundamentalists wholeheartedly reject the application of these laws. The fact that radical Islamic groups constitute mainly domestic movements operating against state authority within the boundaries drawn by Western colonial powers does not mean that they necessarily accept the existing Middle Eastern state order.[37]

Radical Islam has been increasingly manifested by an expansion of the use of political violence or terrorism, especially against non-military targets as a means to undermine that state order. Hence, as Hrair Dekmejian writes, 'confrontation is an important part of the world view of Islamic fundamentalists and many conventional Muslims'.[38] And, it is the duty of all true believers to participate in jihad, or holy war, against infidels.[39] This combination of factors has resulted in a notion of 'historical determinism which considers the ultimate triumph of Islam as prescribed by God'.[40]

The invasion of Afghanistan, a Muslim country, by an atheistic power, the Soviet Union, provided radical groups with a cause and a variety of clerics responded with calls for a jihad against the invaders. This turned the insurrection into a holy war for both Afghans and Arab recruits. That the mujahideen were able to defeat the Soviets elevated the status of the radical groups (who argued that their victory was based on

God's will). Many of these groups would also assert that they played a major role in the downfall of the Soviet Union because of its defeat in Afghanistan.[41]

By the late 1980s, there were repeated clashes between the Afghan and Arab mujahideen as more radical fighters joined the rebel side. Many of the foreign-born mujahideen became convinced that if native Afghans did not join the call for jihad then they were apostates and could no longer be considered Muslim. As a result, these people were subject to the laws of futuhat, or conquest.[42] This led fundamentalist mujahideen to engage in a variety of atrocities, including executing prisoners, rape, and the practice of selling women and children as slaves.[43] These actions angered local mujahideen who were often related or ethnically linked to the populations. It also made it less likely that Afghan Army troops would desert or surrender.[44]

Islam is not a monolithic religion and is instead divided into a variety of sects and is influenced by scores of national cultures. In addition, Islamic fundamentalism developed in a region of the world that was previously known most for 'both religious tolerance and the prevalence of traditional religious practices'.[45] Still, as Graham Fuller and Ian Lesser point out 'Islamic fundamentalism' (an imprecise and poor term for analytical purposes) has been the single most anti-Western force over the past two decades especially with the withering away of communism. Muslim states have, furthermore, provided the West with several dramatic 'hate figures' unparalleled almost anywhere in the world: Gamal Abdel Nasser, Muammar al-Qadhafi, the Ayatollah Khomeini, and Saddam Hussein among the most arresting examples in Western demonology.[46] The latest of these figures is, of course, Osama bin Laden.

Osama bin Laden

From the ashes of the mujahideen that formed to 'liberate' Afghanistan from the Soviets, Osama bin Laden, or Usamah bin Mohammad bin Awad bin Laden, formed the core elements of what has become al-Qaeda. This organization has been responsible for many of the more prominent terrorist acts of the 1990s and 2000s. From his 1993 affiliation with the killing of US service personnel in Somalia to the subsequent destruction of the World Trade Center towers on 11 September 2001, the organization that he founded in 1988 has formed the nucleus of a world wide ring of terrorists bent on the forced realization of their minority views. The context of this alliance of terrorists lies within a narrow interpretation of the Quran that calls for the rise of Muslim culture via jihad.[47] This doctrine amounts to a concept of 'total war' in which all means are acceptable, as documented through severe interpretation of the Quran, in order to achieve the desired goal of the indoctrination of Shariah into all cultures.[48]

Osama bin Laden was born in 1957 in Riyadh, Saudi Arabia into the wealthiest class of society affording him the benefits that such wealth allows for.[49] Growing up as one of 57 children, he inherited millions when his father, Sheik Mohammed Awad bin Laden, died in a plane crash near San Antonio, Texas in 1968.[50] His education and early formation were a product of his father's death, his affiliation with the Muslim brotherhood, and a series of lessons with Islamic scholars.[51] He took these lessons with him to the King Abdul-Aziz University where he earned degrees in public administration and economics.[52] During his time at the University, bin Laden used his free time to further his education with travel. The 1979 Soviet invasion of

Afghanistan coincided with one of these trips giving bin Laden his first relationship with the United States.[53]

Bin Laden was one of the Arab Islamic warriors who traveled to Afghanistan, bent on defending their fellow Muslim brothers from the perils of the Soviet occupation. bin Laden's immense personal wealth and his ties to the Middle Eastern social elite placed upon him a unique role. He became a conduit for funneling money from the Middle East into the resistance movement in Afghanistan.[54]

As the United States continually increased its involvement in the Afghan conflict, bin Laden was quickly becoming an important figure in the movement of money into the conflict and the training of volunteers in the various camps he had set up throughout the region.[55] Through Maktab al-Khidamar (MAK), the organization with which bin Laden was affiliated, he became involved with Pakistan's state security services.[56] Pakistan's Interservice Intelligence agency (ISI) was heavily funded by the United States. Ahmed Rashid stated in 1999:

> With the active encouragement of the CIA and Pakistan's ISI, who wanted to turn the Afghan jihad into a global war waged by all Muslim states against the Soviet Union, some 35,000 Muslim radicals from 40 Islamic countries joined Afghanistan's fight between 1982 and 1992. Tens of thousands more came to study in Pakistani madrasahs. Eventually more than 100,000 foreign Muslim radicals were directly influenced by the Afghan jihad.[57]

The Afghan war served as a proving ground for Islamic fundamentalists throughout the Middle East. The system of bringing new volunteers and funding from around the world into the organization set up by bin Laden did not end with the Soviet withdrawal. Bin Laden had splintered from MAK by 1988 to form his al-Qaeda (The Base). This new organization was to utilize the talents he honed in organizing Muslim extremists in order to continue the fight of a Muslim Holy war. This new organization would act as a 'holding company for globalized terror'.[58]

Osama bin Laden, along with top lieutenants such as Dr. Ayman al-Zawahiri of the Egyptian al-Jihad and Muhammed Atef – who is thought to have been killed in the American air campaign over Afghanistan – formed the nucleus of the new al-Qaeda organization. Most of the members of the organization were the same Arab 'freedom fighters' that had joined the mujahideen to defeat the Soviets in Afghanistan.[59] These soldiers chose to expand the jihad against the West and bin Laden continued to provide the logistical support and leadership that they needed in such places as Kosovo and Chechnya. Bin Laden noted that 'I discovered it was not enough to fight in Afghanistan, but that we had to fight on all fronts against communism or western oppression. The urgent thing was communism, but the next target was America ...'.[60]

Osama bin Laden is different than most other Islamic religious leaders. He does not focus on the individual sects of Islam as much as he encompasses the whole. His view is of a Pan-Islamic society in which all of Islam is marked by its devotion to the tenets of the Quran.[61] He views this society as having been shamed and humiliated by the Western nations, as led by the United States. Consequently, his focus is that of bringing back honor to Islam, as a whole, by shaming the West. He blames the West for all the ills that have befallen this great Muslim society, and most importantly, he blames the West for the failure of Muslim culture to live by the rules set out in the Quran. Consequently, the destruction of the West should 'release' the hold it has taken upon Muslim nations worldwide for it is the West that chooses to go against the rule of Islam. Bin Laden summarized this notion in the following manner: 'You are the nation who, rather than ruling by the Shariah of Allah in its Constitution and Laws, choose to invent your own laws as you will and desire. You separate religion from your policies, contradicting the pure nature which affirms Absolute Authority to the Lord and your Creator.'[62] It is the driving need to 'rescue' Islam that gives bin Laden and his followers their sense of purpose. It is the success of the mujahideen in Afghanistan that makes them feel like they are truly acting with God's purpose.

Al-Qaeda has proven to be very dangerous indeed. Bin Laden's 1996 declaration of war against the United States, his 1998 fatwa to all Muslims and his 1998 announcement of the International Islamic Front as the unifying force behind the cooperation of terrorist organizations towards a 'common cause' have served as media announcements in the continual struggle for the hearts and minds of young Muslims around the world.[63] The successes that al-Qaeda has achieved are one of purpose. This purpose is to make popular a dogma of religious extremism with bin Laden and al-Qaeda as symbols of resistance to Western influence.[64] His stated goal is to instigate an uprising of Muslims from around the world: 'If the instigation for jihad against the Jews and the Americans ... is considered a crime, then let history be a witness that I am a criminal. Our job is to instigate and, by the grace of God, we did that, and certain people responded to this instigation.'[65]

The time period between the fall of the Soviet backed regime and the subsequent fall of the Taliban regime marks the integration point between these 'foreign mujahideen', as represented by Osama's al-Qaeda, and the local mujahideen under the influence of the Taliban. This relationship served a duel purpose in providing a base for al-Qaeda operations and training, and legitimacy through a show of arms for the Taliban regime.

The Taliban and al-Qaeda

A variety of anti-Western militant Islamic groups emerged during the 1980s and 1990s, however, what set al-Qaeda apart was the degree of independence from state influence. While many militant Islamic groups such as HAMAS, Hizballah and the Palestine Islamic Jihad are closely linked with a variety of state sponsors, including Cuba, Iran, Iraq, Libya, North Korea, Sudan and Syria,[66] al-Qaeda enjoyed a degree of financial independence that allowed it access to the resources obtained by groups with state sponsors, but it avoided the political control often exercised by state-based regimes. The eventual location of the al-Qaeda leadership within Afghanistan provided the organization a base for training and operations and maximum political freedom.

While al-Qaeda developed from the Arab mujahideen, the Taliban (which literally translates as 'students') evolved from the Afghan refugee camps in Pakistan where many youths attended madrassas or Islamic schools run by Sunni Muslims of the Deobandi sect. Because of generous outside support, the majority of the Deobandi madrassas were outside of the control of the Pakistani government.[67] They formed the core of the 10 to 15 per cent of the 45,000 Pakistani madrassas which advocated militant Islam or 'jihadi' ideologies.[68] The Deobandi madrassas proved very popular since the sect combined the traditional, conservative tenets of Islam with the strict

Pashtunwali code of personal honor which was practiced by most ethnic Pashtuns in both Afghanistan and Pakistan.[69]

The Taliban initially received widespread popular support from the Afghan population in the mid-1990s, since the organization seemed devoted to correcting the worst abuses of the mujahideen warlords. The Taliban was able to bring peace and stability to regions that had been wracked by 15 years of civil war. Since the group was predominately Pashtun, they enjoyed the support of the majority of Afghans opposed to rule by the ethnic Tajik President Rabbani. The Taliban also initially disavowed any desire to rule Afghanistan until after they captured Kabul in 1996.[70] However, as they consolidated their control of Afghanistan, they imposed a strict interpretation of Shariah and ruthlessly suppressed any dissent.

With the fall of Mazar-i-Sharif in 1998, the Taliban effectively controlled 90 per cent of the country and its only serious rival for power, the United Front or Northern Alliance, a coalition of mainly ethnic Tajiks and Uzbeks, was effectively bottled-up in the north of Afghanistan. Bin Laden developed a number of contacts with militant Islamic leaders in Afghanistan during his experiences as a logistics planner during the Soviet occupation.[71] In fact, a number of Afghans joined bin Laden when he established a base of operations in Khartoum, Sudan in 1992. Under pressure from the United States and Saudi Arabia, Sudan expelled bin Laden in 1996 at which time he returned to Afghanistan, just as the Taliban came to power.

A Terrorist State

Although the Taliban's immediate concern in 1996 was the consolidation of power in Afghanistan, the regime, led by the reclusive one-eyed Mullah Mohammad Omar, also began to extensively support militant Islamic groups around the world. In addition to providing a base for al-Qaeda, the Taliban regime provided both overt and tacit support to a variety of terrorist organizations. By 1998, there were bases for groups involved in terrorist activities in Tajikistan, Uzbekistan, China, Bangladesh, Kashmir, Pakistan, Saudi Arabia and the Philippines.[72] The Taliban also provided training for soldiers who fought alongside Muslims in Chechnya and Kosovo. Meanwhile, bin Laden was able to recruit and train approximately 5,000 al-Qaeda members. Some of these recruits would be dispatched to undertake terrorist operations in the West (or form sleeper cells for future operations) while the al-Qaeda leader maintained a standing force of about 2,000 troops in Afghanistan as a sort of personal militia which supported the Taliban's military operations.[73]

Bin Laden remained quite popular with the Taliban leadership and took pains to ensure that he stayed in their good graces. He paid for the construction of houses for Mullah Omar's family and for those of other top Taliban leaders.[74] He also provided other funds that the Taliban used for military equipment or infrastructure construction, including road building. Al-Qaeda troops also fought alongside the Taliban in their continuing campaign against the Northern Alliance and in offensives to suppress the Shiite Hazaras of Afghanistan.

When the United States demanded that the Taliban surrender bin Laden in the late 1990s, the Taliban initially used the terrorist leader as a 'bargaining chip' and tried to negotiate diplomatic recognition and expanded US aid in return for bin Laden's surrender. When these discussions failed to come to fruition, the Taliban allowed bin

Laden to quietly disappear from public view in Kandahar in an effort to shield him from covert action by the United States.

The Taliban received substantial support from the ISI as the Islamabad government sought to use the Afghan regime as a tool to undermine Indian control of Kashmir. For instance, the Taliban provided a base for the Harkat ul-Mujahideen, one of the main terrorist groups in Kashmir and in return, the Kabul regime received military and financial aid from Pakistan.[75] With Pakistani and continued Saudi support, the Taliban were able to expand their external operations and reinforce their internal control over the country.

The ISI provided the Taliban with intelligence, weapons and training. The Pakistanis also served as the main diplomatic conduit for the Taliban. Pakistani support for the regime, even in light of Kabul's terrorist connections, further provided a sense of empowerment to the Taliban (especially as the regime faced a series of crises with both Iran and later the United States). One result of this confidence was that by 1998, as Ahmed Rashid points out, 'Afghanistan was now truly a haven for Islamic internationalism and terrorism and the Americans and the West were at a loss as to how to handle it'.[76]

US Policy

With the 1991 agreement to stop arms shipments and military supplies, the US policy toward Afghanistan shifted back to its more traditional benign neglect. The United States supplied humanitarian aid, but did not provide substantial support for the Rabbani regime. After the Taliban seized power, the United States continued to recognize Rabbani as the legitimate president of Afghanistan, but it also provided food and other humanitarian assistance to the Taliban regime.

The US policy of avoidance ended with the 7 August 1998 terrorist attacks on the American embassies in Nairobi, Kenya and Dar es Salaam, Tanzania which were traced to al-Qaeda. The attacks led the Clinton Administration to redouble its anti-terrorist efforts and marked the beginnings of a shift away from the view that bin Laden and al-Qaeda were a criminal issue.[77] The administration increasingly viewed Osama bin Laden as a hard security or military threat, instead of a law enforcement concern, and subsequently launched cruise missile attacks on three suspected al-Qaeda bases in Afghanistan and a facility in Sudan. The attacks, which killed 26 people in Afghanistan, infuriated the Taliban and reinforced their unwillingness to negotiate his handover to the Americans.[78]

The trend toward the growing recognition of the security threat posed by al-Qaeda accelerated with the attack on the *USS Cole* in October of 2,000.[79] Within the Administration, Secretary of State Madeleine Albright and Secretary of Defense William Cohen pressed strongly for military action against bin Laden and his al-Qaeda terrorist network while Attorney General Janet Reno strongly dissented.[80] However, intelligence problems and a military coup in Pakistan in 1999, forestalled the implementation of most of the Administration's plans.[81]

The unwillingness of the Clinton Administration to take strong action against al-Qaeda or to exert significant pressure on the Taliban regime emboldened bin Laden. It also led the Taliban to believe that they could defy the United States with little serious consequences. This combination of under-appreciation would lead bin Laden to plan even more daring and powerful attacks on the United States, while it encouraged the Taliban to be dismissive and contemptuous of US threats in the aftermath of 11 September.

Conclusion

The United States, in its efforts to contain Soviet expansion, developed a policy habit in which Washington tended to abandon the client when the Soviet threat was no longer pertinent. Afghanistan is no exception to this. The lack of strategic concern for the Afghani plight once the Soviets withdrew caused within the United States' abandonment of Afghanistan. This, in turn, exacerbated a situation in which Islamic fundamentalism was already an integral and historical component of part of the existing domestic political landscape. When millions of dollars of US supplied military aid was added to the equation, without an equal amount of economic and infrastructure support, it was little wonder that the destabilizing impact of US policy was exacerbated.

The combination of growing Islamic militancy, substantial foreign military aid and existing ethnic and religious conflict, may not have necessarily forced Afghanistan into Taliban rule, with its subsequent support of the al-Qaeda organization, but it definitely weakened the potential for a peaceful resolution of the ongoing Afghan civil war. Once great power interest in the country ended, the different factions within the mujahideen were left without the leadership necessary for the transition to a broad-based national government. This allowed the Taliban to gain ascendancy.

The impetus towards anti-Westernism was accelerated by Islamic 'crusaders'. The dependence upon these militant Islamists and the subsequent internationalization of their goals can be attributed to the global community's willingness to support their short-term actions and needs in combating the Soviets in Afghanistan. The failure of American policy towards these foreign mujahideen was not a tactical failure, but rather a strategic failure based on a lack of appreciation for their potential threat and their growing anti-Americanism. The US commitment to Afghanistan should be analyzed in the context of the bipolar superpower conflict which constrained America's decision making apparatus at the time. What appeared to be a logical marriage then would have naturally been illogical without the Soviet expansionist threat.

The US strategic failure is rooted in the failure of policymakers in successive administrations to understand the long-term impact of US support for the mujahideen. One potential cure for this failure would have been a recognition of the need to separate the mujahideen cause against communism from broader patterns of anti-Westernism among Islamic militants and to concentrate military support for the politically moderate Afghan resistance groups. Concurrently, the United States should have sought a more stable political settlement as opposed to an essential abandonment of interests in the region. Finally, the Clinton administration in particular failed to adapt to the growing militancy of the Taliban and al-Qaeda and underestimated the security threat posed by the combination of a global terrorist group with a national territorial base for operations.

In respect to the future of US interactions within Afghanistan, the United States and other Western powers need to reinvest in their broad commitment to support the ideals that proved victorious in the Cold War, including democracy and free market capitalism.

Only long-term commitments to economic development can eventually alleviate the poverty of the region and consequently, the attractiveness of a militant perversion of Islam which blames hardship and poverty on the 'hedonistic' tendencies of the West. The failure of the United States to invest in a stable government within Afghanistan, once there was no need to counter Soviet aggression, can be directly attributed to the rise of the Taliban. If that investment had been made, a wholly different outcome could have been expected. This is truer now than it was then. The fledgling democracy that is currently forming in Afghanistan will not succeed without a direct investment in its future by Western powers. Only through such investments can the region overcome the legacy of strife and conflict which have fueled the rise of militant Islam and the likes of bin Laden, al-Qaeda and the Taliban.

Notes

1   Anthony Arnold (1983), *Afghanistan's Two-Party Communism: Parcham and Khalq*, Stanford: Hoover Institution Press, 47.
2   Raymond Garthoff (1984), *Detente and Confrontation: American Soviet Relations From Nixon to Reagan*, Washington, DC: Brookings Institute, 921.
3   Galeotti attributes much of the impetus behind the decision to invade to Yuri Andropov who was engaged in a campaign to succeed the increasingly ill and senile Brezhnev. Andropov envisioned a success in Afghanistan as a means to secure his future while the other Soviet leaders present, including Foreign Minister Andrei Gromyko and Defense Minister Marshall Andrei Ustinov, envisioned that a quick victory and the restoration of order in their southern neighbor would allow the Kremlin to return its attention to more pressing global matters; Mark Galeotti (1995), *Afghanistan: The Soviet Union's Last War*, London: Frank Cass, 10–12.
4   Thomas T. Hammond (1984), *Red Flag Over Afghanistan: The Communist Coup, the Soviet Invasion and the Consequences*, Boulder: Westview Press, 60.
5   Ibid., 62.
6   These funds were distributed over a six-week period by CIA officers based in Kabul; Robert Gates (1996), *The Ultimate Insider's Story of Five Presidents and How They Won the Cold War*, New York: Simon and Schuster, 142–9.
7   Rowland Evans and Robert Novak (1978), 'Ignoring the Dangers of the Afghan Coup', *The Washington Post* (8 May).
8   John Lewis Gaddis (1982), *Strategies of Containment: A Critical Appraisal of Postwar American National Security Policy*, New York: Oxford University Press, 350–52.
9   US, White House (1980), 'The President's State of the Union Address', press release (23 January).
10 Ibid.; as a sign of Carter's anger, he asked the various US officials involved in relations with the Soviet Union to draw-up lists of potential action. While the staffers assumed Carter would pick-and-choose from the various lists, he instead incorporated all of the suggested punitive actions in his response. This was a response that even Brzezinski thought too provocative at first; David Skidmore (1993–94), 'Carter and the Failure of Foreign Policy Reform', *Political Science Quarterly*, 108/4 (Winter), 723–4.
11 The first shipments consisted of 'several thousand' World War II era Lee Enfield rifles which were already in common use by Afghan tribes. These would be followed by weapons made in Warsaw Pact countries, such as AK-47s, in order to provide 'plausible deniability' to the US; Bearden, 20.

12   Ronald Reagan, quoted in Charles Krauthammer (1986), 'The Reagan Doctrine', *The New Republic* (17 February).

13   Quoted in Alan J. Kuperman (1999), 'The Stinger Missile and US Intervention in Afghanistan', *Political Science Quarterly*, 114/2 (Summer), 227.

14   Olivier Roy (1991), *The Lessons of the Soviet/Afghan War*, Adelphi Papers 259, London: Brassey's, 35. US support was generally matched by the Saudis; Kathy Evans (1992), *The Guardian* (2 January).

15   During the first use of the American-supplied Stingers on 25 September 1986, five mujahideen fired missiles and shot down three Soviet helicopters; Kuperman, 234–5.

16   Scott R. McMichael (1991), *Stumbling Bear: Soviet Military Performance in Afghanistan*, London: Brassey's, 84, 89.

17   William McManaway (1990), 'Stinger in Afghanistan', *Air Defense Artillery* (January–February), 3–8; and William McManaway (1989), 'The Dragon is Dead!', *Air Defense Artillery* (July–August).

18   Diego Cordovez and Selig S. Harrison (1995), *Out of Afghanistan: The Inside Story of the Soviet Withdrawal*, New York: Oxford University Press, 199.

19   Ibid., 198–9.

20   Michael Dobbs (1988), 'Soviets Say 13,310 Soldiers Died in Afghan War', *Washington Post* (26 May).

21   From 1947 to 1979, the US provided a total of $532.87 million in aid to Afghanistan; US, Agency for International Development (AID) (1979), 'US Overseas Loans and Grants, 1979', Washington, DC: GPO.

22   See Riaz M, Khan (1991), *Untying the Afghan Knot: Negotiating Soviet Withdrawal*, Durham, NC: Duke University Press; and Selig S. Harrison (1988), 'Inside the Afghan Talks', *Foreign Policy*, 72 (Fall), 31–60.

23   Quoted in Rosanne Klass (1988), 'Afghanistan: The Accords', *Foreign Affairs*, 66/5 (Summer), 933.

24   For an overview of the agreement, see UN, Department of Public Information (1991), 'Statement by Secretary-General Javier Perez de Cuellar' (21 May).

25   Selig S. Harrison (1988), 'So Far it Looks Like Another Win for the Islamic Fundamentalists', *The Washington Post* (17 April).

26   Barnett R. Rubin (1989/1990), 'The Fragmentation of Afghanistan', *Foreign Affairs*, 68/5 (Winter), 153.

27   Amaury De Riencourt (1982/1983), 'India and Pakistan in the Shadow of Afghanistan', *Foreign Affairs*, 61/2 (Winter), 430.

28   Ahmed Rashid (2002), 'Osama bin laden: How the US Helped Midwife A Terrorist', in Fredrik Logevall, ed., *Terrorism and 9/11: A Reader*, Boston: Houghton Mifflin, 51.

29   Milton Bearden (2001), 'Afghanistan, Graveyard of Empires', *Foreign Affairs*, 80/6 (November/December), 24.

30   Samuel P. Huntington (1993), 'The Clash of Civilizations?', *Foreign Affairs*, 72/3 (Summer), 40.

31   G. Hossein Razi (1990), 'Legitimacy, Religion, and Nationalism in the Middle East', *The American Political Science Review*, 84/1 (March), 76.

32   Hilal Khashan (1997), 'The New World Order and the Tempo of Militant Islam', *British Journal of Middle Eastern Studies*, 24/1 (May), 12.

33   R. Hrair Dekmejian (1995), *Islam in Revolution: Fundamentalism in the Arab World*, 2nd edn, New York: Syracuse University Press, 22.

34 See Henry Munson, Jr (1988), *Islam and Revolution in the Middle East*, New Haven: Yale University Press; or Emmanuel Sivan (1985), *Radical Islam*, New Haven: Yale University Press.

35 Khashan, 10.

36 Graham E. Fuller and Ian O. Lesser (1995), *A Sense of Siege: The Geopolitics of Islam and the West*, Boulder: Westview Press, 153–4.

37 Under fundamentalist Islamic doctrine, the concept of futuhat, or wars of liberation, which result in the spread of Islam allows for the confiscation of property of non-believers, the execution of males and the enslavement of women and children; see Akram Diya al 'Umari (1991), *Madinian Society At The Time of The Prophet*, trans. Huda Khattab, Riyadh: International Islamic Publishing House.

38 Rubin, 155, 158.

39 Zahid Hussain (1992), 'Snub for Hard-Line Afghans', *The Times* (28 January).

40 Khashan, 6.

41 Fuller and Lesser, 2.

47 Gaber Asfour (1998), 'Osama bin Laden: Financier of "Desert" Islam', *New Perspectives Quarterly*, 15/4 (Summer), 39–40.

48 David Zeidan (2001), 'The Islamic Fundamentalist View of Life as a Perennial Battle', *Middle East Review of International Affairs*, 5/4 (December).

49 Patrick Bellamy, 'Osama bin Laden: High Priest of Terror', online at http://www.crimelibrary.com/terrorists/binladen.

50 Ibid.

51 Ibid.; Asfour; also see http://www.fas.org/irp/world/para/mb.htm for an overview of the Muslim Brotherhood.

52 Bellamy.

53 'The New Powder Keg in the Middle East', *Nida'ul Islam* (October–November 1996).

54 'The Myth, the Reality: The Mission and Method of Osama bin Laden', *CNN*, online at http://www.cnn.com/CNN/Programs/people/shows/binladen/profile.html.

55 US, CIA (1996), 'Usama bin Laden: Islamic Extremist Financier', CIA assessment.

56 Michael Moran (1998), 'Bin Laden Comes Home to Roost', *MSNBC News* (24 August).

57 Ahmed Rashid (1999), 'The Taliban: Exporting Extremism', *Foreign Affairs*, 78/6 (November/December), 22–35.

58 Ruth Wedgewood (2002), 'Al Qaeda, Military Commissions, and American Self Defense', *Political Science Quarterly*, 117/3 (Fall), 357–72.

59 Jim Wooten (2002), 'Beyond bin laden: From Surgeon to Terrorist: The Second Most Wanted Man in the World', *ABC News* (2 October).

60 'Hunting bin Laden: Who is Osama bin Laden and What Does He Want?', *PBS Frontline*, online at http://www.pbs.org/wgbh/pages/frontline/shows/binladen/who/edicts.html (interview from April 1995).

61 Ibid.

62 'Full Text: bin Laden's "Letter to America"', *The Observer* (24 November 2002).

63 Michael Doran (2002), 'Somebody Else's Civil War', *Foreign Affairs*, 81/1 (January/February 2002), 22–42.

64 Michael Doran (2002), 'The Pragmatic Fanaticism of al Qaeda: An Anatomy of Extremism in Middle Eastern Politics', *Political Science Quarterly*, 117/2 (Summer), 177–90.

65 Osama bin Laden interview, *ABC News* (23 December 1998).

66 See US, Department of State, Office of Counterterrorism (2002), *Patterns of Global Terrorism, 2001*, Washington, DC: GPO (May).

67 Deobandism is closely linked with the conservative Wahhabi creed of the Saudi Royal family and therefore, the madrassas received significant financial support from the Saudis during the Soviet occupation.

68 John Echeverri-Gent (2001), 'Pakistan and the Taliban', *Miller Center Report*, 17/4 (Fall), 26–30, reprinted in Fredrik Logevall, ed. (2002), *Terrorism and 9/11: A Reader*, Boston: Houghton Mifflin Company, 107.

69 Ahmed Rashid (2001), 'Afghanistan: Ending the Policy Quagmire', *Journal of International Affairs*, 54/2 (Spring), 398.

70 Rashid, 'The Taliban: Exporting Extremism', 24.

71 During the Afghan insurgency, bin Laden primarily served as a supply coordinator where he raised funds for the mujahideen and oversaw supply efforts, tunneling and road construction operations. He did fight in several battles and was wounded during the siege of Jalalabad.

72 Zalmay Khalilzad and Daniel Byman (2000), 'Afghanistan: The Consolidation of a Rogue State', *The Washington Quarterly*, 32/1 (Winter), 72.

73 Rashid, 'Afghanistan: Ending the Policy Quagmire', 399.

74 For a more extensive overview of the ties between bin Laden and the Taliban, see Ahmed Rashid (2000), *Taliban: Militant Islam, Oil and Fundamentalism in Central Asia*, New Haven: Yale University Press.

75 Sumit Ganguly (2000), 'Pakistan's Never-Ending Story: Why the October Coup Was No Surprise', *Foreign Affairs*, 79/2 (March/April), 4.

76 Rashid, *Taliban*, 60.

77 US, White House (1998), *Combating Terrorism: Presidential Decision Directive 62*, Fact Sheet (22 May); US, White House (2001), *Press Briefing by Jake Siewart* (5 January).

78 M.J. Gohari (2000), *The Taliban: Ascent to Power*, London: Oxford University Press, 141.

79 For an overview of administration reaction to the *Cole* attack, see US, Department of Defense (2001), *USS Cole Commission Report* (9 January).

80 Albright and National Security Advisor Sandy Berger specifically advocated for the use of special operations forces to kill or capture bin Laden.

81 In 1998, Clinton signed three Memoranda of Notification to allow the military to specifically target bin Laden, including shooting down civilian aircraft if bin Laden or his top aides were aboard. In addition, after the 20 August 1998 missile attack on bin Laden's camp in Afghanistan, Clinton authorized three new attacks, but intelligence problems prevented verification of bin Laden's whereabouts. Meanwhile, arrangements with the government of Benizar Bhutto of Pakistan for the capture of bin Laden through CIA operations fell apart after the prime minister was toppled in a military coup; Barton Gellman (2001), 'Broad Effort Launched After '98 Attacks', *Washington Post* (19 December), A1.

Chapter 2

The Fight Against Terrorism in Historical Context: George W. Bush and the Development of Presidential Foreign Policy Regimes

Neal Allen

Introduction

President George W. Bush has responded to the events of 11 September by setting new priorities in foreign policy, and attempting to increase presidential power within the American political system. This response to crisis parallels previous changes in how America responds to the world, and how it formulates that response at home. The president is articulating a new set of national commitments that have the potential of altering both the content of American foreign policy and the institutional arrangement and capacity of American government. This essay puts these new commitments in the historical context of presidential foreign policymaking, elaborating the connections between Bush's attempts to set lasting national goals, and that of other similarly situated presidents. The War on Terror, and the institutional change it has set in motion, may result in a significant transformation of the presidency, and the American political system more generally.

In addition, this essay provides an assessment of the possible historical significance of the Bush War on Terror at the midpoint of his term in office. While any such first appraisal is tentative, historical comparison helps to identify the post-11 September developments that could have long-term importance. I link Bush to the history of presidents and foreign policymaking through a theory of presidential foreign policy regimes, defined as the commitments, constraints and capabilities crafted by creative presidents. My proposed regime structure takes much from the cyclical model Stephen Skowronek outlines in *The Politics Presidents Make*, but I outline a separate foreign policy regime cycle, existing alongside the domestic regime cycle Skowronek identifies. The foreign policy cycle is not directly tied to partisan affiliation, and has two regimes: the McKinley/Theodore Roosevelt regime establishing a substantial but limited American colonial commitment, and the Cold War regime crafted by Franklin Roosevelt and Harry Truman.

Since 11 September George W. Bush has begun to construct a new presidential foreign policy regime, setting new commitments for American overseas involvement. He is creating institutions to support his new regime commitments, and attempting to further increase the power of the president over national policy. I first set out my theory and historical analysis, and then discuss Bush as a possible regime-creating president in the area of foreign policy.

A Theory of Presidential Foreign Policy Regimes

If George W. Bush is successful in altering the long-term commitments and institutional structure of American politics, his war on terrorism will become the third presidentially created foreign policy regime, becoming part of a cyclical pattern going back over a century. The connections between Bush and previous transformative presidents can be understood through a punctuated equilibrium model. Stephen Skowronek puts forth such a model for the presidency in *The Politics Presidents Make*,[1] placing the president at the core of the process of regime construction and breakdown. He argues that certain presidents, like Andrew Jackson and Franklin Roosevelt, create a set of policy directions and institutional arrangements that endures as a stable equilibrium until the next transformative president is elected.

An extension of Skowronek's basic argument to foreign policy yields a different kind of regime cycle. Taking a regime to be a set of commitments that motivate and constrain politics and political behavior, a survey of presidents from McKinley forward yields a regime analysis of the presidency similar in many respects to Skowronek's, but following a different track through the twentieth century, and having different core characteristics. While Skowronek argues that Thomas Jefferson formed the first regime, and successor commitment structures were constructed by Jackson, Lincoln, FDR and Reagan, I argue that the foreign policy regime process did not begin until the 1890s, and only two regimes have motivated American foreign policy since then. The McKinley-Theodore Roosevelt regime of limited international engagement and economic expansionism, and its successor, the Franklin Roosevelt-Truman Cold War regime, originated and were maintained under different conditions and in different ways than concurrent domestic regimes.

A presidentially created foreign policy regime is not tied to a specific political party, unlike Skowronek's domestic policy regimes. Successors to regime-creating presidents adhere to his commitments and institutional arrangements, regardless of party. Truman was instrumental in creating the Cold War regime, and his Democratic and Republican successors continued his policy of opposition to international communism. If Bush is successful in creating an anti-terrorism regime, future Republican and Democratic presidents will adhere to the policies and institutional arrangements he established in response to 11 September. The foreign policy regime cycle also differs from the domestic cycle because in foreign policy presidents have more flexibility to craft policy, and are less restrained by partisan arrangements. Aaron Wildavsky maintained in his classic essay 'The Two Presidencies'[2] that presidential-congressional relations were of a different kind in foreign policy than domestic policy, with the president more powerful in foreign policy. I find a similar difference in the creation of regime commitments.

The two core components of any cycle of regimes are conflict and creative power. A change of regime occurs when a conflict arises which cannot be resolved within the current set of received political commitments, and an actor or group of actors in the political system is able to create a new regime structure which is able to resolve the conflict and set politics on new foundations. This particular kind of regime creation sequence is not unique to Skowronek's analysis; it forms the core of other theories that view American politics as a punctuated equilibrium system. In analyzing electoral politics, Walter Dean Burnham[3] argues that realigning elections occur when a particular conflict is not resolvable within the existing party system, and an activated electorate establishes a new equilibrium with the parties on different footing than before. Bruce Ackerman applies a punctuated equilibrium analysis to constitutional politics, claiming that constitutional change occurred during the Founding, Reconstruction and New Deal because the existing constitutional arrangements were inadequate to resolve the conflicts of contemporary politics.[4]

Presidential foreign policy making also functions according to a punctuated equilibrium model, but in a markedly different manner. The divergence between domestic and foreign policy regimes in American politics occurs because of the differing nature of conflict and the different set of resources possessed by the president in each case. Scholars like Burnham, Ackerman and Skowronek show that in domestic politics, conflict arises within the domestic political system and is resolved through the transformation of that system. But in foreign policy, the chief opposition to the president comes from outside American politics, and his resources are much greater owing to the nature of foreign policy-making and the lack of institutional constraints he faces.

This outward orientation in foreign policy enhances the president's symbolic role as representative of the American nation-state. The head of state function is more prominent than in domestic politics. Instead of acting as head of government, negotiating with Congress and other domestic political actors over the content of public policy, the president is representing America and American values to the world. The symbolic and rhetorical resources that come from this patriotic, outward-oriented part of the presidential role support the president's greater capacity to create governing regimes in foreign policy. George W. Bush has drawn on the head of state role to recast himself as the personification of the war against terror. The mass and elite support he has gained from this role transformation has been used to create a conception of terrorism and how it should be opposed, secure victories in Congressional elections for his party, and expand the institutional power of the presidency. If these changes endure, he will have created a regime along the lines of the two previous presidentially created foreign policy regimes.

The McKinley/Roosevelt Regime

The presidency of William McKinley is the starting point of the cycle of presidential foreign policy regimes because it marks the first time since the end of the wars with Great Britain that the United States committed itself to sustained involvement in international affairs. American foreign policy commitments in the nineteenth century, when they existed, were to protect the nation from European domination and gain additional contiguous territory for the United States. The transformation in American foreign policy that started with the Spanish-American War constituted the first national commitment to sustained foreign involvement. Begun and principally accomplished under McKinley and completed and solidified under Theodore Roosevelt, the new regime carried with it both substantive and institutional changes. The construction of this first regime established commitments of greater internationalism and enhanced presidential power that would last until the next transformation in the 1940s.

William McKinley's mandate for presidential leadership came about from the intersection of the growth of American economic power and the opportunities available for American expansion, both politically and economically. Under his leadership, and that of his successor, the United States became a player in international colonial politics, and became a staunch supporter of American economic interests overseas. Both strands of the new presidential foreign policy regime had roots in earlier eras: the United States had taken on colonial responsibilities in Alaska and Hawaii over the previous decades, and had exerted influence on politics in Latin America. Promotion of the interests of American business interests oversees goes back at least to Jefferson's conflict with the Barbary pirates. But the McKinley/Roosevelt regime systematized and extended these commitments, expanding the power and authority of the presidency in the process. By the end of Roosevelt's term in office, according to Fareed Zakaria in *From Wealth to Power*, even though he exercised power of foreign policy previously considered congressional, 'the expectations of congressional and presidential behavior had changed so much that Roosevelt's relationship with Congress, like McKinley's was generally cordial and productive'.[5]

In the context of system-wide commitments, the actions against Spain stand not just as the entry of the United States into the international colonial system. The forcible acquisition of current colonies like Puerto Rico in the Caribbean and Guam in the South Pacific, along with controlling influence in Cuba and the Philippines, is the military manifestation of what Emily Rosenberg refers to as 'the promotional state'. In *Spreading the American Dream*, she identifies five components of the promotional state, deriving from 'liberal-developmentalist' ideology:

> (1) Belief that other nations could and should replicate America's own developmental experience; (2) faith in private free enterprise; (3) support for free or open access for trade and investment; (4) promotion of free flow of information and culture; and (5) growing acceptance of governmental activity to protect private enterprise and to stimulate and regulate American participation in international and cultural exchange.[6]

America under McKinley, according to Zakaria, took 'the most dramatic extension of its interests abroad since the annexation of Texas'.[7] By fully committing the United States to systematic involvement abroad, McKinley constructed the first presidential foreign policy regime. In order to forge such commitments, he and Theodore Roosevelt expanded the power and authority of the presidency. In their drive to carve out a substantive leadership role for themselves in the fractured American political system, presidents find new ways of gaining and using power.

In the case of William McKinley and Theodore Roosevelt, this expansion of presidential power took two forms. First, they used the commander-in-chief power in ways not seen since the Civil War, and never seen in previous American history except when hostile forces occupied American soil. Responding to calls for the United States to come to the defense of Cuba and other Spanish colonies, McKinley committed American forces to actions in two hemispheres, gaining Congressional approval for his decisions.[8] Roosevelt later followed McKinley's lead by using troops in Latin America and exhibiting the new American navy around the world.

A related development was McKinley and Roosevelt's practice of making fundamental American foreign policy commitments without the specific congressional approval needed in previous eras. Not only in the case of the Spanish-American War, but also in China and throughout the Western Hemisphere the two regime-creating presidents set the form of American international policy. A case in point is Theodore Roosevelt's direct defiance of previous deferential norms governing president-Congress relations with respect to acquiring the territory needed for the Panama Canal: 'If I had followed the general consultative method I should have submitted an admirable state paper, occupying a couple of hundred pages detailing the facts to Congress and asking Congress consideration of it … I took the Canal Zone and let Congress debate, and while the debate goes on the Canal does too.' Roosevelt's own characterization of his action concerning the canal shows an intentional expansion of presidential capacity in furtherance of new policy goals.

The McKinley/Roosevelt regime, consisting of substantial but limited international involvement and promotion of American international interests, was the dominant idea in American foreign policy until the onset of the Second World War. Its most important test was Woodrow Wilson's attempt to take the United States into the League of Nations, which foundered in the Senate. In his failure, Wilson showed the limits of the presidential foreign policy regime, demonstrating that the regime was not reconcilable with international obligations outside narrow conceptions of imperialism and economic promotion. This first foreign policy regime would continue in its limited form through the more isolationist years of Republican rule, until the Second World War and Franklin Roosevelt would create the conditions necessary for regime change.

The Roosevelt/Truman Regime

The best parallel to the Bush anti-terrorism regime is the Cold War regime created by Franklin Roosevelt and Harry Truman. After World War II ended Truman was confronted by a communist adversary fundamentally opposed to the values and existence of the United States of America, just as Bush confronts an international terror network whose mission is to remake the world in a way antithetical to American and Western values. Truman drew on the public role and institutional resources built up by his predecessor to craft a foreign policy regime to oppose Soviet expansionism. The new regime had as its component parts all of the familiar parts of Cold War policy. Soviet expansionism was to be opposed in all conceivable forms, in all places across the world. The idea of containment, which defined the primary aim of United States foreign policy as the limitation of the spread of communism, became the motivating ideology.[9] A key step in the move toward containment was the later-famous telegram by George Kennan, American diplomat in Moscow, which crystallized in the minds of American government officials the image of the Soviet Union as a threat to national security.[10]

While the Cold War regime would have been an impossibility without the consensus among political elites and masses supporting it in the post-war years, Harry Truman's decisions and actions were vital in forming and solidifying the commitments that would define American foreign policy for the next four-and-a-half decades. Truman inherited a system left in flux by the end of the war and ambiguous agreements and understandings between Roosevelt and Stalin. By creating, with the Western European powers, the North Atlantic Treaty Organization, setting a precedent for action motivated by the domino theory by aiding Greece and Turkey to contain communism in the Balkans, and finally by committing the American troops to the defense of South Korea, Truman set American priorities in foreign relations. He supplemented these substantive actions with groundbreaking reorganization of the executive national security apparatus. In

1947 Congress granted Truman's request to combine the War and Navy departments, set up the National Security Council, and convert the nascent foreign intelligence-gathering apparatus into the Central Intelligence Agency. These reforms enlarged the resources available to Truman and his successors in their waging of the continuing conflict with the Soviet Union.[11]

After Truman, all American presidents until George H.W. Bush governed under the Cold War regime in foreign policy, with its motivations and limitations. Presidential election contests were increasingly marked by agreement over US foreign policy goals, with the Kennedy – Nixon race particularly notable for the consonance of candidate positions, with both Democrat and Republican firmly within the Cold War consensus. While Cold War commitments usually ran parallel to and supported the New Deal regime in domestic politics, Johnson's presidency stands as an example of what can happen when a president's domestic and foreign policy commitments come into conflict. Johnson's attempt to extend the social democratic ideals he inherited from the regime-builder FDR ran aground as his adherence to the Cold War regime drove him toward increasing personal and fiscal commitment to the war in Vietnam.

While post-Vietnam policy marked an easing of tensions with the Soviet Union, and Reagan's rhetoric and arms buildup evidenced an increase in combativeness, presidential Cold War politics always took place within the bounds established by the Truman Doctrine in the 1940s. According to LaFeber in *The American Age*:

> From Truman to Ronald Reagan, presidents repeatedly revived the Truman Doctrine's specific words to justify their polices in such places as Lebanon, Southeast Asia, and Central America. As Senator J. William Fulbright wrote in the 1970s, 'More by far than any other factor the anti-communism of the Truman Doctrine had been the guiding spirit of American foreign policy since World War II.'[12]

While Franklin Roosevelt may have bequeathed to Harry Truman a fluid, uncertain international situation, he left his successor with a strong precedent for easier presidential decision-making in international affairs. As Bruce Ackerman and David Golove have shown in *Is NAFTA Constitutional?*,[13] FDR and Truman recast the constitutional arrangements governing foreign policy formation in their successful attempt to transform American commitments after World War II. Overturning the precedent of the Senate's rejection of the League of Nations during Wilson's presidency, FDR used the executive-legislative agreement to gain approval for a variety of measures defining post-war American commitments in foreign relations, culminating in the approval of membership in the World Bank and International Monetary Fund with the ratification of the Bretton Woods agreement in 1945.[14] The vital difference between treaties and executive-legislative agreements is that treaties require a two-thirds vote of the Senate, while executive-legislative agreements only require a majority of both houses. The latter device frees the president from the difficulty of gaining 68 votes in the Senate, thus allowing results like the passage of the North American Free Trade Agreement in 1993 by a vote of 61 to 38. Ackerman argues this change in constitutional process came about through FDR's 'piecemeal presidentialism'. By gaining approval for international commitments of increasing importance, 'each time the Administration convinced a majority of the Senate to join the House in support of an executive agreement, it created a new precedent for further expansion'.[15]

The Cold War regime continued through Republican and Democratic administrations until the collapse of communism eliminated its reason for existence. Neither George H.W. Bush's New World Order or Bill Clinton's limited humanitarian intervention rose to the level of regime commitments. The institutional capacities created to fight Soviet communism remained, however, and have been revitalized and expanded by George W. Bush in his response to terrorist threats.

George W. Bush and the Creation of an Anti-terrorism Regime

Before 11 September, George W. Bush continued the case-by-case foreign policy of his two immediate predecessors. He retained most Clinton Administration international commitments, with the exception of a withdrawal from direct intervention in the Middle East peace process. Bush began to move American foreign policy to a more unilateralist position, withdrawing from the Kyoto global warming talks and abrogating the Anti-Ballistic Missile treaty with Russia, but created no new alliances, institutional structures or commitments. The attack of 11 September broke this continuity, and began a creative process led by the presidency. The attacks on New York and Washington certainly transformed American foreign policy, but transformation does not necessarily constitute a new regime in American foreign policy, or a presidentially created one. It is of course too early to judge the lasting significance of Bush's War on Terror, but it fits the pattern of a presidentially created foreign policy regime. The months after 11 September witnessed a transformation of American foreign policy commitments, and an expansion of presidential capacity to set those commitments and carry out policy. This transformation was certainly precipitated by the exogenous shock of the 11 September attacks, but President Bush has been the dominant actor in responding to that crisis with new substantive commitments and institutional changes.

At least for the time being, the War on Terror has reoriented most American foreign policy commitments, much as the Cold War did in the post-war period. Bush has outlined a policy of opposing terrorism with military force everywhere it exists, and also taking military action against foreign governments that harbor and support terrorists. This commitment, called for the time being the Bush Doctrine, also includes the assassination of terrorist and foreign leaders implicated in terrorism against Americans. This new commitment quickly came to fruition with the war in Afghanistan, an operation pursued under a broad grant of authority by Congress to the president, and at a time and place chosen in the White House, not the Congress.

The Bush Doctrine is much like the Truman Doctrine, pledging the United States to act anyplace in the globe to combat a particular enemy. What separates these regime-level commitments from less lasting ones is the broad, amorphous definition of the enemy. Terrorism, like communism, can stretch to include a variety of groups, movements and social phenomena. Also al-Qaeda terrorism, like Soviet expansionism, is avowedly opposed to American interests and values, and directed at international expansion. Thus the Bush and Truman Doctrines differ from regional commitments like the Monroe Doctrine and its imperial extension by McKinley and Roosevelt, and from commitments specific in time and place like the Gulf War and peacekeeping operations.

Many existing American operations have now been recast as anti-terrorism, and expanded to encompass the new priorities. The best example is Columbia, in which our support for the government in its civil war against the narcotic-financed rebels has morphed into a fight against terrorists opposed to American interests abroad. Bush is also moving the United States into conflicts that previously were not on the agenda for American involvement, like the ongoing Russian campaign against the Chechnyan rebels operating out of Georgia.

Bush has elaborated the necessarily ambiguous concept of the war on terrorism through a substantive expansion of the new regime commitments beyond fighting terrorism narrowly defined. In his 2002 State of the Union address, Bush called Iraq, Iran and North Korea the 'Axis of Evil', because of their attempts to acquire and develop nuclear, chemical and biological weapons. This shift in rhetoric, along with the move against Iraq, could mark another significant departure from previous American policy if it carries with it a commitment to act against such states outside of international organizations. The Administration's recent national security strategy document at least on paper commits the United States to multilateral and unilateral preemptive attack upon threatening nations. A move from containment to preemption could in the long term be as significant as the Cold War shift from cooperation with the Soviets to containment.

Also like the Cold War regime, the nascent anti-terrorism regime extends foreign policy priorities into the domestic arena. The war on terrorism has immigration, public health, and local law enforcement connections. The new set of commitments, while sparked by the threat of international terrorism, has become a public safety regime as well. The institutional manifestation of this new public safety regime is the recently created Department of Homeland Security, an aggregation of agencies from the Coast Guard to the Secret Service to Aviation Security. This recent development is exactly the kind of institutional change that regime-creating presidents bring about, with the executive now possessing enhanced powers over personnel and funding of the new department. When presidents create foreign policy regimes, they gain new powers and means of setting policy.

A particularly controversial expansion of presidential authority has been the proposed creation of military tribunals within the Defense Department to try foreign terrorism suspects, along with the detention of citizens as unlawful combatants without constitutional protection. By superseding the congressionally-created civilian justice system, which in the past has tried terrorism suspects like the first World Trade Center attackers, Bush has expanded the reach of the presidency in foreign affairs to pursue the new priorities he has set. Bush has also expanded American public relations efforts abroad, and proposed sending thousands of Americans abroad as part of a new 'USA Freedom Corps'. The federalization of aviation security, with its attendant bureaucracy, is another result of the extension of foreign policy priorities into domestic affairs.

The 11 September attacks are often compared to the Japanese attack on Pearl Harbor, because both attacks caused enormous numbers of casualties and led the United States into war. But the war on terrorism does not have a foreseeable endpoint like the German and Japanese surrenders. Bush is thus best understood in comparison to presidents that led the nation into long-term foreign commitments. With the overthrow of the Taliban government in Afghanistan, the War on Terror has changed quickly from a traditional war with a foreign state to a long-term commitment to expansive foreign policy goals. Here new commitments to resist terrorism are similar to the commitment to limited colonialism of McKinley and Theodore Roosevelt, and to the Cold War regime of FDR and Truman. Comparison between the Bush Administration and these regime-creating predecessors yields three tests of the existence of a stable presidentially created foreign policy regime. A war with Iraq speaks to all three of these tests.

First, the substantive commitments of the regime-creating president must become a bipartisan consensus, with later presidents of the opposing party as adherents to the regime. The Democrat Woodrow Wilson continued the colonial involvement of his Republican predecessors, and Republicans Eisenhower, Nixon, Reagan and Bush founded their administrations on Cold War commitments. If a new regime has been established after 11 September, a core component of it is the 'Bush Doctrine', a commitment to treat a foreign government that sponsors terrorism as an enemy that must be destroyed. In recent months this doctrine has been extended to include countries like Iraq that could potentially provide chemical, biological and nuclear weapons to terrorists.

For a presidential foreign policy regime to exist, elected officials across parties and institutions must also accept the conceptual framework that underlies regime commitments. Thus it is clear in retrospect that Truman created a Cold War regime because his contemporaries and predecessors in Washington accepted his conceptualization of international communism as Soviet expansionism, and that Soviet expansionism must be opposed in all its forms. Future developments in American policy toward Iraq will demonstrate how much latitude other political actors give President Bush in defining the necessarily ambiguous concept of terrorism. It is one thing for Democrats in Congress to support war against an Afghanistan that harbored and supported terrorist organizations that attacked the United States, and another for them to support war with Iraq because of the possibility that it might acquire and distribute weapons of mass destruction.

Second, the regime must support large-scale military actions, like the occupations of the Philippines in the first part of the twentieth century, and the Korean War. Iraq is the anti-terrorism counterpart to Korea. It would mark a shift and expansion of the regime commitments, with the United States intervening abroad against a nation that has not yet attacked America. Also a war against Iraq will test how transferable the broadened anti-terrorism regime is to other nations and international organizations. Like Korea, the manner in which the United States ends such a war will set a precedent for future US-led construction of governing arrangements for another country.

Third, the new institutional arrangements the president has crafted to meet new challenges must remain after the initial crisis period. Here worth watching is the success of Bush's aggregation of power to the executive branch with his treatment of accused terrorists and terrorist accomplices, and his creation of a Homeland Security Department. In the two previous presidential creations of foreign policy regimes, presidents seized new authority to act abroad, with Theodore Roosevelt seizing the Panama Canal, and Truman committing America to the opposition of Communists in Greece. The next few months of debate and policy on Iraq also will partially demonstrate whether Bush has brought about a similar extension of presidential power, and a new presidential foreign policy regime.

If Bush succeeds in transforming American foreign policy and governmental structure in response to terrorism, he will reinvigorate the presidency as the dominant order-creating actor in the political system. In an era where political parties lack the mass connections to stimulate domestic regime construction, foreign policy remains an issue area susceptible to the creative leadership of the president. But it is worth noting the regime-creating success in foreign policy does not always carry with it domestic and electoral success. Harry Truman set the commitments and institutional arrangements that would define American politics for over 50 years, but had mixed success at the polls. His election in 1948 was much like Bush's 2000 victory, with support drawn mainly from his party's core supporters. His second term fell victim to the needs of the regime he created, with the Republicans gaining support from Cold War ideology after the communist takeover of China. To avoid a similar fate, George W. Bush must skillfully confront the challenges posed by the conceptual and institutional structure he has crafted in response to 11 September and the long-term terrorist threat.

Notes

I would like to thank Peter Trubowitz, Bartholomew Sparrow and Peter Jenkins for comments on earlier drafts of this paper.

1   Stephen Skowronek (1997), *The Politics Presidents Make: Leadership from John Adams to Bill Clinton*, Cambridge, MA: Belknap Press.
2   Aaron Wildavsky (1975), 'The Two Presidencies', in Aaron Wildavsky, ed., *Perspectives on the Presidency*, Boston: Little, Brown and Co.
3   See Walter Dean Burnham (1970), *Critical Elections and the Mainsprings of American Politics*, New York: W.W. Norton.
4   See Bruce Ackerman (1991), *We the People: Foundations*, Cambridge, MA: Belknap Press and Ackerman (1998), *We the People: Transformations*, Cambridge, MA: Belknap Press.
5   Fareed Zakaria (1998), *From Wealth to Power*, Princeton: Princeton University Press, 174.
6   Emily S. Rosenberg (1982), *Spreading the American Dream: American Economic and Cultural Expansion*, New York: Hill and Wang.
7   Zakaria, 163.
8   Ibid., 158–60.
9   Bartholomew H. Sparrow (1995), 'The Presidency and the World: Adjusting to the Post-Cold War Era', in Michael Nelson, ed., *The Presidency and the Political System*, 4th edn, Washington, DC: Congressional Quarterly Press, 557.
10   Walter LaFeber (1995), *The American Age: US Foreign Policy At Home and Abroad*, vol. 2, New York: W.W. Norton, 449–52.
11   Ibid., 458–9.
12   Ibid., 455; quote from J. Fulbright (1972), *The Crippled Giant*, New York: Random House, 6–24.
13   Bruce Ackerman and David Golove (1995), *Is NAFTA Constitutional?*, Cambridge, MA: Harvard University Press.
14   Ibid., 90–91.
15   Ibid., 93.

Chapter 3

Why Bush Should Explain 11 September

Kristin Andrews

Introduction

There were various initial reactions to the terrorist attacks of 11 September 2001, and among those reactions were some contradictions. There were those who demanded an explanation for the attacks, and others who condemned attempts to explain as immoral or unpatriotic. Though President George W. Bush did make some rhetorical remarks that, I believe, masqueraded as explanatory, it appears that he agrees with the latter set.

The arguments against generating explanations are based on moral considerations. Those who are critical of explaining 11 September defend their position by pointing to the depraved character of those who offer explanations, or by declaring that it is unfair to criticize a victim. The tone of the discussion is explicitly moral. However, upon close examination we shall see that these moral arguments against explaining the terrorist attacks do not hold up, and that there are, in fact, no moral barriers to offering an explanation. In addition, there are good pragmatic reasons for explaining the terrorist attacks. Given a president's moral obligation to protect US citizens from outside forces, it turns out that President Bush, contrary to his current position, is morally obligated to seek an explanation for the attacks.

Looking toward the remarks Bush made in the days following the terrorist attacks, I believe he chose not to provide the country with the explanation many were asking for. The rhetorical remarks he did make, such as 'America was targeted for attack because we're the brightest beacon for freedom and opportunity in the world'[1] were not explanatory, as we will soon see. Rather, his statements suggested that the acts of terror were unimaginably evil, and since unimaginable, they must be inexplicable as well. Instead of answering people's why-questions, Bush chose to answer how-questions: 'Americans are asking, why do they hate us? They hate what we see right here in this chamber – a democratically elected government. Their leaders are self-appointed. They hate our freedoms – our freedom of religion, our freedom of speech, our freedom to vote and assemble and disagree with each other.'[2] While many were looking for a reason that led people to feel such hatred of America and American freedoms, Bush only describes the nature of that hatred. An explanation of 11 September should tell us why the United States was the target of such horrific acts, and what drove people to choose a path of murder and suicide in the name of politics and religion.

Bush's statements, however, do not do that. His remarks are more like an assertion that the attacks are inexplicable than they are an attempt to explain why the United States was targeted. There is a temptation to respond to acts of horror by thinking that they are inexplicable, and this temptation was evident in Bush's remarks. These were events that could not be accounted for, and which most could never understand.

To be explanatory, Bush's remarks would have had to address the question, for example, of *why* the terrorists would choose to attack the United States rather than some other country with a democratically elected government, freedoms and so forth, and that is just the question his remarks lead me to ask next. Arguably, there are countries that are more democratic than the United States – or at least as democratic – and countries in which people have just as many freedoms. Bush's 'explanation' makes no attempt to answer the question 'Why us rather than them?' What is missing is the causal history that led to the attacks of 11 September.

This unwillingness to provide US citizens (and others around the world asking similar questions) with an explanation for the worst terrorist attack on American soil is not warranted. Whereas many have been taking the position that one ought not attempt to explain the acts of one's enemy, it will be argued here that there is an obligation to do just that. An explanation of the events leading up to 11 September will help to better understand terrorism, and will better assist Americans and the international community in reducing the levels of global terrorism. Discovering the causes of terrorism, and constructing an explanation that takes into account those causes will demonstrate where the causal chain can most easily be broken, and this is essential to avoiding future acts of terrorism. Without an understanding of where terrorism arises, America and the West will be doomed to fight a continuing battle, rather than achieving the decisive victory Bush claims as his goal.

To make this case, we shall first look at the critics' positions. Several closely related arguments against explaining the terrorist attacks have been suggested. Some worry that a search for the root causes of terrorism would result in feelings of sympathy for the perpetrators and an inclination to blame the victim. Others seem to think that if we understand the motivations of terrorists we will be driven to forgive, or worse, to justify terrorist activities.

Whereas the arguments behind these worries are not strong, there are good pragmatic arguments in support of finding an explanation for 11 September. Before we can examine these, some groundwork on the nature of explanations must be done.

Explanation

There is a large philosophical literature base dealing with explanation that can be traced back to the ancient Greeks. My analysis of Bush's need to explain 11 September benefits from more recent work done on the topics of scientific[3] and psychological[4] explanation.

Before looking at what an explanation is, it will help to see what it is *not*. First, it is clear that an adequate explanation for an act cannot just cite the actor's attitude. To claim that the United States was attacked simply 'because they hate us' is unenlightening. Of course *they* hate *us*; people who like *us* do not try to kill *our* citizens. Claims that the terrorists are monsters or madmen or animals also fail to explain. Even madmen typically have reasons for their actions. It makes sense to ask why John Hinckley, Jr tried to assassinate Reagan. The response is not just that he was insane, but also that he believed that by killing Reagan he could win the heart of Jody Foster, and he valued her love more than Reagan's life. This explanation provides an answer to the why-question.

When attempting to find an explanation for an agent's intentional actions, we are looking for a psychological explanation. Unlike scientific explanations, psychological ones require reference to an agent's belief states and desires. In addition, a psychological explanation usually refers to a relevant psychological law which causally relates beliefs and desires on the one hand, and behavior on the other.[5] Both beliefs and desires are necessary for a good explanation, because one without the other will not be sufficient for action. Suppose I believe that investing in a particular company would make me wealthy. Will I invest? Perhaps not; if I do not *want* to become wealthy, I will not act to become so. The particular beliefs I have allow me to satisfy the desires I have, and because I cannot satisfy a desire if I do not know how to do so, both beliefs and desires are a necessary part of an explanation of behavior.

Another feature of psychological explanation that philosophers point to is the requirement that such explanations 'make sense' of behavior.[6] A successful psychological explanation will make the action intelligible; we will be able to recognize the connection between the psychological state of the actor and his behavior. This idea is connected to the view that we are able to explain others' actions by engaging in a mental simulation of them. We use our own practical reasoning mechanisms in order to pretend, imagine, or simulate being the other person, and ask ourselves which sets of beliefs and desires would lead to the target behavior.[7]

If we accept that a psychological explanation must fulfill both these criteria, that it includes reference to a belief and a desire that together serve to make sense of the behavior to be explained, then it is clear that none of Bush's public remarks following the terrorist attacks came close to offering an explanation. His explanation for the attacks was limited to the attribution of fairly general beliefs to the terrorists: *they* believe that *we* have a democratically elected government, *they* believe that *we* have the freedom of religion, speech, and so on. And he identified an attitude the terrorists had toward these ideals, namely hatred. These beliefs and the attitude do not provide us with the desire, nor do they alone serve to make sense of the behavior. Without the necessary elements, we do not have an explanation. In his 20 September 2001 remarks, Bush did not provide an answer to the question 'Why do they hate us?' Rather, he chose to answer a different question: 'How do they hate us?'

To give an explanation of the events would be to determine what the terrorists hoped to achieve by their actions. What are their desires, and what are their beliefs? Though Bush said that the terrorists hoped to frighten us, this does not make sense of their behavior, either. Rather, that answer leads us directly to a new why-question: Why do they want to frighten us? Bush's comments beg asking this question because his purported explanation does not make sense of the behavior; he does not make the behavior intelligible to his listeners. When an answer to a why-question leads us immediately to ask another one, there is good reason to suspect that an explanation has not been proffered in the first instance.

Why Bush Should Not Explain 11 September

Though Bush's remarks after the attacks did not help to explain them, it could be argued that the White House had good reason to avoid offering an explanation. There are at least two types of reasons that could be given for the position that Bush ought not offer an explanation for the terrorist attacks. One harkens back to the position presented at the beginning of the chapter: there is no further explanation, so Bush *could not* provide an explanation.

This claim is not very plausible. Though it might be nice to think that we live in a world in which horrible events do not belong and so are without reason, it just is not so. That sort of thinking ignores a fundamental feature of the world, namely that every event has a cause. There does exist a causal explanation for the attacks, and because humans are involved in that cause, the explanation will refer to the beliefs and desires of those individuals, as immoral and as incorrect as those beliefs and desires may be.

The second concern is more credible. This is the moral argument that offering an explanation puts America in greater danger, and that we ought not offer an explanation because the consequences will be harmful or because it is unfair. There are different ways of defending this view, which, though related, deserve mention in turn.

Sympathy

Since providing an explanation for 11 September would require that the terrorists' beliefs and desires be taken into account, giving an explanation might be viewed as showing sympathy towards the terrorists. The current campaign would be weakened if one were to develop terrorist sympathies, and one's moral character would certainly be threatened. But does it follow that one must feel sympathy for people whose behavior one can explain?

Following 11 September some people tried to seek an explanation for the terrorists' hatred of the United States and their willingness to die for their beliefs. These attempts to understand were largely condemned by conservative media outlets. For example, consider the response to Susan Sontag's 24 September 2001 essay published in *The New Yorker*. Sontag criticized the mainstream media's lack of analysis of the attacks, and the refusal to acknowledge that American foreign policy with regard to Iraq might provide *part of* an explanation of the attacks. She wrote: 'A few shreds of historical awareness might help us understand what has just happened, and what may continue to happen.'[8] Specifically, she took exception to the claim that the terrorists were cowardly, suggesting: 'Where is the acknowledgment that this was not a "cowardly" attack on "civilization" or "liberty" or "humanity" or "the free world" but an attack on the world's self-proclaimed superpower, undertaken as a consequence of specific American alliances and actions?'[9]

In response to this essay, Sontag was portrayed as no better than a terrorist by right-wing publications. For example, the *New Republic* published an article beginning 'What do Osama bin Laden, Saddam Hussein and Susan Sontag have in common?'[10] And *Human Events Online* offered their condemnation as well, saying: 'As we move further away from the horrors of 11 September the liberal cries about "moral equivalence" — the idea that the United States shares the blame for the terrorist attacks — become more common and more explicit.'[11]

The implication is that Sontag was so sympathetic with the terrorists that she herself was no better than one. Why was she seen as sympathetic? Because she articulated the motivations behind the terrorists' immoral actions.

A moment of reflection will show that understanding someone's motivations does not necessitate a sympathetic response to that person. If we were to attempt to explain the terrorist attacks, one place to look would be toward Osama bin Laden's public statements. Though it is difficult to listen to his repeated condemnation of US culture, rights for women, and his rationalization for killing innocent civilians, his comments must be heard in order to formulate an explanation.[12] However, hearing bin Laden's diatribe would not generate sympathy for him in the West. It would take a heroic act of imagination to see bin Laden's point of view and fully develop an explanation for his actions.

Understanding someone's motivations does not require being sympathetic to those goals. In fact, most cases in which people attempt to explain immoral actions are not taken to be showing sympathy for the perpetrator. Sociologists, surely, should not be accused of endorsing murder, truancy, or drug abuse when they offer explanations of these activities. When a documentary filmmaker recreates the causes of horrific actions by explaining to the audience the motivations of the perpetrator, we do not respond with feelings of outrage. Nor do we accuse the filmmaker of immoral sympathies. Just as we can explain the causes of thunderstorms and landslides without having a normative attitude toward them, we can also explain the actions of terrorists without feeling the slightest bit of sympathy.

Blaming the Victim

If part of the explanation for 11 September includes a description of current states of affairs, living conditions around the world, and aspects of US foreign policy, perhaps there is a worry that offering an explanation that included these facts would amount to a condemnation of the United States. Some seem to think that identifying US foreign policy as part of the explanation for the terrorist attacks amounts to blaming the victim.

One need only look toward the response to recent activities on university campuses around the nation to see the controversy that rose from frankly discussing the possibility that the terrorists were motivated by US foreign policy. According to the Defense of Civilization Fund's report *Defending Civilization: How Our Universities are Failing America and What Can Be Done About It*:

> Polls across the country, coupled with statements from public officials and citizens, have been remarkably uniform in their condemnation of the terrorist attacks … . In contrast has been reaction from the Ivory Tower. While there are no doubt numerous exceptions, a vast number of colleges and universities – public and private, small and large, from all parts of the country – have sponsored teach-ins and other meetings which have been distinctly equivocal and often blaming America itself.[13]

What is interesting about this document is the lack of discrimination shown in choosing the examples. Sixteen pages of quotes, references to teach-ins, and administrative decisions are given in order to demonstrate the dangers that exist within US universities.

Most of these cases involve looking at US foreign policy for a cause of the terrorist attacks, and working from that assumption in an attempt to determine what to do next.

Here are just two examples from the report:

> Professor of art, University of North Carolina-Chapel Hill, shows a slide show of her artwork, 'Places the United States has Bombed' at a teach-in entitled: 'What is war? What is peace?'[14]

> We should 'build bridges and relationships, not simply bombs and walls.' Speaker at Harvard Law School.[15]

The authors of the report make no distinction between those faculty members who sponsor teach-ins on US foreign policy and those who say they were cheering when the Pentagon was attacked. All are portrayed as enemies of civilization who claim that the United States is complicit. The claim is that university professors and students are determined to blame the United States for the terrorist attacks.

To blame a victim is to claim that he engaged in some behavior that not only caused him to be the subject of violence, but also that his behavior was itself unjustified or immoral. The idea is that the victim could have avoided the attack were he to take certain precautions, and that he *ought* to have taken those precautions. It was once fairly usual to hear a woman's rape being blamed on her style of dress or behavior. The victim was blamed for wearing the short skirt, or acting 'flirtatiously'. Today such claims would be soundly (and rightfully) criticized by those who point out that *even if* the woman's short skirt caught the eye of a rapist, women are under no moral obligation to avoid dressing in a particular way. Though the short skirt may have been relevant to the subsequent rape, and played a role in the causal chain leading up to it, if the woman were raped on the way to work, her decision to work also played a role in the causal chain. No enlightened person ever suggested seriously that women should be blamed for their rape because they chose to leave their house and go to work, because women *ought* to be free to leave their houses, even though if all women stayed locked away the number of rapes would presumably drop.

The line of reasoning that leads one to conclude that we ought not try to explain acts of terror is based on a confusion of these issues. The argument seems to go along these lines:

1   to explain the terrorist attacks is in part to identify the role played by US foreign policy;
2   any act leading to an immoral act shares the blame;
3   therefore, to explain the terrorist attacks is to blame the United States.

Assuming the truth of premise (1), this argument fails at premise (2). Just as society did not blame Jody Foster for the assassination attempt on Reagan, even though her decision to act in *Taxi Driver* was part of the causal chain that led to Hinckley's crime, society need not blame the United States for the terrorist attacks just because US foreign policy was part of the causal chain leading to 11 September. If we were right to withhold blame in the Foster/Hinckley case, then premise (2) is false, because we need only one counterexample to falsify a universal claim.

Though the above argument is clearly unsound, it is still widely accepted. However difficult it may be, it is important to distinguish between identifying US policy as playing a role in the attacks and blaming the US policy for the attacks. There is a huge difference between saying 'the chickens have come home to roost' and that US foreign policy was part of the cause for the terrorist attacks. What is the difference? The later purports to be a factual claim that is purely descriptive, and the former is normative. In order to get from a description of events to claims about moral equivalence or complicity, an evaluative premise is needed to connect the facts to the values.

Not all causes of immoral acts are themselves wrong. Jody Foster is not responsible, because there is no way she could have predicted that a bizarre act would be the result of taking the role, and so far as I know she violated no moral principles in doing so. Thus, if the United States is identified as part of the explanation for the terrorist attacks, nothing follows from that about whether those US policies are immoral. Whether the United States should be deemed culpable for its foreign policy is a completely different issue, and should be evaluated separately from the purely descriptive explanation that would include reference to past and present US policy.

The view that we ought not to explain the terrorist attacks, because an explanation of those attacks would be akin to blaming the victim is completely misguided. The United States would only be open to moral suspicion if those acts that entered into the causal chain leading to 11 September are independently morally questionable. So, it may be that there is a danger in explaining 11 September because the White House is afraid of its policies abroad coming under scrutiny, because the administration believes its actions are morally questionable, or seen as morally questionable by others. This worry could lead to the denial that US foreign policy has any role to play in setting the scene.

Explanation and Justification

The general problem seems to come from the widespread difficulty we have distinguishing between an explanation and a justification. Articles offering an explanation of the terrorist attacks based on US support of Israel, its stationing of troops in Saudi Arabia, or the US support of UN sanctions against Iraq were seen by many as tantamount to an endorsement of the attacks. This concern may have been on India's External Affairs Minister Yashwant Sinha's mind when he said: 'India's view is that when you are fighting a war against terrorism, one should not weaken the cause by trying to get into the root causes or the underlying causes of terrorism.'[16]

Even if the critics are right and US policy in these areas is immoral, an explanation citing these policies and describing their immorality would not justify the terrorist attacks. In order argue that the attacks were morally justifiable, one would have to make an additional argument to the effect that the attacks were a just response to immoral US foreign policy, and there is no plausible way of defending that claim.

In other cases we can easily explain an event by citing the causes and mental states that led up to it without condoning those causes and mental states. For example, critics of capital punishment can explain why a criminal was executed by citing as part of the explanation the criminal's own wrong-doing and the laws of the state. This explanation does not amount to an endorsement of capital punishment laws, nor does it serve to undermine the arguments they might have against the death penalty.

The terms 'explanation' and 'justification' are often used interchangeably in common parlance; indeed, some dictionaries define one in terms of the other. However, the sense of explanation with which we are concerned here is quite different from a justification. Before looking at the differences between the two, it is important to note that there are structural similarities between them, which may help account for the confusion. A justification, like an explanation, can include reference to one's belief and desire. I may justify my speeding to a police officer by saying that I believe my friend is about to give birth, and I want to get her to the hospital. This is an explanation for my speeding, but it becomes a justification given the unstated value claim also being asserted. That premise is that getting someone to the hospital in time for her to give birth is more valuable than driving at a legal speed. In casual conversation our arguments are often enthymematic; we tend to leave out the key premise in an informal argument, especially when that premise is widely accepted. Because the police officer probably also believes that there are cases in which it is acceptable to break traffic laws (and this is one of them) there is no need for me to make explicit the value premise of the argument. Whereas an explanation for an act merely refers to the scientific laws, states of affairs, and beliefs and desires behind someone's action, a justification is given to defend those desires, and to support the truth of the beliefs. The reason to provide a justification for an action is to show that the action is morally permissible or pragmatically reasonable.

It is clear that there is quite a distance between an explanation and a justification of the attacks. In fact, there are two additional levels of argument one must give in order to reach a justification from an explanation of this sort: first it must be shown that the behavior that explains is immoral, and then it must be shown that the act to be justified constitutes an appropriate response to the immoral action.

Though there may be some danger in developing an explanation for 11 September it is not because an explanation will serve to justify the attacks. This danger comes not from any intrinsic problem with offering explanations, but because of the widespread difficulty people have distinguishing between an explanation and a justification. That is, people may see any US admission that American foreign policy was part of what motivated the attack against us as an admission of guilt, though of course it need not be.

We have seen that there are many worries one might have about explaining an immoral action. I hope to have shown that none of these concerns are warranted. If there exist strong arguments against explaining an event (other than the concern that your own immoral acts will come to light), I am not aware of them. But just because there is not an argument against Bush's providing an explanation for 11 September, it does not follow that he ought to provide an explanation.

Why Bush Needs to Explain 11 September

To defend the claim that Bush ought to explain the events of 11 September let us first return to the topic of scientific explanation. Traditionally, science is considered to be a body of explanations for natural phenomenon, many of which can be used for prediction and control of the physical world. Scientific explanations are useful because they allow us to make the world more comfortable for the humans who live here. Knowing why rain falls allows us to seed clouds and keep our crops watered. And knowing how the body functions allows us to cure disease. Just as technology that allows us to control the physical world comes from scientific explanations, an explanation of horrific human behavior can help us to prevent the behavior.

If we come to understand the psychological and environmental causes of some behavior that we want to modify, then we will gain greater ability to control those behaviors. The normative aspects of the behavioral sciences are predicated on this thesis, as is medical science. Doctors, when given the option, would choose to treat the cause of a disease rather than simply dealing with the symptoms. Treating symptoms is better than doing nothing, and in many cases it is the first response, but for long-term treatment of chronic ailments, getting to the cause of the illness is essential to curing the patient.

However, knowing a cause does not by itself guarantee the elimination of the target behavior. We must also be able to eliminate that cause. For example, suppose it were discovered that truancy is caused in part by growing up in a single-parent family. In order to solve one problem, truancy, we would have to first solve another. If the secondary problem is too difficult to solve, then one should turn back to the original problem and look for a fuller explanation. Once we learn more about the myriad different elements that contribute to truancy, we could find alternative and potentially more successful methods for reducing the truancy rate. The more complete an explanation one has for some phenomenon, the more opportunities there are to eliminate that phenomenon by breaking the causal chain.

To fight a war on terrorism without trying to determine the causes of terrorism is like going to the doctor who does not examine the patient for the etiology of her illness. Thus far in the War on Terror, Bush has focused on treating the symptoms. Heightening security at airports, imprisoning suspected terrorists indefinitely, increasing attention to immigrants from Muslim countries and even overthrowing the Taliban government are among the steps taken to avoid future terrorist attacks on US soil. Though these actions may offer some advantage in an attempt to alleviate the symptoms of terrorism, they do nothing toward identifying or modifying the root cause.

Without understanding the motivations behind the terrorist attacks targeting the United States, the act of hunting down individual terrorists does not guarantee that new terrorists will not step in to take the place of those caught or killed. If the war against terror is made into a war against people's motivations, rather than a war against people, then the United States may have a chance of succeeding. Success should be defined not as killing or capturing all terrorists (which would make success impossible), but by reducing the animosity toward the United States by people around the world. As long as there is such extreme hatred toward the United States, there will be terrorists.

There is a pragmatic argument for Bush to explain the events of 11 September, which involves winning the war against terrorism, and defending the security of Americans both at home and abroad along with US allies and innocent people around the world. Because an explanation of behavior will allow one to understand the motivations and environmental conditions that caused the behavior, and because the best way to eliminate a behavior is to sever the causal chain leading up to it, one ought to generate explanations for those behaviors to be eliminated. Further, since the stated goal of the war on terror is the elimination of terror in the world, and because Bush must fulfill his obligation to the American people, he is duty-bound to do what he can within the limits of morality to stop terrorism. Given that there are no good arguments against explaining the terrorist attacks, it follows that Bush must work on developing a thorough explanation for 11 September.

It is important to realize that this argument is directed at the phenomenon of terrorism itself, rather than at the terrorist leanings of any one individual. This is not a proposal for a 12-step plan intended to rehabilitate terrorists. Rather, it is an argument in defense of a method aimed at reducing the creation of new terrorists. Whereas it may be impossible to cure Osama bin Laden of his hatred of the United States and willingness to kill innocent people in his quest, we may still be able to reduce the number of people who are convinced by his rhetoric. Unless he is able to recruit new terrorists, his movement will not succeed. When young people cease regarding terrorist groups as an attractive life choice, then the terrorist leaders will lack the raw materials necessary for carrying out successful terrorist attacks.

If the United States chooses to fight terrorism in this fashion, it will be utilizing the explanatory methodology of the sciences. Doctors who want to cure a disease will attempt to stop it from spreading to healthy cells. When there are a finite number of diseased cells, it is possible to track them down and destroy them. However, when the number of diseased cells grows faster than the doctor's ability to eliminate them, the doctors conclude that the outlook for the patient is bleak indeed.

Once a thorough explanation for the terrorist attacks has been generated, the US government can attempt to fight the war on terror by stopping the creation of new terrorists in addition to its current quest to search out those terrorists who already exist. Both tasks must be accomplished if we are to achieve a positive outcome. However, it is important to realize that neither the generation of the explanation nor the subsequent elimination of new terrorists are easy tasks. While some element of the explanation will be psychological, referring to the terrorist beliefs and desires, others will be environmental. Insofar as the environmental aspect of the explanation refers to US foreign policy, which may make that policy vulnerable to additional analysis by the media, academia, and foreign nations, coming forth with that explanation will not be easy. However, we may find that this willingness for discussion will itself be part of the solution. Openness to public debate and an increased sensitivity to the concerns of other nations may result in fewer criticisms of exceptionalism and more sympathy in the Arab street, and it may do more to improve our image abroad than would any amount of money spent on the Office of Global Communications. If the United States' negative reputation is part of what causes people to become terrorists, repairing this image through examination of our policies is the first step toward eradicating terrorism directed toward the United States.

To be successful in the war on terror, Bush must fight it on more than one front. The current approach, which emphasizes the capture of terrorists in the United States and around the globe, must be augmented by an attempt to reduce the regeneration of terrorists. If two more terrorists are created for every one captured, Bush will not emerge triumphant. Though the United States is attempting to improve its standing in the Islamic world with its funding for projects such as Radio Sawa, which broadcasts Western and Arabic pop music and news into the Middle East, and 'Next Chapter', a news and entertainment show broadcast to Iranians in Farsi, such endeavors will only be successful if the United States knows what the youth in the Middle East need to hear.

With a thorough understanding of the motivations leading to acts of terror, and a detailed explanation demonstrating both the psychological and environmental conditions which cause people to become terrorists, the US government will be well placed to succeed in its current fight. As this is written, however, the emphasis on military action in lieu of any real effort to uncover the deeper causes of terrorism undermines the chances of victory. The presidency of George W. Bush will always be inseparable from 11 September 2001, and in evaluating the President at mid-point with regard to the war on terror, I must conclude that there is substantial room for improvement.

Notes

1   11 September 2001. Quotes from Bush's speeches are taken from the official White House website (www.whitehouse.gov).
2   20 September 2001.
3   Contemporary philosophical work on scientific explanation was derived from C.G. Hempel and P. Oppenheim (1948), 'Studies in the Logic of Explanation', *Philosophy of Science*, (15), 135–75.
4   Current theories of psychological explanation emphasize the importance of belief and desire attribution. For example Daniel Dennett (1987), *The Intentional Stance*, Cambridge, MA: MIT Press and Jerry Fodor, (1991), 'You can fool some of the people all of the time, everything else being equal: Hedged laws and psychological explanations', *Mind* (100), 19–34; both argue that psychological explanation is theory based. To predict and explain human behavior we determine which belief, desire, and law would result in said behavior. See also Stephen Stich and Shaun Nichols (1996), 'How Do Minds Understand Minds? Mental Stimulation Versus Tacit Theory', in Stephen Stich (ed.), *Deconstructing the Mind*, Oxford: Oxford University Press. Others focus on the role of understanding when providing explanations. Rather than taking explanations as providing theories about human behavior, it is argued that we simulate being the person whose behavior is to be explained. The simulation allows us to see things from another's perspective. See Alvin Goldman (1995), 'Interpretation Psychologized', in Martin Davies and Tony Stone (eds), *Folk Psychology*, Oxford and Cambridge, UK: Blackwell Publishers, 74–99; reprinted from *Mind and Language*, 7 (1-2) 1989, 161–85; and Robert Gordon, (1995), 'The Simulation Theory: Objections and Misconceptions', in Davies and Stone, 100–22; reprinted from *Mind and Language*, 7 (1-2) 1992, 11–34; and J. Heal, (1996), 'Simulation, Theory, and Content', in Peter Carruthers and Peter K. Smith (eds), *Theories of Theories of Mind*, Cambridge: Cambridge University Press, 75–89.
5   Fodor; Dennett.
6   Davies and Stone; Heal.
7   For instance, Gordon; Goldman; Heal.
8   Susan Sontag (2001), 'The Talk of The Town', *New Yorker* (24 September), 28.
9   Ibid.
10   Lawrence Kaplan (2001), 'No Choice: Foreign Policy After September 11', *The New Republic* (1 October), 21.
11   *Human Events On-line* (24 September 2001), online at http://www.humaneventsonline.com/articles/09-24-01/briefs.html.
12   Given the statements from bin Laden, we cannot conclude that he has provided us with the thorough explanation for the attacks. Psychologists are documenting the many ways in which introspection is fallible, and the difficulty we have identifying the true causes of our actions. For example, if a person is perceived as kindly, we tend to see her as more intelligent, though we deny that the person's kindness affected our judgment of her

intelligence. See Ziva Kunda (2002), *Social Cognition: Making Sense of People*, Cambridge, MA: MIT Press, for a discussion of these issues. Though people are notoriously bad at explaining their own actions, and giving accurate descriptions of their own mental states and reasons, the professed reasons for the attacks would be taken into account as part of the explanation. This might be what some people see as dangerous.

13   Jerry L. Martin and Anne D. Neal (2002), *Defending Civilization: How Our Universities Are Failing America and What Can Be Done About It*, revised edition, Cambridge, MA: MIT Press, 9.
14   Ibid., 23.
15   Ibid., 14.
16   Allen Thompson (2002), 'Terrorism, Poverty Link Called a Mistake', *Toronto Star* (21 September), A8.

PART II
US DOMESTIC IMPLICATIONS

Chapter 4

National Security, Budgeting, and Policy Priorities: The Role and Importance of Candidate and President Bush

Michael G. Dziubinski and Steve A. Yetiv

Introduction

The 11 September terrorist attacks on New York and Washington fixed the spotlight on the leadership potential of President George W. Bush. While some of his detractors had questioned whether he had the acumen to lead the United States, it would not take long for many observers to acclaim him as a great wartime president, highlighting his individual leadership role in the struggle against terrorists. They praised his steadfastness in the face of the most serious terrorist attack in American history, and also, in light of the crisis, his choices for key Cabinet positions. Indeed, with a former Secretary of Defense as the Vice President, another former Secretary of Defense as the current Secretary of Defense, and a former Chairman of the Joint Chiefs of Staff as the Secretary of State, Bush seemed to have picked an ideal set of advisers for handling the war on terror and for strengthening national defense. Rather than appearing as cold warriors that were out of touch with twenty-first century realities, after 11 September the Cabinet appeared as quite suitable to turn back transnational terrorism.

However, while some observers praised Bush's individual role in shepherding the United States through a difficult period and stressed his individual role in shaping budgetary priorities, we could ask a deeper question about his performance. Under a contrarian view, we could say that budgetary priorities and funding, especially in the defense arena, were shaped not so much by Bush the individual, or by his key advisers, but by a plethora of other factors, including government politics,[1] organizational culture,[2] the military-industrial complex, external threats and domestic politics and pressures.[3] This places the role of the individual in contra-distinction to that of the state, its government and internal processes, and that of the system of inter-nation relations and global processes – a classic set of competing variables.[4]

In the present study, this classic exploration takes the form of a core question: how important is President Bush in general as an actor and in particular on issues such as shaping the budget? Consideration is given to the task during the commencement of war. In the past two decades, scholars of the presidency have argued prominently that presidents have limited power. Different a rguments have been put forth for this conclusion, including the effects of increasing complexity of world affairs, political parties that create democratic gridlock, fragmented government, checks and balances writ large, an uncooperative bureaucracy, an adversarial media, poor public relations skills and poor information and advice.[5] At the same time, the popular imagination is fired by the notion that presidents matter, that they are quite powerful, especially during times of war.[6] Indeed, it is not uncommon to hear political pundits say that the President of the United States is the most powerful individual in the world, quite capable of bringing about desired outcomes. Understanding the role of the president against a range of constraints is vital for explaining, understanding and even predicting outcomes involving presidential behavior and it also can lend some insight into the broader question of the role of individuals in political contexts.[7]

In this article, we seek to explore the question of how critical George W. Bush was, first as candidate Bush, and then as President Bush, in shaping budgetary priorities, the budget and subsequent funding. Such analysis provides another means to assess Bush's leadership, particularly with respect to the war on terror. Examination of Bush's stated defense and national security budget priorities as a candidate, and his ability or inability to deliver on them, offers a preliminary look at what would become Bush's national security doctrine and what would soon influence his conduct of the war on terror. Moreover, these matters have been noticeably absent from analysis of Bush's wartime leadership or the war on terror.

Bush's Budget Proposals

Merely examining budget dollars, and attributing increases or decreases in dollars to either individual leadership or other factors is unlikely to be informative. Rather, it is more useful to examine and compare the language used by President Bush with the budget proposals that followed. This 'language versus dollars' approach can indicate whether language is matched by a plan to allocate resources in the manner specified. This would tend to support the idea of individual leadership as a potent force in shaping the budget. Alternatively, it can indicate situations where language was not matched with budget proposals. This would tend to support the idea that conditions outside of an individual leader's control were stronger determinants of state behavior. This might especially be the case during times of war.

With George W. Bush, it is useful to examine two language/budget figure pairs. The first is Bush's pre-election language regarding the budget, and then the national defense/security portion of his first federal budget proposal. The second is his language which accompanied his first federal budget proposal, and then the resource allocation in the second proposal. In this fashion, the research will be able to uncover if publicly announced policies survived substantive environment changes (namely, moving from candidate to elected official, terrorist attacks and the war on terror which moved Bush from a peacetime to wartime president). If previously enunciated policies can survive these changes, and if the changes themselves do not cause significant alterations in the individual's preference, then this would tend to support the position that individual leadership can be a substantive force. It also permits us to take a closer look at George W. Bush's leadership, which many have applauded after the terrorist attacks, and examine a different angle of his leadership of the war on terror.

Candidate Bush

The first case involves George Bush as a candidate for president. Candidate Bush put forth a well-crafted and forceful message on defense and national security issues in his campaign against the incumbent Vice President Al Gore. His message, articulated in multiple fora, provided both rational arguments on how to manage defense, and in some areas, dollar figures needed to accomplish the stated national security goals.[8] This specificity will allow some direct comparison of the period before and after the campaign. We will also offer comparison through qualitative discussion.

Candidate Bush's message on defense/national security provided a vision of the purpose and importance of the military, and three broad ways to achieve that purpose. His vision was 'that a strong, capable and modern military is essential to defend our nation, advance US interests, and extend our peace'.[9] But his vision also encompassed a perception of the then-current condition of the Department of Defense. He characterized US defense capabilities to be in a debilitated condition, because of over-commitment and insufficient funding. He stated that the US military had undertaken an average of one new deployment every nine weeks, during the Clinton-Gore administration. Further, he stated that US defense spending had declined by nearly 40 per cent in the same period.[10] He characterized US forces as overused and underfunded precisely at a time when they were confronted with a host of new threats and challenges, resulting in a military force unprepared to deal with the threats of a new century. To overcome this condition and meet his vision of the US military, candidate Bush outlined three goals.

Renewal

The first goal was to 'Renew the bond of trust between the President and the Military'.[11] Within the discussion of this goal, he highlighted a range of personnel issues. The first along these issues was low pay, indicating that military pay is an average of 13 per cent lower than comparable civilian pay. He also highlighted military housing, claiming that over 200,000 military families reside in substandard quarters. Further, he introduced military personnel shortages in terms of the missed reenlistment goals, an Air Force 2000 pilot shortfall and Navy personnel shortfalls of 18,000 sailors, among other examples.[12] As a part of addressing these problems, candidate Bush identified some fairly specific, but potentially costly steps. To help narrow the overall difference in compensation between the armed forces and the civilian sector, he stated that he would increase a planned military pay raise by $1 billion. Without specifying amounts, he also indicated that he would increase targeted re-enlistment bonuses and special pay for critical specialties to reduce the pay gap for individuals with skills that are in high demand, such as pilots, computer programmers and engineers. Again, without specifying amounts, he indicated he would improve military housing by renovation or construction of barracks or family housing units or, in other cases, increase basic housing allowances, especially in high cost areas. Finally, in the area of improving military training he promised to correct funding shortfalls in training center facilities, equipment and operations in order to reverse the decline in the quality and level of training of our men and women in uniform.[13]

Returning to the central question of this study, if individual leadership is a significant factor, we should expect a minimum increase of $1 billion in personnel funds over what was already programmed. We would also expect additional funds to address the 200,000 substandard housing units, some of which could be in construction, some in additional housing allowances, and additional funding for training centers and programs.

Protect

The second goal was to 'protect America itself from attack'.[14] Bush highlighted that over two dozen countries have ballistic missiles, a number of which – including North Korea, Iran and Iraq – may ultimately reach intercontinental range. He also noted that arms control agreements needed to be addressed. Further, he contended that the United States was vulnerable to a state or terrorist groups using nuclear, chemical or biological weapons that have proliferated around the world.

To protect the nation, candidate Bush stated that he would deter terrorist attacks against the United States by ensuring that every group or nation understands that if it sponsors such attacks, America's response will be devastating. In order to directly counter the missile threat he would accelerate research on, and deployment of, both national and theater missile defenses as soon as possible. He would further either amend the 1972 Anti-Ballistic Missile treaty to permit deployment of effective national and theater missile defenses, or withdraw from it. To get better threat information he stated that he would make it a priority to strengthen US intelligence resources, focusing on human intelligence and the early detection of threats.[15]

Candidate Bush stated his desire to build and deploy a missile defense system to protect the homeland against missiles fired accidentally, by rogue nations, or in future conflicts. He highlighted the need to improve cooperation with its allies as they face many of the same threats as the United States, and should share in the burden of defense. Although candidate Bush did not provide hard dollar figures in this goal area, he did state unequivocal support to a national and theater missile defense and to increased intelligence capability. This leadership position creates the expectation for substantive increases in the defense budget for missile defense programs; however, intelligence funding is perennially difficult to ascertain, so may not be as visible in the defense budget.

A New Military

Candidate Bush characterized the US military as organized more for Cold War threats than for the challenges of a new century (such as terrorism). He called for a new architecture for American defense to permit the United States to project power swiftly under new conditions, requiring very different kinds of forces from those in the past. These forces would be required to combat adversaries with access to ballistic and cruise missiles, weapons of mass destruction and other technologies that may deny the United States its forward bases and logistics capabilities. These adversaries would likely target airfields and ports critical to the flow of American forces and material, and would choose environments in which to fight where American forces that depend on large amounts of logistical support would be disadvantaged. To meet such future challenges, candidate Bush outlined a review of US military force structure, strategy and procurement to be conducted under the future Secretary of Defense. He would be tasked with creating the military of the future – lethal, agile, easier to deploy. This future military would be equipped with some modernized existing weapons, but seek to replace existing systems with new technologies. To enable this action, Bush noted that he would earmark at least 20 per cent of the procurement budget to address future challenges and increase defense R&D spending by at least $20 billion from FY2002 to FY2006.[16]

Returning to the central question of this chapter, we should expect to see, if we are to conclude that Bush played a vital individual role, some evidence that these goals were reflected in budgetary priorities. It would be even more definitive if we observed, for instance, a planned increase of $20 billion in R&D across five years.

Bush's First Tally

Did Bush's platform translate into real budgetary action? To recapitulate, if individual leadership had a major impact, it would be sensible to expect to see: 1) a minimum increase of $1 billion in personnel funds for a pay raise; 2) additional funds to address 200,000 substandard housing units; 3) funds to accelerate research on, and deployment of, both national and theater missile defenses; 4) earmark(s) of at least 20 per cent of the procurement budget to address future challenges; and 5) an increase in defense R&D spending by at least $20 billion from FY2002 to FY2006 in the budget proposal for FY 2002.

The proposed 2002 budget increase for Department of Defense was $14.2 billion over 2001. In fact, we can easily detect a $1.4 billion increase for pay and allowance increase. However, the other evidence is less clear-cut. The budget proposal has provisions for an increase of $400 million to improve the quality of housing and decrease out-of-pocket housing-related expenses for military personnel and their families. Given candidate Bush's statement that more than 200,000 housing units were substandard, this equates to less that $2000 per unit to upgrade housing or to ameliorate expenses.[17] The budget does propose a total increase of $3.567 billion in R&D for the Department of Defense (DOD)[18] with a $2.6 billion initiative in research and development for missile defense.[19] It also contains proposed specific focus areas of leap-ahead technologies and cost reduction for new weapons and intelligence systems; improvements to the laboratory and test range infrastructure; and efforts focused on countering unconventional threats to national security.[20] However, the original budget document does not provide a projection for the outyears that could substantiate the previously mentioned $20 billion over five years in R&D. Interestingly the DOD portion of the budget allocates $3.9 billion for better retirement benefits for military personnel. This proposal appears to be in response to Congressional actions[21] as it was not in evidence in previous goal statements from candidate Bush.

Overall, the scorecard based on our comparison is mixed. The proposed budget (1) meets the test on the pay issue, (2) does not seem to adequately address the housing issue, (3) provides for a robust R&D effort in missile defense area, (4) identifies focus areas, (5) but does not provide outyear figures for $20 billion in R&D. The $3.9 billion for retirement benefits is not part of the Bush campaign initiatives. A $3.6 billion decrement to the Navy shipbuilding program also appears in the budget.[22] Although candidate Bush indicated the need to choose weapon systems carefully, he had not previously identified the Navy shipbuilding program as the target for reductions.

President Bush

The policies embedded in President Bush's first budget appear to be crafted with a long-term perspective. Highlighting a new approach to budgeting, the budget calls for a moderation of recent rapid growth in spending, paying down the debt and providing tax relief. The largest per centage increase in the budget is in the Education Department (11.5 per cent). It also focuses on Social Security, saving a surplus and directing modernization of the system. Other social services such as Medicare receive attention in an effort to modernize and reform the program. Last in the list of significant efforts is President Bush's attempt to restore the commitment to military personnel and begin transition to a twenty-first century force structure. In fact, defense comes next to last on a list of initiative highlights, just above increasing embassy security, and preceded by social service improvements and tax relief.[23]

Governing Principles

In the discussion of the governing principles of the budget, the budget document highlights the conviction that the government should play a role that is both activist and limited. It notes that the important role of government in fostering an environment in which all Americans have the opportunity to better themselves and their families. This is operationalized in the budget language as: providing good educational opportunities for all youths; allowing families to keep more of their incomes; keeping commitments to the elderly and future generations; keeping the peace; and ensuring that communities have the ability to minister to their local needs.[24] Once again, the reader can note the order of these imperatives; domestic oriented aspects both predominate in order and number. The budget language then provides a set of limiting ideas. It highlights the need 'not to overstep', and to ensure that it keeps the commitments it makes. It indicates that the government must take lessons from the private sector, finding ways to increase efficiency and customer satisfaction, stating the intent to make the government more accountable, thereby increasing Americans' confidence in a government/private sector partnership that would raise everyone's standard of living.[25] To ascertain if President Bush's individual leadership was predominant over external forces, we should be able to see the same principles, albeit with some slight adjustment, repeated in the language of the next budget, all the while accounting and adjusting for the changes in Bush's own budgetary views that were engendered by the 11 September attacks. Overall, as the President outlines the budget as a ten-year plan, the principles should not vary substantially in the next year. However, if we believe that the external environment shapes the policies, we would expect to see a different set of principles enunciated, with the possibility of some minor portions being a continuation of the previous principles.

Allocating the Taxpayers' Dollars

The fiscal year 2002 budget has an extensive discussion of how a surplus is generated and proposes a way to disburse that surplus. It indicates that over the next 10 years, the federal government projects it will collect $28 trillion in revenues from American taxpayers. The President's budget estimated that it will cost roughly $22.4 trillion to continue the government in existence today, including new initiatives outlined previously. This leaves a $5.6 trillion surplus. The budget allocates the entire Social Security surplus for Social Security and debt retirement. It partially justifies the expenditure on debt retirement, as a further cost savings measure in the long term, paying off $2 trillion in debt that matures at and before 2011 over the next 10 years. The budget language estimated that by 2011, Federal debt will have fallen to 7 per cent of gross domestic product (GDP), its lowest level in more than 80 years. It claims that net interest payments on this debt will be less than 0.5 per cent of GDP, less than one quarter of today's share and only 3 per cent of the budget. A portion of the surplus was proposed to fund a return of $1.6 trillion tax dollars to the taxpayers.[26] Whether the arguments above are correct from a policy perspective or not, it is important to note that the focus of the discussion was on domestic issues of debt retirement, Social Security and tax refunds – not on national security or anti-terrorism. The budget allocation discussion further reinforces the domestic, economical focus. The budget language continues to address issues beyond Social Security, paying off the debt and tax refunds, by highlighting Medicare reform and establishing a true financial reserve for future priorities and unexpected contingencies. This financial reserve is noted to be $1 trillion. In the discussion of this reserve, the issue set is broadened slightly beyond purely domestic concerns, adding a mention of the potential for increased defense spending almost in parallel with farm conditions that could require additional resources for agriculture and additional debt retirement.[27]

The principles went on to highlight the need to examine existing programs, looking for ways to redirect resources to their most productive end and the potential of freeing resources to address emerging needs. Ideas such as flattening the federal hierarchy, moving the government toward performance-based contracting, opening government functions to competition, reducing erroneous payments by federal agencies, expanding electronic government, including-procurement, were claimed to have the potential for savings to exceed $100 billion over 10 years.[28]

The budget document recognized that it, like any long-term plan, was subject to alteration due to unanticipated needs. It claimed that by using cautious estimating assumptions, reserving the Social Security surplus for debt retirement and Social Security reform and preserving an additional large reserve beyond the Social Security surplus, the Administration would be able to adjust the budget in the future to meet new requirements as they arise.[29] This coda implied that President Bush's principles would remain as the guiding factors despite trillion dollar emergencies, as an adjustment to the budget would suffice to address the issue.

If we believe that President Bush's leadership shapes the agenda, this allocation discussion builds the expectation that the priorities outlined here will remain much like this in the next year's budget. The importance of retiring debt, protecting Social Security and other social services should remain highly regarded. Even an emergency should not substantially change the inherent importance of the domestic economic well-being. However, if environmental factors were determinant, we would expect wholesale changes to funding priorities outlined here.

Bush's Second Tally

To recapitulate, continued stability in principles and funding would tend to support the premise of leadership as the key contributor to policy, with the adjustment that the events feed back into the leader's views. Meanwhile, substantial shifts in policy and funding would tend to indicate non-individual factors as important, either because they shape individual views or because of an independent set of effects on policy.

The Fiscal Year 2003 budget document highlighted the following priorities/ categories: protecting the homeland; winning the war on terror abroad; returning to economic vitality; governing with accountability; and other priority initiatives. The first category included funding for equipping and training first responders, enhancements to hospitals, medical research, information nets for detection for biological issues, better border control and aviation security issues. The second category supported a defense budget increase and military aid to other allied countries. The third category contained economic stimulus to assist the unemployed, moderates the growth of spending, with the exception of national security and homeland issues to 2 per cent, and balances the budget by 2005 without raising taxes. The fourth category incorporated a set of five management reforms into agencies' budgets and plans, shifting the budget's focus to what is being accomplished, beginning the integration of performance measures in the budget process and seeks reprogramming and reorganization authority to better align programs and resources. The final category included education, National Institutes of Health, community health centers, Medicare prescription drugs, health insurance, breast and cervical cancer screening, compassion and Faith-Based Initiatives and many other social service initiatives.[30]

President Bush's previous theme of moderation of growth in spending survived the change in environment, albeit in a weak form, as evidenced by his attempt to keep spending growth, aside from defense and homeland security, at 2 per cent.[31] His goal of paying down the debt appears to have been excised from the budget, as the phrase 'debt retirement' did not appear, even once, in the 431-page document. The importance of providing tax relief assumed the important role of helping regain economic vitality, versus purely a moral imperative of returning the taxpayers money. The priority focus on education was not entirely lost but now fell into the last category of 'other priority initiatives'. Other social programs such as Medicare received attention short of last year's effort to modernize and reform, and benefited from an approach that looked to incrementally improve the program.[32] We also observed that issues that were previously last in the list of significant efforts, became much more important. Chiefly, the President's attempt to restore the commitment to military personnel and to begin the transition to a twenty-first century force structure assumed both a near-term focus as well as a more important longer term focus on military transformation, with a 12 per cent increase in budget authority.[33]

Overall, we find as we did in the analysis of the previous figure pairs that the scorecard is mixed. However, it appears that most of the previous principles survived the transition in circumstance, with some variation in priority. Funding, however, suffered a substantial shift. For example, the Department of Education benefited from the highest increase in the previous year at 11.5 per cent, but now would be held within the 2 per cent increase for all but defense and homeland security programs. The plan to retire substantial amounts of debt and sustain any emergency through the use of a reserve fund did not survive either.

Conclusion

This chapter has sought to assess the importance of the role of candidate and President Bush in shaping the budget as a means of assessing his leadership and wartime leadership. This research task, no doubt, is complicated by the ever-present challenge of attempting to assess causality when numerous different variables are at play (such as war). Doing so with enhanced rigor would require greater attention to isolating different variables that could explain budgetary priorities and shifts. But that is a task that is more sensibly handled in one or more volumes, and not in a short foray of this kind.

Rather, while we do not want to present our findings as definitive, we do believe that they are suggestive and useful. What we would argue is that in the present case, neither the individual nor the non-individual factors were pre-eminent. Rather, the results appear to indicate an interaction between both factors. When candidate Bush became president his intention to bolster defense was moderated by the need to understand better how to transform US armed forces in order to make them more effective against the emergent adversary. The global environment in which Bush would have to operate post-11 September included an unmistakable transnational element since al-Qaeda represented at its core a transnational terrorist threat. The war on terror in this new environment shaped the budget both independently and partly by shaping Bush's views, views that also had their own inertia and continuity.

Moreover, when the principles in the first budget were challenged by an emergent adversary, the second budget provided funding for current counter-terrorist operations, while retaining force transformation principles and funding. There was by no means a serious break with previous budgetary imperatives, but the 11 September realities accelerated some priorities that were already in motion, while generating their own independent effects. Although funding for education dropped in importance, education did maintain its relative priority within the social services arena.

Ultimately, what may be the most interesting is the combination of factors – individual and non-individual – that produce outcomes. It may be that we find the most sensible answers as to how budgets are shaped and what factors are most germane in shaping them, in the complex mix of factors. But even so, that leaves a more difficult and interesting question: what are the conditions under which some factors or combination of factors will be more important than others in this process? That is a question more suitably tackled in future work.

Notes

1   The government politics model stresses bureaucratic politics as predominant over the influence of particular individuals. See Steve A. Yetiv (2001/2002), 'Developing a Theory of Government Politics: The Case of the Persian Gulf Crisis', *Security Studies*, 11 (Winter).

2   The organizational process model stresses the role, culture, and routine of organizations and their resistance to change, and subordinates individuals to the machinery of organizations. See Graham Allison and Philip Zelikow (1999), *Essence of Decision*, 2nd edn, New York: Longman.

3   On the importance of domestic politics and the discussion of this literature, see Barbara Rearden Farnham (1997), *Roosevelt And The Munich Crisis: A Study Of Political Decision-Making*, Princeton: Princeton University Press, especially chapter 2. Also, see Philip E. Tetlock (1985), 'Accountability: The Neglected Social Content of Judgment and Choice', *Research in Organizational Behavior*, 7, 295–332.

4   In modern times, this analysis was elevated in importance in Kenneth Waltz (1957), *Man, the State, and War*, New York: W.W. Norton. Also, see Harold and Margaret Sprout (1956), *Man-Milieu Relationship Hypotheses in the Context of International Politics*, Princeton: Princeton University Press.

5   On this broad literature, see Marcia Lynn Whicker (1993), 'The Case AGAINST the War', in Marcia Lynn Whicker, James P. Pfiffner, and Raymond A. Moore (eds), *The Presidency and the Persian Gulf War*, Westport, CT: Praeger, 114–16.

6   And scholars no less prominent than Richard Neustadt, as well as more recent thinkers, argued several decades ago that Presidents can be very powerful, especially if they know how to persuade. For references, see Craig Allen Smith and Kathy B. Smith (1994), *The White House Speaks: Presidential Leadership as Persuasion*, Westport, CT: Praeger, esp. 16.

7   On how individuals can shape foreign policy decisions, see Margaret G. Hermann (ed.) (1977), *A Psychological Examination of Political Leaders*, New York: The Free Press. Lawrence S. Falkowski (ed.) (1979), *Psychological Models in International Politics*, Boulder: Westview Press. For a good synopsis of case studies of individual leaders, see David C. Winter (1992), 'Personality and Foreign Policy: Historical Overview of Research', in Eric Singer and Valerie Hudson (eds), *Political Psychology and Foreign Policy*, Boulder: Westview Press, esp. 85–6.

8   'Gov. George W. Bush on the Economy and Taxes', in C-SPAN.ORG Public Affairs on the Web, http://cspanrm.fplive.net:554/ramgen/cspan/ldrive/c2k090600_5.rm, 6 September 2000; George W. Bush (1999), 'Issues – Defense', *in United States Special Weapons Nuclear, Biological, Chemical and Missile Proliferation News*, online at http://www.fas.org/news/usa/1999/09/990923-bush-dod.htm.

9   Ibid., 1.

10 Ibid., 2.

11 Ibid., 3.

12 Ibid.

13 Ibid., 4.

14 Ibid.

15 Ibid., 5.

16 Ibid., 5-7.

17 *A Blueprint for New Beginnings: A Responsible Budget for America's Priorities* (2001), Washington, DC: Government Printing Office, online at http://w3.access.gpo.gov/usbudget/fy2002/pdf/blueprnt.pdf.

18 *Fiscal Year 2002: Analytic Perspectives* (2001), Washington, DC: Government Printing Office, online at http://w3.access.gpo.gov/usbudget/fy2002/pdf/spec.pdf.

19 *A Blueprint for New Beginnings*, 86.

20 Ibid.

21 Ibid.

22 *Fiscal Year 2002: Analytic Perspectives*, 505.

23 *A Blueprint for New Beginnings*, 9.

24 Ibid., 11.

25　Ibid.
26　Ibid., 11–12.
27　Ibid., 13.
28　Ibid., 18.
29　Ibid.
30　US, White House (2002), *Fiscal Year 2003 Budget of the US Government*, Washington, DC: Government Printing Office, 11–13.
31　Ibid., 8.
32　Ibid., 8–9.
33　Ibid., 29.

Chapter 5

The War on Terrorism and President Bush: Completing His Father's Legacy and Defining His Own Place in History

John Davis

Introduction

As one considers President George W. Bush's foreign policy, one cannot escape the inextricable fact that three components of the younger Bush's policies are directly connected to initiatives explored by his father during his presidency. Employing three case studies – the search for stability in the international system, confronting Iraq, and the war on terrorism – this chapter represents an effort to explore this linkage. Similarly, I believe that the results of this examination offer significant opportunities for George W. Bush, including: 1) the President is positioned to redefine and revive – thereby completing – aspects of the legacies of his father; and 2) as a by-product, the possibility exists to define his own place in history.

The First Linkage: the Search for Stability in the International System

The 'new world order' defined, represents an attempt to stabilize the international system following a period of upheaval characterized by a period of a lengthy, major war, and efforts by the 'ordained great power' to reorder the international system under new auspices.[1] With respect to the United States, and beginning with Woodrow Wilson, US presidents endeavored to create an international system based on democratic values. Under President George H.W. Bush, his Administration articulated a vision of the world order that was very much consistent with Wilsonian-Idealism, where collective security and the rule of law were paramount instruments of global security.[2] Similarly, the resulting confrontation with Iraq offered the elder Bush two significant opportunities: 1) to define a post-Cold War vision; and 2) Iraq represented a test case for the imagery associated with the new world order.

In an address to Congress on 6 March 1991, President George H.W. Bush ushered in a period of *Triumphalism*. In fleshing out the vision, Bush spoke of 'guaranteeing an era of perpetual peace'. He also noted that, in the absence of rules to guide postwar stability, and in the wake of victory over Iraq, an era symbolized by an 'enduring peace must be our mission'. On the second point, the President offered the following elaboration and goals: 'A world where the United Nations, freed from Cold War stalemate, is poised to fulfill the historic mission of its founders. A world in which freedom and respect for human rights find a home among all nations.'[3] The Gulf War, according to the President, 'put this new world to its first test', adding 'and my fellow Americans we passed that test'.[4]

According to former National Security Advisor to President Bush, Brent Scowcroft, a key architect of the postwar strategy, the new world order has a supplementary objective: prevent interstate conflict.[5] For Scowcroft, the Administration's postwar strategy fulfilled its purpose. However, in the months immediately after the celebratory environment that swept the United States after the Gulf War, the President's vision lost its luster and became a source of discontent and disillusionment among scholars, who incessantly argued that postwar recommendations were problematic.[6] That is, while the Administration's strategy proved successful in precluding interstate war, the vision did not address the burgeoning ethnic civil wars that simmered throughout the postwar period. Moreover, the President's postwar strategy offered no solutions to the increasing threat of transnational terrorism.

Having allowed these conflicts to fester, and in the absence of counter-terrorist strategy, one pundit opined that 'for the country and the world ... the new world order had no content'.[7] Within the Administration, with the campaign season approaching, and hounded by queries about the details of the new world order which were overwhelming the Bush White House staff, several senior members informed the President that it was time to distance the Administration from this vision. David Gergen, the former Director of Communications, offered the following account:

> In his frequent incantations of a 'new world order', President Bush seemed on the verge of setting forth a new set of doctrines for US policy, and the White House even announced that he would give four commencement addresses in the spring of 1991 fleshing out his vision. Because his staff felt that a public debate over a new order was spinning beyond control, however, the President gave only one of the addresses and then pulled back, returning to a more comfortable, day-to-day management of foreign affairs ... the new world order seemed destined to become no more than a campaign slogan for 1992. A rare moment of opportunity had passed ... . Few outside the White House talk anymore of creating a 'new world order', except in jest.[8]

Once a productive component of Bush's impending legacy, the construction of a new world order emerged as a failure for the self-described foreign policy president. Confronting this reality, the President turned inward to deal with the economy as the presidential campaign approached. In the wake of the shift in the Administration's strategy, the grand coalition that was successful during the Gulf campaign – and a strong symbol of the Administration's multilateral priorities – collapsed, as neo-isolation swept America. As a result, disorder became the phrase employed to describe the international system.[9]

The War on Terror provided the younger Bush with an opportunity to revive discourse on the new world order. Likewise, 11 September presented the President with something equally significant: an opportunity to learn from the mistakes of his father. For George W. Bush, the War on Terror was couched in verbiage that was consistent with the language employed by his father. In making the case against Iraq, the elder Bush argued the time had arrived to confront 'the darker side of human nature' and 'forge a future' for the expansion of democracy and the rule of law throughout the world. Following the tragic events of 11 September, the younger Bush offered his imitation during an address to Congress on 21 September 2001:

Some speak of an age of terror. I know where there are struggles ahead, and dangers to face. As long as the United States of America is determined and strong, this will not be an age of terror; this will be an age of liberty, here and across the world ... . Our nation – this generation – will lift a dark threat of violence from our people and future. We will rally the world to this cause by our efforts, by our courage. We will not tire, we will not falter, and we will not fail.[10]

As with the father, in making the case for the campaign on terror, the son employed the same 'good versus evil' imagery. For the younger Bush: 'The course of the conflict is not yet known, yet its outcome is certain. Freedom and fear, justice and cruelty, have always been at war and we know that God is not neutral between them.'[11]

This statement notwithstanding, there is an irony awaiting public discourse. In an effort to confront post-Cold War stability, George H.W. Bush spoke of ending interstate aggression, but failed to provide solutions for ethnic conflicts and transnational terrorism. The magnitude associated with this failure is clear: the inability of the elder Bush to deal with intrastate conflict sealed the fate of the vision of the new world order. Interestingly, in the campaign against terror, George W. Bush proposed the eradication of terrorism. In opting for this approach, unknowingly, the President confronted an element of intrastate aggression (transactional terrorism which functioned within and between states) that contributed to the withdrawal of his father's vision. Finally, if Bush's post-11 September vision offers opportunities to revive the father's idea of a different world, the strategy will invariably open the Administration up to a series of questions. For example, will Bush complete the eradication of terrorism and pave the way for the survival and the expansion of American values? Similarly, will the younger Bush repeat the error of his father? That is, in the midst of questions regarding the parameters of the post-11 September world, will the President provide answers, or withdraw the vision? In the end, the outcome of the War on Terror will be the defining moment for the legacies of both presidents.

The Second Linkage: Iraq and the Search for Regional Stability

Both the first and second President Bush found their presidencies intertwined again on the subject of Iraq. For the elder Bush, Iraq emerged as a potent foreign policy issue following Saddam Hussein's invasion of Kuwait. In the case of the younger Bush, Iraq developed as a corollary to the war against terrorism: as a member of the 'axis of evil'. This section explores George W. Bush's effort at regime change in Iraq and how this strategy carried an unspoken objective – the revival and completion of George H.W. Bush's legacy.

For the senior Bush, the objectives were rudimentary: the removal of Iraqi forces from Kuwait and the destruction of Saddam Hussein's 'offensive military capabilities', thereby limiting Iraq's ability to make war on its neighbors. Throughout Operation Desert Shield and Operation Desert Storm, the Administration acknowledged that the removal of Saddam Hussein carried consequences that were beyond the parameters of US national security. Similarly, the UN Security Council did not approve of the removal of Hussein, and the Administration maintained that toppling the Iraqi leader would force Arab coalition-partners to end their participation and association with the alliance. Finally, the Administration argued that, without a unified Iraqi opposition, the elimination of Hussein could lead to the 'Lebanonization' of Iraq.[12]

Although these were the stated war aims, President Bush and members of his staff quietly articulated that there were indeed efforts at regime change. Initially, the Administration viewed efforts to topple Hussein as 'nonsensical'. This public face aside, the Administration never expected Hussein to survive the war, and second, Bush privately authorized several plans to remove the Iraqi leader. With respect to the first point, Secretary of State James Baker offered this statement: 'It's important to recall that, while it would have been welcome, Saddam's departure was never a stated objective of our policy. We were always very careful to negate it as a war aim or political objective. At the same time, we never really expected him to survive a defeat of such magnitude.'[13]

On the second point, plans for the regime change – both during and after the Gulf War – consisted of the following: the use of special operation forces to 'assassinate Hussein,' the employment of 'special bunker buster' missiles to destroy hardened strategic command facilities frequented by the Iraqi leader and an overt campaign on 15 February 1991 to enlist 'the Iraqi military and the Iraqi people to take matters in their own hands, to force Saddam Hussein, the dictator, to step aside'. The 'Iraqi people' the President spoke of consisted of the Shiites and the Kurds.[14]

The impact of these strategies proved disastrous for Bush and eventually redefined his legacy. The results of these endeavors represented 'post-victory blues', the notion that in spite of high post-war approval ratings, the President's earlier triumph in the Gulf War was dubbed 'operation desert shame', and the Administration's abandonment of the Shiites and the Kurds was considered reprehensible.[15] With respect to Iraq, two postscripts were influential in defining Bush's legacy. In the first instance, by defeating internal dissent, the Iraqi leader transformed himself from an 'international outlaw into the champion of Iraq's survival as a state, goals to which the Bush administration and most ... of the allies were also committed. It was the cruelest twist of the whole affair. Saddam had, in effect, joined the coalition.'[16] Secretary Baker illustrated the significance of the second point: 'I am reminded of something Tariq Aziz said to me in Geneva: We will be here long after you're gone. It was one of the few things he said that proved to be true.'[17]

In the end, while Bush's legacy took a major hit, there were other less obvious casualties: the president's test case – Iraq – for postwar stability had been derailed, and an Administration that earlier boosted of an era of new internationalism, reversed course talking instead of isolationism as a means to recover from the post-Gulf War verities.

George W. Bush

For the younger Bush, Iraq represented both opportunities and challenges. The opportunities were rudimentary: end the regime of Saddam Hussein, and the Administration could enhance regional stability. However, initially the Administration publicly moved away from its original goal, instead opting for a multilateral approach to force Saddam to disarm. Privately, the White House thought that Iraq would violate the UN Security Council Resolution (UNSCR) 1441 which required unfettered access to suspected weapons of mass destruction (WMD). Second, Saddam Hussein's removal would represent a vindication for the Bush family, and to those advisers that served with the senior Bush, namely Vice President Dick Cheney and Secretary of State Colin Powell.

Returning to the second point, the Iraqi threat posed numerous challenges for Bush. In the preparation for the war against terrorism, bureaucratic rumblings indicated that no consensus existed on a series of critical issues. If the Administration intervened in Iraq, for example, Bush strategists were concerned with the timing of the invasion. Similarly, the President and his advisers had to access how the new phase of the War on Terror would affect the coalition, particularly Arab members, thus the Bush team would have to develop a strategy to manage the regional fallout.

Another dilemma awaiting President Bush involved clarification on how and to what extent the Administration would utilize Iraqi opposition forces. To put this point in context, consider that the elder Bush had rallied the 'Iraqi people' to overthrow the Iraqi leader but, absent US military support, the opposition groups were in no position to defeat Hussein. In the final analysis, the end game was obvious: the Kurds and Shiites were slaughtered by the remnants of Iraq's elite Republican Guard.

Certain of regime change, the younger Bush not only enlisted the Kurds and Shiites to rise up against Saddam, but the President was determined to ensure a united opposition following the transition to a post-Saddam regime. Consistent with this approach, strategists at the Pentagon opted to train elements of the opposition in preparation for any American-led invasion.[18] By taking this approach, the younger Bush silenced the criticism that preoccupied his father – that he would betray the Kurds and Shiites.

The second issue concerned doctrine. The President's 'axis-of-evil' address dramatically altered Administration strategy and provided renewed impetus to remove the Iraqi president.[19] Noting that Iraq's WMDs threatened world peace, Bush launched a new doctrine on terrorism and issued this caveat: the United States would not allow rogue states to hold the country hostage to 'terror weapons'. To protect the homeland against rogue states (Iraq, Iran and North Korea), Bush introduced the doctrine of 'preemption'.[20] According to the President, the United States would employ force to destroy WMDs in a 'preemptive attack' intended to protect the homeland. The doctrine immediately alienated alliance members in the Middle East and caused considerable consternation among NATO allies concerned about American unilateralism.[21] In an effort to defuse the increasing apprehension regarding his Administration's intensions, Bush asserted that future of world peace rests with Iraq: 'As for Mr. Saddam Hussein, he needs to let inspectors back into his country, to show us that he is not developing weapons of mass destruction.'[22]

As to the second Bush-Hussein showdown, according to the President, 'this is personal', noting that the Iraqi leader tried to assassinate his father. Thus, for Bush the stakes were raised considerably. Moreover, there is an important side note to this struggle: Bush intimated that his anger and frustration were directed not only at the Iraqi leader, but former President Bill Clinton for failing to 'appropriately respond' to Iraq's assassination attempt of the elder Bush. To illustrate the President's point, in response to an assassination attempt (in June of 1993) Clinton observed in a speech to the nation that: 'The plan [was] devised by the Iraq Government .... As such, the Iraqi attack against President Bush was an attack against our country and against all Americans.'[23] In a counter-attack, Clinton launched 23 cruise missiles that destroyed one of the four Iraqi intelligence facilities. For the younger Bush, Clinton's use of cruise missiles was unsettling and contributed to the perception of a weak America: 'The antiseptic notion of launching a cruise missile into some guy's tent is a joke. I mean, people viewed that as the impotent America.'[24]

On another issue, the younger Bush utilized the UN as a means to take up the case against the Iraqi leader. Employing similar verbiage as his father, Bush argued that the struggle against Iraq could define the future of the UN: 'Will the United Nations serve the purpose of its founding, or will it be irrelevant?'[25] After making a prosecutorial case outlining Iraqi contravention of post-Gulf War Security Council agreements, the President offered this caveat: 'The purpose of the United States should not be doubted. The Security Council resolutions will be enforced, or action will be unavoidable. And a regime that has lost its legitimacy will lose its power.'[26]

Finally, as of the time of this writing, the military showdown with Iraq has just begun. Of immediate focus for this study is the query: how will the war assist in the evaluation of Bush's legacy? Obviously, until the shooting finishes the jury remains out. However, with the war commencing the outcome of the battle will serve notice on several fronts. For the younger Bush, regime change in Iraq will force the dissipation of the old debate concerning his father's inability to 'remove the Butcher of Baghdad'. Thus, victory would mean the father would have to thank the son for rewriting history. For the current president, with a successful campaign against terror well underway, triumph in Iraq would add to, in my opinion, an already impressive foreign policy resume.

The Third Linkage: the War on Terror

As with the former cases, the War on Terror offered another variable that indicated a connection between the father and son presidents. For the elder Bush, during his tenure as vice president for Ronald Reagan, and then as president in his own right, the issue of terrorism represented a continuing and vexing aspect of foreign policy. At issue then is the contribution of the elder Bush in confronting terrorism during his twelve-year span in the nation's two highest offices.

During the Reagan Administration, the elder Bush's role was mixed, if not controversial. In confronting terrorism, Lebanon remained an area of concern for the Administration, particularly since a US embassy was destroyed, and six months later, 241 US Marines were killed. These events were in addition to the several US citizens who were held hostage by Hezbollah, an Islamic extremist group allied with Iran.

As a member of the National Security Planning Group (NSPG), Vice President Bush participated in a number of critical decisions. That said, as a member of the faction that was adverse to the use of force (Secretary of Defense Casper Weinberger also belonged to this faction), Bush found himself in the untenable position to recommend to Reagan that the United States should *not* launch any military reprisals against Hezbollah for their attacks on US interests, in spite of the overwhelming evidence of their complicity. At the very least, these recommendations damaged Bush's standing among conservatives within the Administration.

In the second term, Bush chaired the committee to combat terrorism. In a speech in February of 1986, Bush issued a report that noted: 'We are prepared to act in concert alone to prevent or respond to terrorist acts. *We will make no concessions to terrorists* [italics in original].' The problem for Reagan and Bush was that one month earlier (17 January 1986) the Vice President, along with National Security Advisor Admiral John Poindexter, in a meeting with the President, provided Regan with a memo that outlined the proposed sale of weapons in exchange for US hostages in Lebanon.[27] The result of this meeting undermined the report of the counter-terrorism task force and Administration policy and laid the foundation for the resultant Iran-Contra Scandal. In the fight against terrorism, the elder Bush, like many other participants in the scandal, appeased terrorists.

Beginning in 1989, Bush reduced terrorism to a low priority for his incoming Administration. Moreover, having been tainted by Iran-Contra, Bush made an astute decision. He had terrorism remanded to interagency deliberations where bureaucratic turf battles ensured that the subject of terrorism would die a slow death and cease to be a major foreign policy issue. According to Michael Ledeen, this attitude was kept in place with the policies of the Clinton Administration and the result was a do-nothing approach that culminated in the horrific events of 11 September 2001.[28]

The events of 11 September thrust the younger Bush into a historic position. In little over a year, the War on Terror redefined American security interests and international relations. The creation of the Department of Homeland Security represented the first of many initiatives that indicated that President Bush was serious about securing the homeland against future terrorist attacks. Staying on the domestic side of the War on Terror, the President created a special military command (USCOM) whose sole purpose was to provide military security for the defense of the United States.

These two initiatives represented the domestic elements of an extraordinary grand strategy in a concentrated campaign to defeat al-Qaeda. President Bush introduced the overall strategy and plans to prosecute the first war of the twenty-first century during a nationally televised address to the nation on 20 September 2001. In this speech, the President argued: 'We will direct every resource at our command – every means of diplomacy, every tool of intelligence, every instrument of law enforcement, every financial influence, and every necessary weapon of war – to the destruction and to the defeat of the global terror network.'[29]

Nearly a month into the second year of the War on Terror, President Bush had scored significant victories. The Taliban had been routed in Afghanistan. In addition, al-Qaeda had been defeated and dispersed and was no longer utilizing Afghanistan as a staging area to export transnational terror. Consistent with the Administration's strategy, the President deployed detachments of Special Forces to the Philippines, Yemen and Georgia, in an effort to defeat al-Qaeda forces in those countries. A CIA-controlled unmanned Predator aircraft patrolling the skies over Yemen launched a Hellfire missile killing six members of al-Qaeda. This attack demonstrated Bush's willingness to employ 'any and all means' to achieve his objective: a post-11 September world free of the threat of terrorism.[30] While it is too soon to view these actions as ending terrorism, at best the Administration can argue that it has contained the terrorist threat in these and other areas of the world for the short-term.

Finally, however, the War on Terror is well underway and victory over al-Qaeda and other terrorist networks is still far off. In the final analysis, Bush has used the failed efforts of the past – including those associated with his father – in order to ensure victory in the present. At issue is the extent to which Bush can claim that the War on

Terror is a central component of his legacy. At the midpoint of his presidency, the President can assert that his Administration has precluded further al-Qaeda attacks on US interests, and American military forces continue to pursue and contain bin Laden and his global terrorist network.

Conclusion

In October of 2002, President Bush uttered the words 'this is personal'. Little did the President know that these words represented an apt description of his legacy at midpoint. Whether known or calculated, it is clear that since the commencement of the War on Terror – with respect to the three areas of stability in the international system, Iraq and terrorism – a connection exists between the presidencies of George H.W. Bush and George W. Bush.

In lieu of the aforementioned connections, how then do we evaluate Bush? Exploring this issue requires an assessment of an incomplete and ongoing process. The assessments link stability in the international system, confronting Iraq and the War on Terror. The research has established a relationship between the two presidencies and these factors, leaving the investigator with a quandary. On the one hand, with respect to the War on Terror, evidence supports the contention that the Administration has a proven strategy; moreover, true to his word, the President has conducted a campaign of global reach. However, in the long term, the need for more clarification remains. In the case of the search for stability within the post-11 September international order, the President has enlisted imagery as a means to define the parameters of the world the Administration is trying to construct absent international terrorism. As envisioned by the President, that world has yet to come into view.

On the subject of Iraq, as the leading threat within the 'axis-of-evil', the Administration has focused global attention on ridding the world of Hussein and his stockpiles of WMDs. With war just underway at the time of this writing, and discussion with Iraqi opposition forces for the post-Saddam Hussein phase having occurred, the Administration is far ahead of the elder Bush. Similarly, the 15–0 Security Council decision on 8 November 2002 tightened the screws on Iraq, setting the stage for what some perceived as an inevitable showdown. In the final analysis, the war will say much about the future potential for international stability.

With respect to the last area of focus, the War on Terror, the Administration has, in my opinion, passed expectations. Though the President spoke of a campaign of global reach, few took Bush at his word. The introduction of US special forces in the Philippines, Georgia and Yemen has produced the desired outcomes – the containment and dispersal of al-Qaeda and affiliated organizations. Consistent with this point, the US/Kenyan military exercises in November 2001 were designed to warn Somalia of acting as a host to fleeing al-Qaeda, and by all accounts these exercises have proven successful.

Finally, the irony of this research endeavor is that, in the final analysis, Bush's legacy is linked to his father's. As the study has identified, a clear linkage exists between the policies of the father and the son. In each area, the son has benefited from the mistakes and successes of the father. In the end, with success in all three areas, Bush has resurrected discussion about his father's legacy and positioned himself to define his own place in history. This leads to a concluding paradox: the outcome of the conflict with Iraq will be a barometer for Bush's long-term legacy. Certain of victory, Republicans have predicted approval ratings reminiscent of the elder Bush. While construing this reality, Republicans may do well to remember the complete story. With the 1992 presidential election approaching and having ignored the economy during a string of foreign policy successes (Panama, the Philippines and Iraq), the elder Bush turned inward to fix the economy. In short, the President's approval rating declined precipitously and issues related to the economy precluded reelection. Finally, as we move from a discourse on Bush's legacy at midpoint to a wider discussion of the long-term evaluation of his presidency, the younger Bush may do well to remember the misfortunes of the father as he seeks a second term.

Notes

1   This definition was employed in my doctoral dissertation, *Unfilled Promises: American Foreign Policy and the New World Order* (unpublished August 2000).
2   Some authors assert that the vision represented a reversal of the Reagan doctrine. Under Reagan, the administration concluded that the UN personified a weak institution and was thus unable to assist with US policy objectives, mainly the rollback of communism. For more on this point and a comparison of the Wilsonian and Bush visions of a new order, see Robert W. Tucker and David Hendrickson (1992), *The Imperial Temptation: The New World Order and America's Purpose*, New York: Council on Foreign Relations Press, 54–9.
3   George H.W. Bush (1991), Joint Address to Congress (6 March), reprinted in *The New York Times* (7 March 1991).
4   Ibid.
5   Interview with Brent Scowcroft (February 2000).
6   Benjamin Schwartz (1994/1995), 'The Vision Thing: Sustaining the Unsustainable', *World Policy Journal* (Winter), 101–21.
7   Stephen R. Graubard (1992), *Mr. Bush's War: Adventures in the Politics of Illusion*, New York: Hill and Wang, 164–7.
8   David Gergen (1991/1992), 'America's Missed Opportunities', *Foreign Affairs*, 71/1 (Winter), 12 and 1.
9   Lawrence Freedman (1991/1992), 'Order and Disorder in the New World Order', *Foreign Affairs*, America and the World Edition, 20–37.
10   George W. Bush (2001), Joint Address to Congress (21 September), reprinted in *The New York Times* (22 September 2001).
11   George W. Bush (2001), Joint Address to Congress and the American People, US Capital, Washington, DC (20 September).
12   James A. Baker, III (1995), *The Politics of Diplomacy: Revolution, War and Peace, 1989–1992*, New York: Putnam's, 442.
13   Ibid., 437–8.
14   On the plans to kill the Iraqi leader, see 'The Plan to Kill Saddam Hussein', *Newsweek* (10 January 1994), 4–5; Janet Seymour (2001), *Operation Provide Comfort*, Montgomery, AL: Maxwell Air Force Base. In another example of the efforts to kill Hussein in command bunkers, see Walter Pincus (1998), 'Saddam Hussein's Death is a Goal Says Ex-CIA Chief; Bush Advisers Hoped That Collateral Damage Would Include Iraqi Leader', *Washington Post* (15 February).
15   For more on this point, see Strobe Talbot (1991/92), 'Post-Victory Blues', *Foreign Affairs*, 71/1 (Winter), 53–69; and Michael Ledeen (1991), 'Operation Desert Shame', *American*

Spectator, 24/6 (June), 12.

16 Talbot, 63.
17 Baker, 442.
18 See Peter Slevin (2002), 'US Pushes for Iraqi Opposition', *Washington Post* (9 August), A20.
19 US, White House (2001), 'President Speaks on War Effort to Citadel Cadets' (11 December), online at www.whitehouse.gov/news/releases/2001/12/20011211-6.html.
20 Randall Mikkelsen (2002), 'Bush Outlines Strategy of Preemptive Strikes', *Washington Post* (20 September).
21 Thomas E. Risks and Vernon Loeb (2002), 'Bush Developing Military Policy of Striking First: New Doctrine Addresses Terrorism', *Washington Post* (10 June), A1.
22 Mike Allen (2001), 'Iraq's Weapons Could Make it a Target, Bush Says', *Washington Post* (27 November).
23 William J. Clinton (1993), 'Address to the Nation on the Attack on Iraqi Intelligence Headquarters', *Public Papers of the President, Administration of William J. Clinton* (26 June).
24 Bob Woodward and Dan Bolz (2002), 'We Will Rally the World: Bush and His Advisers Set Objectives, But Struggle on How to Achieve Them', Part III, *Washington Post* (28 January), A1.
25 US, White House, Office of the Press Secretary (2002), 'Address by President Bush: Remarks at the United Nations General Assembly, 12 September 2002' (12 September).
26 Ibid.
27 Constantine C. Menges (1988), *Inside the National Security Council: The True Story of the Making and Unmaking of Reagan's Foreign Policy*, New York: Touchstone Books, 274–5.
28 See Michael A. Ledeen (2002), *The War Against the Terror Masters: Why It Happened, Where We Are Now, How We Will Win*, New York: St Martin's Press.
29 Bush (2001), Joint Address to Congress and the American People.
30 James Risen and Judith Miller (2002), 'CIA is Reported to Kill a Leader of Qaeda in Yemen', *The New York Times* (5 November).

Chapter 6

The Loyal Foot Soldier: Vice President Cheney in the War on Terror

Jack Lechelt

Introduction

George W. Bush, during the time he was the apparent Republican nominee for president, had always wanted Richard Cheney to be the vice presidential nominee for the 2000 election. Unfortunately for Bush, Cheney had no interest in the position, but he did agree to lead the search that would produce a running mate. Little did Cheney know, the search would lead right back to him.[1] More amazingly, the reluctant Vice President quickly would become the most influential and powerful vice president in the history of the United States.

From the early stages of the Bush presidency, it was evident that Vice President Cheney would be quite influential.[2] With the terrorist attacks of 11 September 2001 and the ensuing War on Terror , Cheney's influence would only increase. President Bush has relied on Vice President Cheney for sound advice and council, and has placed the Vice President in charge of important areas of concern for the War on Terror . Moreover, the President has allowed the Vice President to have unprecedented access to every aspect of the foreign policy process in the Bush White House, and has given Cheney much leeway to take charge of other areas of interest to the Vice President.

It is always important to recognize the personal aspects of the president in assessing the tasks, responsibilities, and roles of the president's aides and staff. A president's preferences and personality are vitally important in attempting to gauge how his team is utilized. Still, it is equally important to recognize the surrounding environment to understand why the vice presidency has become more important. In a global environment that is becoming increasingly interrelated and complex, it is far more difficult for any one country or one person to lead. Furthermore, the expanding size of the federal government makes management increasingly complicated. As the Brownlow Commission recognized in the 1930s, the president needs help – and this will always be the case. The vice presidency can be the help that the president needs: the vice presidency is an office with increasing stature, resources, and a unique perspective that can offer the president one more means of exerting some semblance of control in a difficult environment.

Add to this complexity the horrible attacks on New York and Washington in September of 2001. President George W. Bush was thrust into a situation that presented a ruthless enemy of no particular nation-state, which had connections that stretched across the globe in a myriad of ways. Amazingly, a new method of waging war would have to be developed, and a means of protecting a huge nation of 270 million people would have to be developed – and quickly. Any former governor with no national government experience would have his hands full (and the United States has a penchant for electing state governors). In this new world, President Bush was able to utilize a vice president with an impressive array of national and international political experience. Moreover, Dick Cheney brought to the position an extensive career of White House and national political experience, including his service as Secretary of Defense under George H.W. Bush.

In the following pages, I will discuss the many roles Vice President Dick Cheney has had in the War on Terror, and attempt to explain *why* he is so influential. Although Cheney has spent much time in 'undisclosed locations' since the terrorist attacks, his influence on the War on Terror has not reflected any absence. Indeed, it is paramount to a thorough understanding of the formulation and conduct of America's War on Terror to assess the role of Vice President Cheney, a major architect of the war.

The Roles of Vice President Cheney in the War on Terror

Vice President Cheney has many roles in the Bush Administration's war on terrorism: 1) policy advisor and counselor to the President; 2) policy specialist; 3) policy advocate; 4) ambassador-at-large; 5) public relations specialist; and 6) liaison to Congress.

Without question, upon entering the vice presidency, Dick Cheney brought with him an impressive national government résumé, serving in many important positions: Chief of Staff to President Ford; Representative in the US House of Representatives (with positions in the Republican leadership and service on foreign policy related committees); and wartime Secretary of Defense for President George H.W. Bush. Considering that Cheney would be working with a former governor who had no national or international experience, one could reasonably expect Cheney to greatly assist Bush.[3]

After accepting Bush's offer to serve as his running mate and prior to the Republican national convention, Cheney was also designated to serve as chairman of the Bush transition effort.[4] This greatly enabled him to have a serious impact on who would work closely with Bush and himself: 'the vice president interviewed every cabinet secretary – and succeeded in placing his favorites at the helm of the Defense and Treasury departments.'[5] Cheney is also credited with having a 'direct hand' in selecting Colin Powell as Secretary of State;[6] and Donald Rumsfeld, Secretary of Defense, is an old acquaintance of the Vice President. Finally, Cheney is responsible for finding 'two of the most powerful deputies in the foreign policy team – Stephen Hadley, number two to Condoleezza Rice on the National Security Council, and Paul Wolfowitz, deputy to Mr. Rumsfeld'.[7] In essence: 'Cheney's prominent role in selecting people to staff the top echelons of the Bush administration and his ties to some Washington figures dating back more than 30 years add up to an unprecedented network of plugged-in officials who have at least one thing in common: all have a Cheney connection.'[8]

This 'network' and Cheney's influence in selecting important members of Bush's foreign policy team allow Cheney to be an excellent policy advisor and counselor to the President in the War on Terror . These factors enable the Vice President to have a consummate knowledge of the important activities that are occurring throughout the foreign policy world of the US government. President Bush can rest assured that Cheney is, in fact, 'plugged-in'.

Cheney is also assisted in his efforts to advise and counsel Bush through an impressive staff of foreign policy experts, which have been described as the 'fulcrum of Bush's foreign policy'.[9] With a staff of 50: 'Cheney and his aides have been fully integrated into the national security apparatus.'[10] Furthermore, Cheney's chief of staff, Lewis 'Scooter' Libby, is highly regarded and also serves as Cheney's national security advisor.[11] Finally, 'though greatly outnumbered by the [National Security Council's] 80 professional staffers, the 13 members of Cheney's foreign policy shop are more highly regarded in Washington'.[12] With all of these resources, Cheney has largely avoided specific assignments (except those he wishes to take on) so that he can have a broad foreign policy reach and better provide general foreign policy assistance to the President: 'As a minister without portfolio, he has no territory to defend or institution to protect, which means that "the President doesn't have to run his advice through a filter"', says an aide to the Vice President. 'Cheney's view isn't the State Department view or the Pentagon view; it's Cheney's view.'[13]

Also enabling Cheney to have an important role in Bush's War on Terror are the practices and precedents established under earlier vice presidents and presidents; in particular, the precedents established under President Jimmy Carter and Vice President Walter Mondale have had a major impact on all vice presidents since Mondale.[14] First and foremost, Vice President Cheney has an office in the West Wing of the White House: proximity is power. Second, Vice President Cheney attends the President's daily national security briefings.[15] From 8 a.m. to 9 a.m., the President, Vice President, then-Director/now-Secretary of Homeland Security Tom Ridge, National Security Advisor Condoleezza Rice, and Chief of Staff Andrew Card receive the most sensitive intelligence information – also called the President's Daily Brief (PDB), which are given by the Central Intelligence Agency and Federal Bureau of Investigation.[16] Third, Bush and Cheney have a completely private lunch on a weekly basis: no aides can attend. And fourth, as mentioned earlier, the vice presidency has a respectable budget and staff resources.[17]

Another important resource for Vice President Cheney's influence is President George W. Bush's desire to have an actively involved vice president: Cheney's 'is the last voice Bush wants to hear before making difficult decisions. "What does Dick think?" the President routinely asks'.[18] Much has been made of the fact that Cheney has no intention to run for president himself, which enables Bush to accept Cheney's advice without questioning his motives. Cheney 'has no plan to run for president or for anything', says Mary Matalin, formerly one of Cheney's closest advisers. Adds White House counselor Karl Rove:

> The one thing that differentiates the advice the president gets from Cheney from the advice he gets from everybody else is Dick Cheney has absolutely no agenda except the president's. The president never has to worry about, Is this in Dick's interest or my interest? It elevates the level of trust between the two individuals.[19]

Time magazine's Nancy Gibbs described Bush and Cheney's relationship as the 'partnership of the year': the Bush/Cheney 'inner workings are utterly secret, the Vice President perfectly discreet. He's Bush's personal CIA, with secure lines into corporate boardrooms, foreign governments, both houses of Congress and sleeper cells in every branch of government'.[20]

Beyond the private weekly lunches and daily intelligence briefings, Bush and Cheney spend much of their day together: 'They are together every day; sometimes for most of the day; Cheney attends any important meeting and then often stays behind with Bush alone.'[21] The Vice President also has weekly meetings with Secretary of State Powell, and on 'Wednesdays, he chews over policy at the Pentagon with the president's national security team'.[22] The close contact between Bush and Cheney was hardly impacted by the terrorist attacks on 11 September: although Cheney has often been dispatched to his 'undisclosed location' to ensure the line of presidential succession in case of another terrorist attack, the Vice President has been able to maintain constant communications with the President and has continued to attend important national security meetings through state-of-the-art video communications conferencing.[23] According to Bob Woodward:

> Cheney, Rice, Card, Hughes, Rove and Fleischer could just stop by and ask Ashley [the President's secretary] if [the President] had five minutes or whatever might be needed. The president said it worked the other way around too. 'It makes my job a heck of a lot easier to be able to have access to a lot of people' to get their feedback or reactions. 'It was very likely that a Condi or a Dick Cheney would come in, and I'd say, "What are you thinking now?"'[24]

From the very moment of the attacks, Vice President Cheney has been actively involved in the War on Terror. While President Bush was aboard Air Force One attempting to get back to Washington, Cheney advised the President that it was not safe enough for him to return to the capital, and Cheney advised Bush of the potential need to shoot down hijacked civilian airliners that may be en route to destructive ends. Cheney, after consulting with the President, gave the orders to shoot down United Flight 93 before it crashed in Pennsylvania.[25]

Throughout the War on Terror in Afghanistan (the military effort was formally titled Enduring Freedom), Bush found Cheney's presence and input to be quite helpful; at an early November 2001 National Security Council meeting, the Council was discussing the less than stellar performance of allied opposition forces in the region, which were leading the ground fight against the Taliban and al-Qaeda. Vice President Cheney raised the possibility that the American troop deployment might need to be increased from 50,000 to 55,000. Woodward records the President's reactions to Cheney's input in the following passage:

> The president had not known that Cheney was going to raise these issues, but he had found that when Cheney asked questions it was worth listening to them. He wanted [General] Franks to take them seriously. 'When can you give me some options,' Bush asked Franks, 'along the lines of what the vice president talks about?'
> 'In one week,' Franks said, 'to a very small group.'[26]

President Bush also ensured that Cheney would have total and continuous access to all Administration discussions regarding homeland security; in Homeland Security Presidential Directive (HSPD) 1, which detailed the organization of the newly created Homeland Security Council (HSC), one of the members of both the HSC Principals Committee and HSC Deputies Committee is the Vice President's Chief of Staff, Lewis Libby. Also, 'the Vice President may attend any and all meetings of any entity established under [HSPD 1]'.[27]

With an established relationship based on precedents from previous administrations, Bush's desire to have an actively engaged vice president, and Cheney's breadth of knowledge and experience in foreign policy, Cheney was destined to play an incredibly important role in the War on Terror and this has certainly been the case. Bob Woodward's *Bush at War*, portrays Vice President Cheney as continually and actively present at all important meetings after 11 September.[28] Interestingly, and as an example of Cheney's role as a policy specialist, one of the missions Bush had assigned to Cheney prior to 11 September, was for the Vice President to 'coordinate the US response to domestic terrorism'.[29] On 8 May 2001, Bush announced that Cheney would head the National Preparedness Review task force, which would coordinate 'the efforts of all federal departments and agencies with weapons of mass destruction: chemical, biological or nuclear weapons'.[30]

After the attacks of 11 September, the task of coordinating a more focused response to domestic terrorism was again handed to Cheney, who was able to build upon his earlier work with the National Preparedness Review.[31] Furthermore, 'it was Cheney who recommended to Bush the creation of the Homeland Security Office and suggested Pennsylvania Governor Thomas J. Ridge as the one to head that office'.[32] Cheney also 'put his stamp on the new homeland security office by installing retired Admiral Steve Abbot, a senior aide, as Ridge's chief deputy. Abbot [would] oversee the office's day-to-day operations and the development of the long-term strategy, with the goal of presenting the plan to President Bush for consideration [in spring 2002]'.[33]

Cheney has also become a policy expert and proponent of a strong national defense against possible bioterrorism: 'Mr. Cheney's office has become a mini-research center on bioterrorism. ([Lewis Libby], Mr. Cheney's chief of staff, is called 'germ boy' by other White House aides.)' The possibility of a bioterror attack has been a concern to Cheney for years and, upon touring the Centers for Disease Control and Prevention and meeting with various scientists and Central Intelligence Agency officers, the Vice President presented Bush with numerous suggestions for protecting the nation: 'President Bush had accepted all of Mr. Cheney's suggestions except for one: a call for every single American to be vaccinated for smallpox.'[34] As Vice President, Cheney 'can both counsel the president and plunge into the subjects that interest him, using the full powers of his office to assemble facts and marshal his arguments, without feeling any pressure to justify himself to voters'.[35]

The Bush Administration has for months been attempting to widen the scope of the War on Terror to include a preemptive strike against Saddam Hussein and Iraq. Although Cheney initially quieted Deputy Defense Secretary Paul Wolfowitz in early discussions of broadening the War on Terror to include Iraq, the Vice President has since become one of the administration's strongest advocates for attacking Iraq.[36] In his role of international ambassador, along with that of policy advocate, in March 2002 Cheney traveled to the Middle East in hopes of garnering support for expanding the war to include Iraq.[37] As the Vice President continues to counsel the President on Iraq:

> Cheney's impact on the Iraq debate – or his influence on the president – cannot be overstated, officials and experts said. Cheney is involved in key aspects of the planning for Iraq, from wording the administration's draft U.N. resolution on resumed weapons inspections to what to do with Iraq if Saddam Hussein is toppled. In interagency councils, Cheney has been consumed with whether the Iraqi president has obtained weapons of mass destruction.[38]

It was also Cheney's recommendation that the public case for war against Iraq be made in late summer 2002, as opposed to later in the fall, because the public case *against* war on Iraq was already underway via opinion articles by Brent Scowcroft and James Baker.[39] In a speech to the Veterans of Foreign Wars (VFW) in Nashville, Tennessee on 26 August 2002, Cheney 'presented the administration's most forceful and comprehensive rationale yet for attacking Iraq, warning that Saddam Hussein would "fairly soon" have nuclear weapons'.[40] The Vice President's work regarding Iraq concerns both his role as policy advocate and public spokesperson for the administration:

> Much as the US keeps pulling the rest of the world toward a tougher line on Saddam, so Cheney keeps pulling within the White House. Bush uses Cheney to play that role publicly as well – most remarkably back in August [2002], when Cheney's very tough speech about the threat posed by Iraq helped convince U.N. members that Bush was serious about going after Saddam, alone if necessary.[41]

Cheney's infrequent public appearances and speeches make those rare appearances and speeches all the more valuable to President Bush. Moreover, he is less associated with the 'hawkish' forces in the Administration than is Deputy Defense Secretary Wolfowitz, and if Bush were to make the initial case for regime change in Iraq, then he would limit his own options: Cheney became the natural choice.[42]

More recently, in January 2003, Cheney spoke to a group of Republican activists and stated that removing Saddam from power is an important aspect of the War on Terror: 'Confronting the threat offered by Iraq is not a distraction in the war on terrorism', he told those attending the Republican National Committee's winter meeting. 'It is absolutely crucial to waging the war on terror.'[43] Cheney is highly regarded in dealing with conservative audiences ('a superstar among the Republican faithful'): he campaigned hard for Republicans in the 2004 Congressional elections.[44]

Journalists are not the only people who have caught on to Cheney's influence in the Bush White House and in the War on Terror: foreign government officials have also recognized the importance of the Vice President. With the added complexity of the divide between the more moderate Secretary of State Colin Powell, and the more conservative elements of the Bush administration (Cheney and Bush adhere more closely to the latter), foreign officials know that it is important to work with the Vice President. More specifically, due to Cheney's past leadership of the Defense department during the Persian Gulf War, the Vice President has many established connections in the Middle East region, which has been vitally important in the War on Terror:

> Cheney is most plugged in on the Middle East and Persian Gulf, White House officials say, because no one else in the administration can replicate the depth and breadth of his connections in the region. Cheney and his staff are routinely on the phone with Arab leaders, an unusual channel in addition to the regular State Department contacts.[45]

Moreover, 'visiting foreign leaders almost always hold separate private meetings with Cheney because their ambassadors have told them that such conversations are a necessary addition to sessions with Powell, a relative moderate whose advice does not always prevail'.[46] It was reported that Cheney cancelled a meeting with a foreign dignitary because his government was holding a dissident; realizing the importance of the meeting with Cheney, the government quickly let the man free so that the appointment would be kept. In 2002, as of October of that year, Vice President Cheney had met with 17 prime ministers and presidents.

Finally, Vice President Cheney has served as a liaison to Congress. The Constitution already requires that the Vice President also serve as President of the Senate; still, that task is only important in the case of a tie vote among senators, in which case the Vice President can break the tie. With his official position as President of the Senate, Cheney has a customary office on the Senate side of the Capital; however, as a sign of his importance to House Republicans, he also has an office on the House side of the Capital.[47] Cheney has proven to be a far more important congressional player than just a tiebreaker. From Cheney's work on the transition, Bush had intended that Cheney would build up some political capital 'so he [could] go up to Capital Hill and spend it'.[48] The Vice President also attends weekly lunches with Congressional Republicans and has addressed the concerns of Congressional Democrats, particularly after 11 September.[49] According to Bumiller and Schmitt, 'on Capital Hill', Cheney has been described as the 'administration's chief schmoozer and enforcer, and often gives counsel on national security'.

Table 6.1 provides a summary of Vice President Cheney's various roles in the War on Terror.

Summary Discussion and Conclusion

Clearly, Vice President Richard Cheney is an integral part of President George W. Bush's war on terrorism. Bush and Cheney spend much time together and Cheney is afforded many opportunities to offer useful advice and have an influence on administration policy. Still, to understand that Cheney is an important player in the Bush White House does not explain *why* Cheney is so influential.

Many have credited vice presidential involvement with presidential allowance of involvement: what the President has given, he can take away.[50] Although it is important to recognize a president's personality and desire to have an actively involved vice president, much is overlooked in not appreciating other important explanations of vice presidential involvement. In particular, Joseph Pika has discussed the importance of practices and precedents in understanding the more recent and actively involved vice presidency.[51] The most important president/vice president duo, with regards to practices and precedents, comes from the Jimmy Carter/Walter Mondale administration (1977–81). As discussed earlier, Carter and Mondale established that the vice president would have an office in the West Wing, would be able to access all paperwork and information coming from and going to the president, that the vice president would have a respectable budget and staff, and that the president and vice president would meet on a weekly basis for lunch. All of these precedents have carried through to all following vice presidents.

Also important in understanding the current state of the vice presidency is global and domestic politics. First, as Bayless Manning has pointed out, international issues are no longer neatly divided between international and domestic issues: we now have 'intermestic politics'. Also, there has been an increase in the importance of low policy

Table 6.1   Roles of Vice President Cheney in the War on Terror: examples

Policy advisor and counselor to the President
- Bush asking, 'What does Dick think?'
- Weekly lunches with President, which are completely private and not talked about.
- Continuous daily interaction with President.
- Attends daily national security briefings for President; if not in person, then via videoconference link.
- Strong foreign policy staff, many of whom are also 'counselors to the President'.

Policy specialist
- Created National Preparedness Review, which was forerunner of Homeland Security Office, and was proponent of selecting Gov. Tom Ridge to head office.
- Leads government efforts to protect homeland from bioterror attacks.

Policy advocate
- Strong proponent of taking action in Iraq.
- Traveled to Middle East to gain support for regime change in Iraq.

Ambassador-at-large
- Considered by foreign officials to be the 'go to' Bush official.
- Toured the Middle East and traveled extensively.
- Has many contacts with Arab leaders from work in Gulf War.

Public relations specialist for building public support
- Gave important speech to VFW (08/02) about importance of regime change in Iraq.
- Another speech to GOP activists (01/03) describing the importance of removing Hussein to War on Terror.
- Also highly regarded in conservative community.

Liaison to Congress, particularly Republicans
- Has offices in both House and Senate sides of capital.
- Attends GOP Senate lunches weekly.

(economics and trade), without a decrease in the importance of high policy (national security and military). Finally, there has been an increasing importance in transnational actors like international organizations and multinational corporations. Making this complex environment more unmanageable is the growth of the US government. Although the US government has an increasingly far reach into the affairs of the world, the institutionalization that accommodates such growth makes management more complicated. In particular, standard operating procedures, the stability and longevity of bureaucratic offices, and other components of the 'institutionalized presidency' make management more difficult; that is, the responsiveness of government and bureaucracy to individual presidents has often been forfeited to ensure stability.[52]

President George W. Bush has had to face these difficulties in an entirely unique post-11 September world, in which he must confront enemies in a potentially never-ending struggle. Unlike during the Cold War, when the supposed enemy combatant would be a communist foe that the US has spent decades and billions of dollars preparing to fight, and even unlike the post-Cold War world Bush's father, President George H.W. Bush, and President Clinton confronted, in which it appeared that the United States could operate with a relatively unique free hand, George W. Bush confronts a different environment. He needs help, and for him, help has been realized in Vice President Dick Cheney.

Many have credited Cheney's decision not to seek the presidency with allowing him to be a greater force in the Bush White House: the President does not have to wonder if Cheney is looking out for Cheney's future, or for Bush's present. Regardless of the influence such a fact may have on Bush, it is interesting to note that Dick Cheney, a highly respected Washington insider, does not feel the need to pursue higher elective office; the vice presidency has become an important and influential office in its own right.

Notes

1   Mark Bowden, Ron Hutcheson, and Ken Dilanian (2000), 'How Bush Selected Cheney', *Philadelphia Inquirer* (26 July).
2   See, for example, Abraham McLaughlin (2000), 'A Vice President-Elect with "Big Time" Clout', *Christian Science Monitor* (20 December), 1; Dana Milbank (2001), 'For Cheney, the Future Is Now', *Washington Post National Weekly Edition* (12–18 February), 12; Reuters (2001), 'The Vice-President – Savvy Journeyman at No. 2', *The Australian* (22 January); Peter Grier (2001), 'Cheney's Vice-Presidential Load Is Heaviest Yet', *Christian Science Monitor* (7 March); and Francine Kiefer (2001), 'Behind the Plan, the VP Who's Everywhere', *Christian Science Monitor* (18 May).
3   It was predicted before the Bush administration began that Cheney would wield extensive influence. See McLaughlin, 'A Vice President-Elect with "Big Time" Clout'; James Traub (2001), 'The Bush Years: W.'s World', *New York Times Magazine* (15 January); and Edward Walsh (2000), 'Cheney Lead a Life of Unexpected Turns', *Washington Post* (23 July).
4   John B. Burke (2002), 'The Bush Transition in Historical Context', *PS: Political Science & Politics*, 35 (1), 23–6. See also McLaughlin, 'A Vice President-Elect with "Big Time" Clout'; Edward Walsh (2001), 'Remaking the Role of Vice President; Cheney Expected to Wield Much Power, Influence', *Washington Post* (20 January); and Stephen Hess (2002), *Organizing the Presidency*, 3rd edn, Washington: Brookings Institution Press.

5   Kiefer, 'Behind the Plan'.

6   Reuters, 'The Vice-President – Savvy Journeyman'.

7   Gerard Baker (2001), 'Bush's Constant Friend: Man in the News Dick Cheney: The US Vice-President Keeps a Low Profile but Wields Enormous Influence', *Financial Times* (19 May).

8   Stewart M. Powell (2001), 'Even Outside D.C., Cheney Is Ultimate Insider; VP's Network Keeps Him in the Loop', *San Antonio Express-News* (2 December).

9   Glenn Kessler and Peter Slevin (2002), 'Cheney is Fulcrum of Foreign Policy: In Interagency Fights, His Views Often Prevail', *Washington Post* (13 October).

10 Milbank, 'For Cheney, the Future is Now'.

11 Libby is also an 'Assistant to the President', which is yet another acknowledgement of Cheney's immersion into the Bush foreign policy network.

12 Barbara Slavin and Susan Page (2002), 'Cheney Rewrites Roles in Foreign Policy: Influence "Unique" for Vice President', *USA Today* (29 July).

13 Nancy Gibbs (2002), 'Partnership of the Year: Double-Edged Sword', *Time* (30 December), 86–96. See also Kessler and Slevin, 'Cheney is Fulcrum'.

14 The practices and presidents have been best discussed by Joseph A. Pika (2000), 'The Vice Presidency: New Opportunities, Old Constraints', in M. Nelson, ed., *The Presidency and the Political System*, Washington, DC: CQ Press.

15 Kiefer, 'Behind the Plan'.

16 Walter Pincus (2002), 'Under Bush, the Briefing Gets Briefer; Key Intelligence Report by CIA and FBI Is Shorter, "More Targeted", Limited to Smaller Circle of Top Officials and Advisers', *Washington Post* (24 May).

17 For a thorough discussion of the Office of the Vice Presidency, which includes staff numbers and budgeting, see Bradley Patterson, Jr. (2000), *The White House Staff: Inside the West Wing and Beyond*, Washington: Brookings Institution Press.

18 Susan Page (2001), 'Cheney Takes "Backseat" in a Strong Way', *USA Today* (16 November).

19 Kenneth T. Walsh (2002), 'Cheney Out of the Bunker: The Most Powerful V.P. Ever, Now in the Role of a Lifetime', *US News & World Report* (25 March), 16–20.

20 Gibbs, 'Partnership', 92.

21 Ibid., 86–96.

22 Kiefer, 'Behind the Plan'. See also Gerard Baker (2001), 'Bush's Constant Friend: Man in the News Dick Cheney: The US Vice-President Keeps a Low Profile But Wields Enormous Influence', *Financial Times* (19 May), 13.

23 Roland Watson (2001), 'Cheney Stays Out of Sight But He is Still Calling the Shots', *The Times* (9 October); Powell, 'Even Outside D.C.'; Elisabeth Bumiller (2001), 'Cheney, Shrinking from View, Still Looms Large', *New York Times* (30 November); and Edwin Chen (2001), 'Cheney Busy Behind the Scenes: Vice President is Kept Hidden for Security Reasons', *Los Angeles Times* (12 October).

24 Bob Woodward (2002), *Bush at War*, New York: Simon & Schuster.

25 Dan Balz and Bob Woodward (2002), 'America's Chaotic Road to War: Bush's Global Strategy Began to Take Shape in First Frantic Hours after Attack', *Washington Post* (27 January).

26 Woodward, *Bush at War*, 292. Although Cheney's advice was important to the President, the increased troop deployment was apparently not needed according to Woodward, 314: 'In all, the US commitment to overthrow the Taliban had been about 110 CIA officers and 316 Special Forces personnel, plus massive American airpower'. For an excellent and brief analysis of Enduring Freedom, and the important role that the Northern Alliance played in the fighting, see Kenneth M. Pollack (2002), *The Threatening Storm: The Case to Invade Iraq*, New York: Random House, 298–302.

27 George W. Bush, 'Organization and Operation of the Homeland Security Council', Homeland Security Presidential Directive-1, 29 October 2001, online at http://www.fas.org/irp/offdocs/nspd/hspd-1.htm (15 February 2003).

28 Woodward, *Bush at War*, 255–6.

29 Kiefer, 'Behind the Plan'.

30 Andrew Schneider (2001), 'Domestic Security: Forging a Homeland Defense', *Kiplinger Business Forecasts* (21 September).

31 Woodward, *Bush at War*, 89.

32 Chen, 'Cheney Busy Behind the Scenes'.

33 Eric Pianin (2001), 'Homeland Security Team's Key Members Announced; Top Appointees Have Close Ties to Senior Bush Officials', *Washington Post* (21 November). In early 2003, the Department of Homeland Security (DHS) came into existence, with Tom Ridge serving as its first Secretary. However, according to President Bush's National Strategy for Homeland Security, 'the White House Office of Homeland Security will continue to play a key role advising the President and coordinating the interagency process', George W. Bush (2002), 'National Strategy for Homeland Security', Office of Homeland Security (June), 13. Still, with the existence of the DHS, there are many issues to be ironed out regarding executive branch coordination of homeland security; see Ivo H. Daalder, I.M. Destler, David L. Gunter, James H. Lindsay, Michael E. O'Hanlon, Peter R. Orszag, and James B. Steinberg (2003), *Protecting the American Homeland: One Year On*, Washington: Brookings Institution.

34 Bumiller and Schmitt, 'Cheney, Little Seen by Public'.

35 Ibid.

36 Regarding Wolfowitz, see Page, 'Cheney Takes "Backseat"'.

37 Kevin Whitelaw (2002), 'One Tough Roadshow', *US News and World Report* (25 March), 19.

38 Kessler and Slevin, 'Cheney is Fulcrum of Foreign Policy'.

39 Ibid.

40 Elisabeth Bumiller and James Dao (2002), 'Eyes on Iraq: Cheney Says Peril of a Nuclear Iraq Justifies Attack', *New York Times* (27 August).

41 Gibbs, 'Partnership', 88. For a differing account of Cheney's speech, in which he 'perturbed' the President and possibly 'boxed him in' with his speech on Iraq, see Evan Thomas (2002), 'The Quiet Power of Condi Rice', *Newsweek* (16 December), 24–34.

42 Gibbs, 'Partnership', 90.

43 Will Lester (2003), 'Cheney: Iraq Policy Key to Terror War', *Washington Post* (31 January).

44 Bumiller and Schmitt, 'Cheney, Little Seen'.

45 Slavin and Page, 'Cheney Rewrites Roles'.

46 Ibid.

47 James A. Barnes (2001), 'The Imperial Vice Presidency', *National Journal* (17 March), 815.

48 Gibbs, 'Partnership', 93–4.

49 Eric Schmitt (2001), 'A Nation Challenged: The Vice President; Out Front or Low Profile, Cheney Keeps Powerful Role', *New York Times* (7 October); Kiefer, 'Behind the Plan'.

50 Richard E. Neustadt (1997), 'Vice Presidents as National Leaders: Reflections Past, Present, and Future', in T. Walch, ed., *At the President's Side: The Vice Presidency in the Twentieth Century*, Columbia, MO: University of Missouri Press; Paul C. Light (1984), *Vice-Presidential Power: Advice and Influence in the White House*, Baltimore: Johns Hopkins University Press.

51 Pika, 'The Vice Presidency'.

52 The growth of the institutional presidency is thoroughly discussed in Lyn Ragsdale and John J. Theis, III (1997), 'The Institutionalization of the American Presidency: 1924–92',

American Journal of Political Science, 41 (4), 280–318; for an excellent account of standard operating procedures and their effect on crisis situations, see Model II from Graham T. Allison and Phillip Zelikow (1999), *Essence of Decision: Explaining the Cuban Missile Crisis*, 2nd edn, New York: Longman; finally, the responsiveness/professionalism debate is discussed in Terry Moe (1985), 'The Politicized Presidency', in J. Chubb and P. Peterson, eds, *The New Direction in American Politics*, Washington, DC: Brookings Institution.

PART III
INTERNATIONAL
IMPLICATIONS

Chapter 7

The Politics of the Middle East Peace Process and the War on Terror

Vaughn P. Shannon

Introduction

In 2001, George W. Bush inherited a stalled peace process in the Arab-Israeli dispute, as well as related renewed violence in the area. For several months, the new US president did not appear interested in getting involved in the perennial Middle East dispute. But, 11 September 2001 changed everything in US foreign policy, including the approach to the Arab-Israeli conflict. The priority of addressing global terror threats on the United States and its assets forced a renewed effort to win regional allies to aid in such a mission. Many of those allies in the Arab world sought movement on the peace process in order to give aid in the US agenda. Under such strategic circumstances, the United States has put the cause of a Palestinian state at the brink of reality – a phenomenal event in regional and world affairs, if it actually comes about.

But the same strategic circumstances prodding the United States toward this position of sympathy for the Palestinians also served as a constraint. The amount of Palestinian violence toward Israeli targets that can be defined as terrorism – for our purposes, *premeditated, politically motivated violence perpetrated against noncombatant targets by sub-national groups or clandestine agents, usually intended to influence a target*[1] – has been quite high since the beginning of the latest cycle of conflict in September 2000. This fact makes it difficult for a President 'fighting terrorism' to get too close to those in the cause. Though Arafat has denied involvement or endorsement of the activities, he has been seen as either unable or unwilling to stop the terrorism and, thus, part of the problem. The distancing from Palestinian officials was coupled with renewed sympathy for Israel's own 'war on terror', which effectively stalled or slowed the momentum of the Bush plan for a Palestinian state. Such a position also played well domestically, as the US public and interest group community has largely favored Israel over the Palestinians.

This chapter analyzes Bush policy toward the Arab-Israeli conflict in relation to the American War on Terror. It argues that a 'balancing act' has been struck between strategic needs for Arab and Muslim support for the War on Terror and the strategic and domestic pressures to support Israel and avoid appearing supportive of terror.[2] This tension, which has pervaded US policy toward the conflict for decades, perpetuates inaction but also permits the possibility of innovation. I first discuss the context of US policy toward the Arab-Israeli conflict, then examine how the Bush Administration balanced domestic and strategic considerations after the events of 9/11, from the campaign in Afghanistan to the pending war against Iraq in the spring of 2003. I conclude with prospects and implications of US policy and the creation of a Palestinian state.

US Policy and the Arab-Israeli Dispute: Domestic and Strategic Balancing Act

The Arab-Israeli conflict has been summarized thus: 'At the heart of the problem is the Jews' sense of insecurity and the Arabs' feeling of injustice and dispossession.'[3] There are several components to the Arab-Israeli conflict: that of the Zionist effort to establish statehood in friction against competing Arab interests in the area of Palestine; that of the subsequent conflict between the state of Israel and the Palestinian nationalist movement; and that of the conflict between Israel and its Arab and Muslim neighbors in the region. Since achieving statehood in 1948, Israel faced immediate and enduring hostility that, in conjunction with a history of persecution, has bred intense feelings of insecurity about its existence and safety in the years since. To the degree that insecurity brings occupation (for 'buffer zones' or 'strategic depth') of Palestinian-filled lands in the West Bank and Gaza, the result is increased resentment by those under the permanent military rule of Israel: the Palestinian people. Each side feels the other 'started it', and each side feels they are merely responding to aggression with resistance.[4]

As a whole, the Arab-Israeli conflict is essentially the battle for legitimate control over the area known as Palestine, as defined by the current state of Israel, the city of Jerusalem, and the occupied territories. The 1948 War for Palestine, and subsequent wars and negotiations, are reduced to this fundamental issue: Who rules which parts of this area known as Palestine? Do the Jews get it all? Do the Arabs get it all? Do they share, and if so in what proportion? Importantly, would the answer to these questions be accepted by the relevant parties? Control without legitimacy is coercion or occupation, and is likely to perpetuate hostilities as we see in the Gaza Strip and the West Bank today. What role does the United States play in determining these other questions?

The US position on the conflict has been tugged and pulled by the strategic interest of regional oil access and the domestic interest in support for Israel, leading to decades of a balancing act between pro-Israel sympathies and sensitivity to Arab opinion.[5] The result has been an awkward, situationally-driven patchwork of actions that leaves frustrated observers on both sides to claim 'the United States does not have a Middle East policy'.[6] I next elaborate on the strategic and domestic factors that influence US policy, and discuss the implications for policy that result.

Strategic Influences

From theoretical standpoint of realism, the dominant approach to international relations analysis, states define threats to security and interests, and pursue power and policies aimed at increasing influence and reducing such threats.[7] There are two general US strategic concerns in the Middle East: geopolitical stability and terrorism. Perceived threats to vital regions, resources, allies – those things that sustain state power – are an important determinant of policy.[8] The 'Great Game' has been well documented in history, as world powers vied for control of vital trade routes, sea lanes, and oilfields in the Middle East.[9] Out of concern for relative position and the security and prosperity of the state, the argument here is that the United States and others would seek to confront threats and safeguard those material resources deemed vital. In the case of the Middle East, oil is that resource, and one constant of US policy underlying its approach to the

Arab-Israeli conflict is the determination to maintain the stability of the region and promote the free flow of fair-priced oil from the Gulf.[10]

After 9/11 particularly, a second strategic priority has been the pursuit and disruption of terrorist networks with 'global reach', especially but not exclusively al-Qaeda. Confronting the capabilities and causes of terror in the region presents the United States with new motivation to bolster relationships in the region for intelligence, law enforcement and military action. Much of this chapter, then, is dedicated to examining that process.

Domestic Influences

Others have shown the power of domestic politics explaining US policy. The source of domestic political influence comes in many forms, but can be summarized by institutional and societal inputs: Congressional-Executive relations, interest groups, and broader electoral politics, as well as the decision-makers' perspectives and beliefs.

A running theme in the history of US policy in the Arab-Israeli conflict involves a pro-Zionist/pro-Israel Congress clashing with an Executive interested in balancing considerations. While Congress is subordinate to the President in power and decision-making, all executives have dealt with the reaction their policies will have on the Hill. Most decisions about foreign relations are made in the Executive branch. Nonetheless, Congress has the will and ability to serve as a check on presidential power on this particular issue. In lock-step behind Israel by huge margins on most any issue, the US Congress does not hesitate to produce resolutions of support and appropriations and legislation aimed at publicly declaring support for Israel and cautioning the sitting president not to stray too far from this course.

How the US Congress came to be so pro-Israel may have a lot to do with interest groups. The most noted interest group related to US foreign policy is AIPAC, the American Israel Public Affairs Committee. Its electoral connections and financial and organizational strength are unparalleled by anything constituting an 'Arab' or 'Palestinian' lobby. From 1978–2000, one study concludes, Israeli Political Actions Committees (PACs) outspent Arab/Muslim PACs 99 to 1 in Congressional contributions.[11] The 'Jewish' lobby includes other groups, such as the Conference of Presidents of Major American Jewish Organizations, composed of 38 groups that formulate and express the 'Jewish position' on foreign policy, including the Arab-Israeli conflict.[12]

There is a growing Arab lobby present in the United States as well, but nothing comparable. The National Association of Arab-Americans (NAAA) was founded in 1972, based on the AIPAC model.[13] The Council on American-Islamic Relations (CAIR) and American Muslim Alliance (AMA) have emerged to raise awareness on issues relevant to the Islamic world. There are also related interest groups that factor in situationally-based or economic interests. Oil companies, such as the Arabian American Oil Company (ARAMCO), constitute among the earliest of formal lobbies regarding the Middle East, sympathetic to policies yielding regional stability. These different interest groups attempt to frame foreign policy in terms of American national interests when confronting US policy elites.

Beyond the formal groups, foreign policy is also influenced by the electoral politics surrounding the 'informal' lobby defined as 'pro-Israel' or 'pro-Arab'. The Jewish population in the United States is about six million (roughly 3 per cent of the total US population), for instance, and while few of these are members of formal interest groups the vast majority are considered pro-Israel in sympathies. Add to this that an estimated 90 per cent of American Jews live in twelve key electoral states, such as Florida and New York, the status of pro-Israelis as a political force is consequential, with some considering it 'one of the largest veto groups in the country'.[14] This is particularly salient for Democrats, the traditional home of the Jewish vote. Nonetheless, candidates from both parties are susceptible to election-year concerns about courting, and not alienating, votes. As Berggren suggests: 'When it comes to Israel, partisan politics stops at the water's edge. Both parties are unequivocally pro-Israel.'[15]

The pro-Israel domestic influence extends past the Jewish lobby. There is a coalition of conservative Christians and neo-conservative policy-makers siding strongly with Israel on most any issue.[16] On the religious right, some 55 million evangelical Christians are claimed to support Israel due to a perceived 'powerful spiritual connection between Israel and the Christian faith' and belief that Palestine constituted 'covenant land' that God bestowed upon the Jews.[17] In response to two attacks in Tel Aviv by Palestinian terrorists in early 2003, the Christian Coalition of America (the largest Christian grassroots organization in the United States) issued a statement saying that 'the enemies of America and the enemies of Israel are one and the same and seek the wanton goal of killing Westerners for their twisted cause'. They vowed to urge Americans 'of all faiths to stand by Israel and urge our government to understand that the Palestinian Authority is devoted to the destruction of the State of Israel'.[18]

No such parallel exists in the power of the Arab or Muslim voting community, where the vote is less potent or more diffuse. The four to six million estimated Muslims in the United States have not had a cohesive, single-issue record on the Arab-Israeli conflict, for example. Nonetheless, one study suggests that George W. Bush's narrow Presidential victory in 2000 could be attributed to the increasingly organized, bloc-voting constituency of Muslim-Americans.[19] As a whole, however, the 'balance of power' in the domestic arena has tilted toward Israel, with public opinion, the media, and formal and informal aspects of the Israel lobby providing pressure and cover for elected officials.[20]

As for the American voting public, there has historically been support and sympathy for Israel over the years, and much more so than for the Palestinians. Though the numbers have fluctuated at times, in 2003 the overall favorable ratings of Israel were at a highpoint according to Gallup polling. Polls showed Israel's favorable rating at 64 per cent, and 58 per cent said their sympathies were more with the Israelis than the Palestinian Arabs, compared to 13 per cent who said they had more sympathy toward the Palestinians.[21]

A final consideration influencing policy is the decision-makers themselves. Those in the area of political psychology and constructivism emphasize the personal or shared 'constructions of reality' that serve as a lens for viewing the foreign policy environment, and thus insight requires knowing how decision-makers view the world rather than how the world 'is' objectively.[22] From this perspective, each decision-maker's viewpoint may be unique, in terms of perceptions of actors, perceptions of US interests (definition of threats and strategic priorities), and values. While each decision-maker is heavily constrained by the strategic and domestic parameters already discussed, there is room for free will and innovation in US policy that sometimes leads to new turns in policy based on the party, personality or perceptions of individual presidents and their advisers.

Some say the Bush Administration has swung 'to the right' under the influence of 'neo-conservatives' who support Israel as a democratic ally in a strategic and hostile region.[23] Stanley Hoffman refers to this 'loose coalition of friends of Israel' as 'well ensconced in the Pentagon', and a senior US official was quoted saying 'for the first time a US administration and a Likud government are pursuing nearly identical policies'.[24] The Bush Administration put Elliot Abrams in charge of US Mideast policy at the National Security Council, lending credence to the charge of neo-conservativist influence. Having publicly decried the Oslo process and 'land for peace' scenarios, Abrams is strongly pro-Israel. He also was a staunch advocate for 'regime change' in Iraq well before the events of 9/11. He has also been said to push for Arafat's ouster from power as part of Palestinian 'reform', a view backed by Rumsfeld and Cheney and eventually adopted by Bush as a condition for a Palestinian state.[25]

The result of these various influences depends on whether strategic and domestic factors reinforce or conflict with each other. Policy is contextual to the broader domestic and strategic situation, meaning that the US approach to the Arab-Israeli conflict is often a means to an end rather than an end in itself. I now turn to analyzing George W. Bush's policy towards the Arab-Israeli conflict, considering the strategic and domestic influences that at once pushed for innovation (calling for a Palestinian state) and constrained real movement toward implementing his declared vision.

The Bush Approach Before 9/11

George W. Bush inherited a moribund peace process. His predecessor had worked furiously to negotiate a deal between Israel and the Palestinian Authority, headed by Yasir Arafat.[26] The heady optimism of the Oslo peace process begun with a handshake on the White House lawn in 1993 had by early 2001 given way to pessimism, distrust and violence. Peace talks gave way to a Palestinian uprising, the 'al Aqsa intifada', which included terrorism aimed at Israeli settlers, civilians and military targets in Israel and the occupied territories of the West Bank and Gaza Strip. Israel responded with violence and collective punishment, and the result was a mounting death toll on both sides.[27] With the failure of the Clinton-led peace talks and the renewal of violence, each side was less willing and less politically able to make concessions in the face of each other's bloody killing of their own constituents.

In this climate, the new US president George W. Bush took office at about the same time as Israel's elected hardliner Ariel Sharon. Both incoming regimes would shape the conflict in their own way, at times at odds with each other, other times in conjunction. Sharon, like other leaders of the Likud Party, framed the conflict in terms of 'peace with security', demanding an end to violence prior to talking about peace. It implied a large security perimeter, an expansive view of Israel's control of Jerusalem, continued security presence in Jewish settlements and, traditionally, opposition to any independent Palestinian state with its own army.[28] In the US political context, the rise of a conservative administration had mixed implications. Less beholden to the Jewish lobby or Jewish vote, Republicans had been more willing and able to challenge Israel when interests dictated. Nonetheless, a conservative strain of American sympathy to Israel influenced decision-making.

Bush's early policies indicated pro-Israeli politics and lack of interest in the peace process and its aftermath. In one of his first actions as president, George W. Bush had instructed aides to begin exploring the process of moving the US Embassy in Israel from Tel Aviv to Jerusalem. During his campaign, Bush vowed to 'begin the process' of moving the embassy to Jerusalem 'as soon as I take office'. But Bush postponed the move, even when 'recommended' by congressional legislation, citing the delicate negotiations between Israel and Arafat over the status of the city.[29] There were also efforts to remove anti-Israel language from the draft declaration of the upcoming UN racism conference in 2001. The UN World Conference Against Racism, Racial Discrimination, Xenophobia and Related Intolerance (UNWCAR) preparatory committee included language equating Zionism with racism. Secretary of State Colin Powell strove to have the language removed and, failing this, decided not to attend the UN conference.[30]

In terms of the Israeli-Palestinian tinderbox, the Bush administration was decidedly hands-off in the first several months. In May 2001, the Mitchell Report was released, with conclusions about the new conflict and recommendations for where to go next in terms of dialogue and confidence-building measures. The emphasis of the report was on encouraging the two parties to: 1) end the violence; 2) rebuild confidence; and 3) resume negotiations.[31]

After taking criticism for the hands-off approach to the conflict, Bush sent Tenet to produce a signed agreement that would bring together the previous cease-fire agreements and set the stage for the implementation of the Mitchell Report recommendations. The resulting Tenet Plan, which Israel accepted 'with some reservations' and the Palestinians gave 'conditional approval',[32] called for Israel and the Palestinian Authority to: 1) resume security cooperation, including eventual joint patrols, to replace the adversarial posture on the ground; 2) take immediate measure to enforce adherence to Israel's unilateral cease-fire, including Palestinian arrests of those committing acts of terrorism; 3) provide information on terrorist threats to each other and the United States, and take operations to prevent attacks; 4) prevent persons from using areas 'under their respective control to carry out acts of violence'; 5) forge 'an agreed-upon schedule to implement the complete redeployment of IDF forces to positions held before September 28, 2000'; and 6) develop a timeline for the 'lifting of internal closures' and 'reopening of internal roads', bridges, airports, and border crossings.[33]

Despite the agreement on the terms and the cease-fire, the violence persisted, and the Palestinian leadership seemed either unable or unwilling to stop it. Many groups and individuals in the occupied territories claimed a right to resistance, suggesting the Palestinian uprising to be 'legitimate self defense' against Israeli military occupation of the West Bank and Gaza Strip since 1967.[34] On 9 August 2001, a Palestinian suicide bomber blew himself up in Jerusalem, killing 15 and wounding 130. In response, Israel seized the Palestinian headquarters in Jerusalem while launching rocket attacks on Palestinian police stations in Gaza and Ramallah.[35] Sharon placed the blame on Arafat for any terrorism emerging out of the territories under the administration of the Palestinian Authority (PA). With each strike and counterstrike, the PA's capacity to administer was weakened and the trappings of statehood nurtured under Oslo crumbled, under the Israeli belief that Arafat was either unwilling or unable to stop the violence. The United States stayed on the sidelines.

9/11 and the War on Terror

The events of 11 September 2001, altered US thinking on the Arab-Israeli conflict as it did for most any policy issue. Hijackers, later identified as tied to the terror group al-Qaeda, had forcibly gained control of four US passenger jets, running two of them into New York City's World Trade Center and one into the Pentagon.[36] The death toll for the day was estimated at about 3,000. Al-Qaeda had emerged in the late 1980s from the Islamic resistance to the Soviets in Afghanistan. Its leader, wealthy Saudi Osama bin Laden, directed the organization's attention toward the United States for its support of the Saudi regime and stationing of American forces on Saudi soil since the Gulf War. An Islamic organization bent on installing its brand of fundamentalism in Saudi Arabia and elsewhere in the Middle East, al-Qaeda and its leader bin Laden increasingly saw the United States as an obstacle to its goals. A series of terrorist attacks on US bases and embassies from Saudi Arabia to Kenya and Tanzania, were linked to bin Laden's umbrella network organization, and in 1998 bin Laden declared war on the United States, calling for attacks on all Americans, military or civilian.

After the embassy bombings of 1998, which killed some 300 people and wounded another 5,000, the United States turned up pressure on al-Qaeda and the Taliban who provided the group safe harbor to train and plan in Afghanistan. But aside from sanctions on the Taliban and a one-time strike against al-Qaeda camps in Afghanistan on 20 August 1998, the United States had not fundamentally reordered its foreign policy orientation – not until 9/11.

The American response after the events of 11 September was a reordering of foreign policy priorities to fight an extended War on Terror. This new war was defined by Bush in a couple of terms; namely that 'either you are with us, or you are with the terrorists', and that the United States would not distinguish between those who carry out acts of terror and those who harbor them.[37] In terms of who the terrorists were, the first immediate answer was al-Qaeda, a transnational umbrella network considered to be operating in over 60 countries. Beyond bin Laden's group, it was murkier whether the war included all other terrorism, but US officials left it at the slightly narrowed but ambiguous notion of terrorist organizations with 'global reach'. The target list also would expand to include state sponsors of terror – first the Taliban of Afghanistan (who gave aid and comfort to bin Laden), but also in the Bush Administration crosshairs was Iraq.[38]

Addressing a transnational network like al-Qaeda required cooperation on all facets of counter-terrorism: disrupting financial flows, intelligence gathering, criminal investigation, and the potential use of force.[39] As with his father before him, the strategic priority of the post-9/11 world necessitated a new coalition of countries in the Middle East and beyond to assist in military campaigns, intelligence, defense, and criminal investigation. Bush assembled regional support for use of airspace and bases to conduct operations to root out the Taliban and smash al-Qaeda bases, camps and operations in Afghanistan, which it did with surprising speed with the help of internal Afghan rivals to the Taliban, notably the Northern Alliance. But, with bin

Laden having apparently escaped capture, and al-Qaeda being dispersed globally, the United States continued to need the help of other countries in pursuit of those the United States identified as a threat, or those who would harbor such elements.

What this meant for US policy toward the Arab-Israeli conflict was a newfound need to curry favor with the Arab and Muslim world, both for image management and to foster a new coalition. First, the United States devoted great attention to winning over the 'Arab street', to counter al-Qaeda's rhetoric about the United States as an imperial infidel power insensitive to the plight of Muslims, including the Palestinians,[40] and both enabler and lapdog to the Zionists.[41] When US operations against al-Qaeda and the Taliban commenced 7 October 2001, bin Laden tried to link the cause with Palestine, vowing 'neither America nor the people who live in it will ever taste security or safety until we feel security and safety in our land *and Palestine*'.[42] Any US movement on the issue of the Palestinians, then, would hope to quell al-Qaeda's recruitment and try to avoid a 'clash of civilizations'.[43] If the United States sought further action in the region, it was deemed important to garner regional support the likes of which Bush's father obtained for the Gulf War.

An 'American Balfour Declaration': Calls for a Palestinian State[44]

The new strategic priorities of the United States in the region lent itself to new policy thinking regarding the Arab-Israeli conflict. Jordan's Foreign Minister said plainly: 'it will be difficult to line up Arab support without a commitment to solving the Israeli-Palestinian dispute once and for all'.[45] This view was shared not just among the Arab states but European allies as well.

The initial US response to the need to cultivate support in the War on Terror and prospective action on Iraq was a true landmark in American policy: the first explicit acknowledgment that there should be a Palestinian state since the original debate over Palestine in 1947.[46] While claiming they had decided matters prior to 9/11,[47] the decision was in part driven by the new imperatives, including the 'battle for the hearts and minds' of the Middle East. It also followed Sharon's public warning that the United States not 'appease the terrorists' as Hitler was appeased, implicitly comparing Bush to Neville Chamberlain in a way that did not sit well with the American president.[48]

The idea of declaring support for the creation of a Palestinian state was floated first in early October, about the same time the United States began Operation Enduring Freedom, the military campaign against the Taliban and al-Qaeda in Afghanistan. Bush formally declared the US stance to the UN General Assembly on 10 November, suggesting the United States sought 'a day when two states, Israel and Palestine, live peacefully together within secure and recognized borders'.[49] The two-state idea was formalized 12 March 2002, with the passage of UN Security Council Resolution 1397. This resolution, which passed 14–0 with one abstention, affirmed the two-state vision of Israel and Palestine living side by side 'within secure and recognized borders'.[50] It also demanded a cessation of all acts of violence, and called upon leaders to implement the Tenet Plan, the Mitchell Report, and resume negotiations.

All previous attempts to endorse a Palestinian state in the formal language of a Security Council resolution had been vetoed by the United States, thus this marked a watershed event, however symbolic in nature. Some observers suggested the move was taken in return for 'good will' from Arab states ahead of Vice President Cheney's regional visit to push for support in taking action against Iraq.[51] The courtship of the Arab world for US plans, included the need to 'accelerate US pressure' on Israel for acquiescing to an independent Palestine.[52]

This departure in American policy rhetoric sparked controversy and political commotion from predictable quarters. After the UN speech, a US Senate delegation emerged from a meeting with leaders of the American Jewish community with a letter to the President that declared 'our shared commitment for the enduring security of the state of Israel, our close ally in the fight against terrorism' and stating frankly their opinion that 'no solution can be imposed upon the parties', finally urging the President to 'remain steadfast in standing with our ally, Israel'.[53] It is notable, then, that beyond the rhetorical support, the United States had not departed from its 'procedural bias' of implementing the two-state vision.[54] That is, the United States had not unilaterally recognized the Palestinian state, nor did it even lay a specific, explicit time-line for its creation. Instead, the United States returned to the old stance of suggesting that such details be negotiated. At this point, the symbolism of the new approach outstripped the substance, creating questions amidst the domestic backlash to Bush's proposal about the sincerity of the United States to enforce this vision.

Another reason that the US approach to the issue of Palestine slowed was the War on Terror. Defining the world in the Bush Doctrine in zero-sum terms, the 'with us or against us' approach tended to label all terrorism as equally bad or evil. The rhetoric of terrorism lumped together various conflicts and violence, including those by Palestinians fighting the Israeli occupation.[55] Too much sympathy and assistance to the Palestinians, who in the new uprising witnessed new levels of terror against Israeli civilians, would be awkward on the domestic front both in selling the war on terrorism and in relation to Israel and its sympathizers. Bush became entangled in his own rhetorical webs, finding it difficult to work with Arafat so long as Arafat was perceived to be linked to terror, for fear of the domestic backlash of an apparent double standard.

Palestinian Terror and US Policy Toward Arafat

To the extent that Arafat's Palestinian Authority was responsible for the protection of areas such as Jenin and Bethlehem, continued terrorism emanating from these areas was seen as a sign of either Arafat's inability or unwillingness to stop it. Either way, this was an awkward time for an American president rallying the world in a War on Terror to be embracing the Palestinian leader.

When Israel sent troops and tanks into Palestinian cities on 29 March after a suicide bombing that killed 27 people at the start of the Jewish Passover holiday, the initial US response was to support a UN resolution urging Israel to withdraw its troops, reaffirming his commitment to a Palestinian state on the same day that Israeli troops invaded more West Bank towns. Within days, however, Bush received domestic criticism for his actions, with one Congressman calling diplomatic missions to the Palestinians 'a bow to the bombers'.[56] Bush took pains to address the terror issue, suggesting 'to those who would try to use the current crisis as an opportunity to widen the conflict: stay out'. Meanwhile, Israeli collective punishment and killing of civilians escaped such labels, though Bush called on restraint and withdrawal. Bush sent Powell to urge Israel to stop building settlements in Palestinian areas, but did not mention a timetable for Israel's withdrawal or for an end to settlements.[57] Sharon defied the President's urging to withdraw 'without delay', claiming he had to address terrorism, accusing Arafat of establishing 'a regime of terror in the territories under his control'.[58]

Bush appeared to back away from his demand for an immediate Israeli withdrawal, claiming Sharon had met the US timetable by withdrawing from some Palestinian areas, and that Israel had the right to try to root out five Palestinians blamed for the murder of an Israeli cabinet minister. This was simultaneous with a speech by Vice President Cheney at an Israeli Independence Day reception, saying 'Our friendship is strong and enduring, and it can never be shaken.'[59] The Congress passed resolutions expressing solidarity with Israel and condemning Arafat. The resolutions reminded the President of the position of Congress, that – in the words of Democratic House Minority leader Richard Gephardt – 'we stand with Israel historically and morally'.[60]

After meeting with Saudi, Moroccan, Jordanian, and Israeli leaders, Bush declared that Israel must negotiate an end to its occupation of Palestinian areas in the West Bank. The Saudi Crown Prince Abdullah had presented a peace plan at the Arab Summit of March 2002, and sought to push the President to embrace it. The plan, however, was 'totally unacceptable' to the Likud government, in that it provided for a Palestinian state with full sovereignty. Bush gave the plan some public support, without committing to it, suggesting to Sharon that Israel get used to the 'new reality' of the legitimacy of the two-state option.[61] Sharon said that under stringent conditions, he would agree to creation of such a state, at one point calling it inevitable; but he insisted that Israel could not negotiate with Palestinians before the terror ended and their leadership underwent reforms.[62] This latter point suggested the view held by Sharon, and soon Bush, that Arafat had to go.

Administrative attention and frustration turned on Arafat, seen as an obstacle to ending tensions and violence in the area. The pressure on Arafat to control the terror was poised to shift to pressure to remove Arafat from power. Sensing the pressure and this shift, Arafat's Fatah group announced an urge to the end to suicide attacks. This was an effort to distance themselves from the al-Aqsa Martyrs Brigades, the unofficial but affiliated group that emerged in the new *intifada*. It was also a reassertion of the Palestinian Authority as the legitimate security force of the Palestinian people, as opposed to the 'armed militias' of Hamas and the Martyrs Brigades.[63]

On 10 May Israel ended the six-week offensive against Palestinian militants across the West Bank with claims of success. As Bush set to announce a plan for an interim Palestinian state, extremists set off two bloody bombings in two days, one killing nineteen and another killing seven.[64] In response, Sharon decided to reoccupy all Palestinian Authority territory in an open-ended stay 'as long as terrorism continues'. Washington warned Israel against toppling Arafat but also sharpened criticism of him, calling him 'ineffective and untrustworthy'.[65]

The bombing had a profound impact on Bush's thinking, and changed the substance and tenor of his proposal. The proposal called for the establishment of an independent Palestinian state, but there was a catch. Bush urged the Palestinians to 'elect new leaders not compromised by terror'. Despite Arafat's condemnation of the attacks, the perception at the White House, as in Israel, was that Arafat had encouraged or permitted these activities.[66] What had changed was the emphasis on replacing Arafat. The suicide bombings the week prior confirmed to Bush a view of Arafat as unwilling or unable to control terrorism that some say dates back to 1998.[67] 'The violence did change the character of this speech', one official said. 'It also crystallized again the fact of the disappointments that we've had with the Palestinian leadership.'[68]

While Bush clearly placed the onus on the Palestinians, he said that once security began returning to the region, Israel would have to withdraw its forces to the positions they held prior to the outbreak of violence in September 2001, and would ultimately have to end the occupation. 'Occupation threatens Israel's identity and democracy', he said. Once violence subsided, Bush insisted Israel would also have to end all settlement activity, as discussed in the Mitchell Report. Israel would also have to allow Palestinians more 'freedom of movement' and release frozen Palestinian assets.[69]

Bush sought to distinguish the plight of Palestinians from the view of the terrorism and the alleged link to Arafat. The proposal reflected the balance of appealing to Arab sympathies while taking a hard line on terrorism, consistent with the War on Terror, and a hard line on Arafat, consistent with the Israeli view, and Bush's own beliefs, about the Palestinian leader's intentions. Bush's speech was seen by many as a retreat from the ambitious tones of prior months: suddenly, Palestinian statehood came with many strings attached, to a degree that some questioned its tenability. Many in the Arab world were disappointed, and saw the new language of the US position as consistent with the Israeli perspective. The call for new leaders, a functional democracy, constitution, and market economy – prior to statehood, mind you – was a tall order that, as one observer notes, had not been accomplished by any Arab state after a half-century of independence.[70]

The official Arab response to the Bush plan was ambiguous, but the reaction from the 'Arab street' was hostile and skeptical.[71] Egypt, Saudi Arabia and Jordan had tried to persuade Bush to set a time scale for Palestinian statehood and an end to Israel's 35-year-old occupation and settlement of the West Bank and Gaza Strip, in return for full Arab ties with the Jewish state.[72] As for those directly affected, both Israel and the Palestinian leadership emphasized aspects that best matched their views. Israel praised the parts condemning Palestinian leadership and calling for change, but was silent on the issue of a sovereign or provisional Palestinian state. Having previously rejected the idea of Palestinian statehood, Sharon had been forced to consider the eventuality, should the US press the issue.[73] Arafat lauded Bush's speech, downplaying the call for 'change' and noting Bush did not mention Arafat by name. His interpretation was aimed at others in power, and so he continued with reform and a call for elections, while rallying international support for his leadership as the elected President of the Palestinian Authority. Arafat's cabinet quit in September 2002 to avoid a no-confidence vote in the Palestinian National Assembly. Arafat appointed a new cabinet, endorsed by a 'reform-seeking' Assembly, on 29 October, to serve until elections were held.[74]

Further signs of a US hard line on Palestinian terror, and sympathy toward Israel, came on 2 November 2002, when the State Department added Hamas, Islamic Jihad, PFLP, and Hizb'allah to the list of groups associated with bin Laden. This made the groups targets of an Executive Order directing the US Treasury Department to sanction foreign banks that fail to freeze assets of groups on the list.[75] Those raising monies for such groups and their causes came under new pressure, which culminated in eight arrests in February 2003, including a Florida professor charged with running the North

American fundraising operation of Palestinian Islamic Jihad.[76] Several individuals in the United States were indicted on charges of trafficking with terrorist states Libya and Syria, linked by US officials to Hamas or Palestinian Islamic Jihad. Attorney General John Ashcroft vowed to 'pursue the financiers of terror as aggressively as we pursue the thugs who do their dirty work'.[77] The targeting of terror groups focused on Israel signaled the War on Terror was wider than al-Qaeda, but also that the United States and Israel had developed a relationship of mutual interest in the region. While Arab states balked, Israel was fast becoming a willing partner in the US agenda.

Sharon had thought 9/11 would bring the United States more into the Israeli perspective regarding terrorism and the Palestinians. After a rocky start dating back to the reference to appeasement, there were signs that the United States and Israel were converging in their views and priorities. Sharon sought to firm up the relationship and persuade the United States about the terrorist links in the Palestinian territories. Israel asserted at one point that al-Qaeda operatives had established a presence in Palestinian-ruled areas of the Gaza Strip and in Lebanon.[78] They claimed senior al-Qaeda officials sought to enlist Palestinian support and membership, a charge admittedly not backed with evidence.[79]

But al-Qaeda fueled the fires by beginning to target Israeli and Jewish targets with terror. On 28 November, a suicide bombing of a Kenyan hotel used by Israelis killed eight and wounded 80 others. At the same time, missiles were fired at an Israeli airliner nearby, missing their targets.[80] The attacks were confirmed to be the work of al-Qaeda, serving as the first direct attack on Israelis by bin Laden's network. The al-Qaeda network vowed more attacks against Israel and the United States. Leading al-Qaeda member Sulaiman Bu Ghaith declared 'the Christian-Jewish alliance will not, God willing, be safe from attacks'.[81]

Arafat sought to refute the link to al-Qaeda, and publicly told Osama bin Laden to stop claiming he was fighting for the Palestinians. Saying bin Laden's agenda is 'against our interests', Arafat's public disavowal hoped to reassure the United States and avoid an Israeli pretext for more operations in the name of the War on Terror. In fact, Israel sought to frame its incursions in the occupied territories as a 'second front' of a pending war on Iraq, seeking 'proper resources' to confront terrorism in the area to ensure 'decisive victory'.[82] But Arafat had more concerns than the kiss of death from al-Qaeda; a looming American confrontation with Iraq would bring out anti-Americanism within the Palestinian population, risking further isolation by the United States as it sought friendly assistance in its campaign.

As for progress in the implementation of a plan for a Palestinian state, little changed since Bush's proclamation in June 2002. The demand for Palestinian reform guaranteed some time would pass, and the United States was in no hurry. Arafat continued to make gestures of reform, and scheduled elections that could spark change in Palestinian leadership. Israeli and US attempts to seek successors to Arafat caused ordinary Palestinians to rally to their leader.[83] Palestinians grew frustrated with their situation throughout the 1990s and the new *intifada*, and public opinion surveys indicated that support for both Arafat and the bombers was slipping. Most Palestinians considered Bush's call for a new Palestinian leadership 'high-handed US meddling in their affairs'.[84]

Palestinian Authority Interior Minister Abdel Razek Yehiyeh presented Israel with a security plan to end the violence, including returning civic order and taking control over the Palestinian security forces in the territories.[85] Despite these measures, the prospect for a resumption of some semblance of peace talks under Sharon was dashed by the sudden dissolution of his coalition government. On 30 October 2002, the Labor faction of the Sharon government resigned in protest over items in the 2003 budget that increased spending on settlements.[86] Sharon, unable to save his government, called for early elections on 28 January 2003. Under such circumstances, any progress in negotiations was unlikely. Bush's end game was not a peace settlement but regional stability for the Administration's agenda regarding terrorism and Iraq. Showing interest in the Arab-Israeli conflict was a means to these ends. But, as time and again before, the competing pressures and needs for Israeli and Arab support made US policy equivocate and drift for fear of alienating either side. The United States, which has usually preferred moderate parties and candidates as more amenable to negotiating with the Palestinians, this time backed Sharon. Bush personally moved to postpone the publication of the 'road map' being drafted by the United States, European Union, Russia and the UN (known as the 'Quartet') until after the Israeli elections, as a favor to Sharon.[87] Leading up to elections, the militant al-Aqsa Martyrs' Brigades, an armed offshoot of Arafat's Fatah faction, set off attacks killing 22 in Israel. Claiming it was retaliation for the demolitions of Palestinian homes, it had the effect of strengthening the hardliner Sharon.[88] Pre-election violence by Hamas also likely boosted Sharon's support, rallying Israelis into a hard line against terrorism.[89]

Likud won 38 seats of the Knesset (31.7 per cent), compared to Labor's 19 (15.8 per cent). While Sharon was required to muster a coalition (which Labor refused to join), the decisive defeat signaled the Sharon approach to the Palestinian problem would continue.[90] The re-elected Sharon sounded much like Bush, open to a Palestinian state in theory, but not before the removal of 'terrorist leadership' in the Palestinian Authority. Neither Bush nor Sharon would deal with Arafat politically, since he was considered an affiliate of terror.[91] This also had the effect of dragging out the process and stalling any progress, as Arafat signaled an eagerness to talk to anyone about peace.[92] He also promised to appoint a prime minister in accordance with the demands of the United States and the rest of the Quartet.[93]

European leaders and others wanted a timetable adopted and to have the 'road map' published and publicized, worried that a war against Iraq without concomitant vigorous Middle East peace negotiations, would inflame the region for the apparent double standard in pursuing one war while ignoring the region's 'other war'. Perhaps a kiss of death to the American attempt at showing 'neutrality' or Arab sympathy, Sharon declared that among the Quartet mediators, only the United States sees 'eye to eye' with Israel.[94] Bush would finally hint at revealing the road map, well after Israel's elections, in March 2003. In doing so, he would attempt to link the process to a postwar (Iraq) vision of a new Middle East.[95]

From Afghanistan to Iraq

In the meanwhile, the United States had largely fought and won the first battle of the War on Terror, without much help from the Arab world. Operation Enduring Freedom, combining US air power and special forces with local armies in Afghanistan, ousted the Taliban from Kabul and set up an interim successor through a UN conference, all by the end of 2001. By the spring of 2002, the operation was one of 'mopping up' and pursuit of the still-elusive Osama bin Laden and associates.

Increasingly, emboldened by its success in Afghanistan, the United States turned to its next priority in its vision of a War on Terror: Iraq. The Bush administration had been careful to define the 'war' more broadly than merely al-Qaeda and the events of 9/11. Some in the US Administration were convinced that Saddam Hussein, as a sympathizer to some terrorism while allegedly possessing weapons of mass destruction, was an unacceptable combination. As early as February 2002, the Bush Administration made the decision to 'oust Saddam Hussein'.[96] The discussion of just when and how divided the administration between unilateralist hawks – Cheney and Rumsfeld – and internationalist Powell, who made the case for going to the UN for the legitimacy of the mission. The latter joined a chorus of domestic and international voices concerned with the 'day after implications' of a unilateral, preemptive war on Iraq.[97]

The internationalists won for a time, with the United States taking the case to the UN demanding Hussein be held accountable for his material breach of Security Council Resolutions pertaining to weapons of mass destruction. The Council passed Resolution 1441 ordering inspections back in Iraq, and threatening 'serious consequences' if Iraq did not fully comply.

The United States was skeptical that this process would yield disarmament, and spent the fall of 2002 and winter of 2003 building forces in the Persian Gulf and courting support for the eventual use of force. They had little success. As with his father before him, Bush sought to wage war against Iraq in midst of a jittery region. Unlike his father, the junior Bush appeared to be hurtling toward confrontation with or without the region, the UN, or the world – all this with less legal justification than the elder Bush, who at least was responding to an Iraqi act of aggression.[98] Middle East states were reluctant to participate or endorse a war started by a Western superpower against an Arab or Muslim fellow state. Jordan's King Abdullah said that a US attack on Iraq would be catastrophic for the Middle East.[99] Thousands of people took to the streets in Arab capitals to protest against a possible US war on Iraq, labeling President Bush a 'butcher'. Most Arab countries opposed war against Iraq fearing it would further destabilize the Middle East, and advocated instead a peaceful solution to the crisis over Iraq's alleged weapons of mass destruction.[100]

Vice President Dick Cheney visited the Middle East in early 2002 to solicit support for US plans to oust Saddam Hussein from power. The Bush Administration already offered a major missile sale to Egypt and an increase in foreign assistance to Jordan, but the concern for the Palestinian issue would not go away, nor was an Arab state politically able to side with the United States in a war on an Arab country while the 'other war' (Palestinian) continued to be ignored by the United States.[101] Bush did as his father had done, promising action on the Arab-Israeli problem after dealing with Iraq, but this time the sale was not effective.

Israel the Ally

Israel's inclusion on Cheney's tour of the Middle East indicated an interest in coordinating on issues such as the defense of Israel and whether Sharon would retaliate if attacked by Iraq as it was in the 1991 Gulf War. Some in the Bush administration, disappointed with the half-hearted support it received from old allies like Saudi Arabia, began to think the United States, with Israeli intelligence assistance in the region, could tackle the Iraq issue alone.[102] Israel Defense Forces units and security officials began training and coordinating with the United States for the contingencies of war.[103]

Sharon again sought to exploit the circumstances to show Israel's support and the ring of terrorism allying against them. Hizb'allah, operating out of Lebanon and long an Israeli foe, had been heard using incendiary threats in reference to a possible US invasion of Iraq, suggesting they may take actions against Israel or other assets in the region.[104] Sharon accused Iraq of transferring chemical and biological weapons to Syria to hide them from UN inspectors – though his comments were based on unconfirmed information and involved no evidence to support the allegation.[105] Al-Qaeda chimed in with the claim that an attack against Iraq was aimed to 'protect the Jewish occupiers and achieve their expansionist dream of setting up a (Jewish) state between the Nile and Euphrates'.[106]

The Palestinian leadership sought to dampen the pro-Iraq sentiments of their populations, which had gone unabated during the 1991 Gulf War. While Hamas and Islamic Jihad continued vocal support for Hussein, the Palestinian Authority sought a prudent course to downplay any link with Iraq that could sour US relations or invite Israeli action.[107] Nonetheless, there were some rallies linking support for Iraq by members of the Palestinian Authority, according to Israel's Ministry of Foreign Affairs. Israel focused on Iraq's ties to Palestinian terrorism against Israel, suggesting Iraq has given substantial financial and military aid to the Palestinian Liberation Front (PLF) and the Arab Liberation Front (ALF), both pro-Iraqi organizations. An article published in the *Al Quds* magazine in June 2002 stated that 'Saddam Hussein's popularity is growing due to the millions of dollars he contributes to Palestinian families hurt by the al-Aqsa intifada'.[108] And indeed, Hamas publicly gave support to Iraq, urging 'the Iraqi leadership to open the door for Muslim volunteers' and calling the pending American-led attack 'not against Iraq' but 'against the Islamic nation'.[109]

A New Chapter

In its pressure to be consistent in the War on Terror, Bush had begun to mute criticism of Israeli tactics against the *intifada*, much to the scorn of the Arab world and regional allies.[110] Picking up on the Arab resentment, and still wanting for international and regional legitimacy in the coming war with Iraq, the United States came out in successive displays of concern for the Arab-Israeli conflict in early 2003. In February, Bush made a grandiose speech about the postwar (with Iraq) vision for a new Middle East that would include an independent Palestinian state. 'Success in Iraq,' he offered, 'could also begin a new stage for Middle Eastern peace, and set in motion progress towards a truly democratic Palestinian state.'[111] Linking Iraq to Palestinian terror, the argument was that once the patron is gone, Palestinian terror would be reduced, and willing Palestinian moderates could reign in an independent Palestine. The United States also began to rebuke Israel for its tactics in its fight against the uprising. After Sharon said the Palestinians would negotiate only after they were 'beaten', US officials said they would no longer give unequivocal support for Israel's actions. Secretary of State Powell publicly scorned Sharon, adding that 'if you declare war against the

Palestinians thinking that you can solve the problem by seeing how many Palestinians can be killed, I don't know that that leads us anywhere'.[112]

Still, the United States could not muster Arab and Muslim support for the war against Iraq, with Saudi Arabia and NATO ally Turkey refusing to participate, leaving only Kuwait, Bahrain and Qatar for bases of operation. Numerous demonstrations in the Muslim world in opposition to the United States and its plans to invade Iraq continued, and leaders from those countries warned that any attack would destabilize the region and fuel more anti-American terrorism and retaliation.[113] The Arab League announced 'the complete rejection of a strike against Iraq', though some like Kuwait provided US base support pivotal to a ground invasion.[114] With little help from regional allies, nor much of the world, the United States had a choice to continue a diplomatic approach or go to war without the desired support. It chose the latter, with Bush announcing on 17 March 2003 that Saddam Hussein had 48 hours to leave the country or face military action.

At the same time, under pressure from the United States and other Quartet members, the Central Council of Arafat's PLO approved his nomination of moderate Mahmoud Abbas to the new post of prime minister. The Central Council also called on Palestinian militants 'fighting Israeli occupation and settlement not to target Israeli civilians inside Israel' so as not to give Israel a reason 'to continue its annihilation war against our people'.[115] As an alternative to Arafat's removal, it seemed possible Israel and the United States would instead accept an alternate voice in the negotiations in the form of a powerful prime minister.[116] Bush announced on the eve of war with Iraq that he would unveil the so-called 'road map' for Middle East peace once a new Palestinian prime minister with real governing authority took office. Having spoken to Egyptian President Hosni Mubarak and Jordan's King Abdullah II just before the speech, it indicated Bush still sought to minimize the negative regional consequences of going to war with Iraq, consequences for the United States as well as for regional allies. Arafat resisted forfeiting control over peace policies and security decisions, but the reform-minded Palestinian Parliament passed a measure that bestowed some such powers upon Abbas. Once again, the Palestinian state was conditional, this time on a new prime minister in a 'position of real authority'. However this would be determined, Bush held out the promise that 'immediately upon confirmation, the road map for peace will be given to the Palestinians and the Israelis' for input. This at once promised some advancement but also heralded another round of haggling, delay and obstruction by the parties involved. Bush's call for 'concrete actions to achieve peace' could ring hollow depending on whether the United States is willing to push the plan through.[117]

At the time this goes to press, it is too early to see the results of the war against Iraq, or of the road map to a Palestinian state. The Palestinian Parliament passed the measure creating the position of Prime Minister on 18 March, the day of Bush's deadline for Iraq before war.[118] Thus the end of this episode is the beginning of many more significant events that could push the Arab-Israeli conflict down a new road to peace or the old road of violence.

The Future

What does not need to be changed is continued aid and support to moderate regimes in the Middle East. Countries like Egypt, Jordan and Israel should continue to receive US aid and assistance in a larger framework of encouraging a 'New Middle East' much different than that envisioned by bin Laden and others, but still one that transcends the status quo of perennial conflict and division. All sovereign states, including Israel, deserve the guaranteed protection against aggression that the United States has long granted it.

Given the Islamic-based terror that threatens Israel, the United States, Egypt, and Saudi Arabia, among others, there is a consensus focal point for continued cooperation to prohibit the rise of such forces in the greater Middle East. These forces already deem the United States and these aforementioned states to be evil and violently met. Sadat was assassinated by Egyptian Islamic Jihad, who killed him for making peace with Israel but also in their desire for a fundamentalist regime in Cairo. Saudi Arabia too faces such internal threat, the likes of which came to power in Iran. These targeted states must meet this challenge directly and cooperatively.

This continuity of purpose requires a keen focus on the priorities the United States espouses: regional stability and countering terrorism. Such a focus makes plain the need to rally the region to the US cause. Rather than taking for granted 300 million Arabs and some 900 million Muslims in the world, who control 60 per cent of world gas and oil reserves,[119] these constituencies need to be sincerely heard. The resentment against America is widespread well beyond al-Qaeda, and provides some fertile ground for recruiting terrorists, and constrains regional states from greater support of the United States.[120] The United States must expend resources to ensure that the violence against America does not similarly grow to match that resentment.[121] A new approach to the Arab-Israeli conflict must be soon, significant, and sincere.

It is my belief that the fate of Palestinians, Israel and the United States would all be improved with the creation of a Palestinian state. The difficulties in negotiating under present circumstances, with Israel's system providing government-toppling political power in the hands of small, reactionary parties; and Arafat's constraints under similar right-wing hardliners to win a state on their terms, suggests the idea of letting all matters be negotiated (the US 'procedural bias') will guarantee no settlement will occur. Two possible alternatives exist: as Tom Friedman suggests, two 'civil wars' may be necessary, to root out extremists in the Palestinian and Israeli camps who pose a barrier to the two-state solution.[122] The feasibility of this plan is questionable, however, asking each side to battle their own for the sake of the other.

Alternatively, the United States and the international community could unilaterally recognize a state of Palestine under West Bank and Gaza. Abandoning the procedural bias, the US action would be virulently opposed by Israel,[123] and would sour relations between the two countries to a degree. Nonetheless, the unipolar United States is in a position to take such actions, and Israel's dependency on US aid places it in a position difficult to challenge the United States. Unlike the previous proposal, this one is practically easier but politically difficult for an American president to take.

Interest group theory suggests that special interests prevail when there is no powerful counterbalance and when the general public is disengaged. Israel's peril in relation to its patron is that the latter may be changing. Long have everyday Americans been largely unaware of the Arab-Israeli conflict beyond the news spots that treat it as an 'ancient' ethnic conflict. But 9/11 has awakened them to the US role in the region and may spawn questions about the costs of that role. A *Newsweek* poll on 6 October 2001 found 52 per cent of Americans responding that US aid to Israel was 'too much'.[124] This may mean that the tilt toward Israel, at the expense not just of Palestinians but of Americans too, without the Cold War strategic context to justify the relationship, may lead to a change of heart, and a change of policy.

This does not suggest abandoning Israel or throwing its fate to the winds. The United States should still support Israel and its security. Rather, the suggestions provided here reflect an outcome I believe would benefit Israel as much as it would the Palestinians and the United States. It would clarify the distinctions between the nationalist resistance violence by everyday Palestinians from the fundamentalists bent on pushing Israel into the sea. A new Palestinian state would then have the power and responsibility to clamp down on the latter, to the PA's political benefit, since Hamas and others are political rivals to Arafat and other secular nationalists. The rejectionists would then face the combined will and resources of a supportive Israel, United States and other moderates in the region. Israeli security would be clarified by distinct borders, and it would be free to defend such borders as a sovereign state may, without the international stigma that has undermined Israel's reputation over the course of its existence.

A more long-term alternative 'change' in the US approach to the Middle East and Arab-Israeli conflict would involve extricating itself from it altogether. This seems politically and strategically impossible at this point, nor is it desirable under the current state of US interests and affairs. But to the extent that the United States has increasingly become entwined in the Middle East and its conflicts, the first and foremost reason has been the strategic value of oil and of the region as its fundamental source of supply and reserves. Many similar conflicts have transpired in, say, sub-Saharan Africa without such American resource investment of blood and treasure. This suggests that either by policy or nature, oil will someday come to matter less, and matter not, to the United States and the industrial world. Whether alternative energy sources precede (by choice) or follow (by necessity) the future end to the finite supply of oil, there will come a time where this chief pillar of US policy in the Middle East will dry up with it. By then, if the Arab-Israeli conflict has not been solved, the United States may lose interest, as the broader population questions the value of entangling alliances in a region holding no more interest to the United States. Reducing oil dependency, in short, is an inevitable future (be it 100 years or more) that both Israel and the oil-rich regional states may fear, loathe, and had best prepare for.

These are profound political, military, and moral considerations that have been wrestled with for years already. The tragedy of 9/11 brings new impetus to the cause, and the Bush Administration has made indications that it indeed is a new day, calling for a Palestinian state 'within three years' under certain conditions. Whether the United States musters its influence to coax lasting change remains to be seen. The legacy of the US president to end the Arab-Israeli conflict, even if it gives way to a moderate/fundamentalist conflict already afoot, would be historic – if the political will that this book demonstrates would be required, is present in the decision-makers of US foreign policy.

Conclusion

US policy toward the Arab-Israeli conflict reflects continuity and change. The events of 9/11 undoubtedly reordered US priorities, motivating the superpower to fight terrorism and stabilize this region so vital to a US definition of interests. Like the Gulf War a decade before, another President Bush sought to lead in the Arab-Israeli peace process not for its own sake, but in a broader strategic context of American actions against al-Qaeda, Afghanistan, and Iraq. This at first translated into a courtship of the Arab and Muslim world, with the momentous declaration of US support for an independent Palestine. But the War on Terror served simultaneously as a constraint on US relations toward the Palestinian cause. The pervasive terrorist violence by Palestinians forced Bush to take a hard line toward Arafat and perpetrating groups, in the name of consistency with the US principles in the War on Terror. Palestinian statehood thus became conditional on reform in the Palestinian Authority and the promise to end the violence, much in line with the Sharon view.

US policy also reflected continuity in that a balance of strategic and domestic influences characterized the American approach, leading once again to a slow, deliberate, stalling policy that is ambiguous enough that it may not lead to real change. The Bush Administration is pro-Israel for domestic and strategic reasons: Israel has cooperated with the United States on the War on Terror to a greater extent than the Arabs Bush had courted. Bush was personally affronted by Arafat, a sentiment intensified by the context of terror precipitated by 9/11 and the continued terror acts in the occupied territories. Bush domestically had a freer hand to create new policy tracks, but he remained cognizant of the domestic pressures that confined his behavior so as not to alienate Israel or its supporters.

The promise of Palestinian statehood thus far has been rhetorical, and its realization is by no means secured. The war against Iraq and numerous confounding stumbling blocks in the peace process provide room to question whether the 'road map' ever becomes reality. But what Bush accomplished rhetorically is a shift in the debate – de-legitimating any one-state solutions or those not giving Palestinians independence. This is an historic shift with which even Sharon has had to reconcile. The implementation is in question and may take time. But it is a moment the Bush Administration should not let slip by. A two-state vision would help the image of the United States greatly, defusing a regional argument for anti-Americanism by leading the way to the creation of a homeland for Palestinians. This would ameliorate the violence and conflict based on nationalism and the scourge of oppression, which has taken a toll on Palestinians and Israelis alike. While it would not likely ameliorate more extremist terrorism, such as that of Hamas (which still claims to seek the elimination of Israel and the establishment of an Islamic Palestine), a Palestinian state would be an empowered ally to join both the United States and Israel against fundamentalist extremism. What began out of strategic necessity in the War on Terror could very well be President Bush's crowning achievement and legacy in the Middle East. Only time will tell if this was a time of momentous change or of another cycle in the never-ending Arab-Israeli conflict.

Notes

1   This definition is that of the US government; see Paul R. Pillar (2001), *Terrorism and US Foreign Policy*, Washington, DC: Brookings Institute, 13. While terrorism is a contested concept, this definition focusing on terror as a method is a useful approach that I employ in this chapter, and one used by the editors in this book.

2   This term is the title of a book analyzing US policy toward the Arab-Israeli conflict over time. See Vaughn Shannon (2003), *Balancing Act: US Foreign Policy and the Arab-Israeli Conflict*, Aldershot, UK: Ashgate Publishing.

3   George W. Ball and Douglas B. Ball (1992), *The Passionate Attachment: America's Involvement with Israel, 1947-Present*, New York: W.W. Norton, 11.

4   On these images, see Daniel Heradstveit (1979), *The Arab-Israeli Conflict: Psychological Obstacles to Peace*, New York: Columbia University Press, and David K. Shipler (1986), *Arab and Jew: Wounded Spirits in a Promised Land*, New York: Penguin Books. For a look at Arab views, see also Yehoshafat Harkabi (1972), *Arab Attitudes to Israel*, New York: Hart Publishing, and Daniel Pipes (1998), *The Hidden Hand: Middle East Fears of Conspiracy*, New York: St Martin's, the latter of which goes so far to say that 'conspiratorial anti-Semitism and overwrought fears of Israeli expansionism perpetuate the Arab-Israeli confrontation' (28).

5   The 'national interest' versus domestic interest contrast is made by many works, including Steven Spiegel (1985), *The Other Arab-Israeli Conflict*, Chicago: University of Chicago Press; Ball and Ball (1992); and Abraham Ben-Zvi (1993), *The United States and Israel: The Limits of the Special Relationship*, New York: Columbia University Press.

6   Ronald J. Young (1986), *Missed Opportunities for Peace: US Middle East Policy*, Philadelphia: American Friends Service Committee, 7.

7   For the seminal realist statement, see Hans J. Morgenthau (1978), *Politics Among Nations*, New York: Knopf. For a discussion of the 'strategic' or 'national interest' approach to the Arab-Israeli conflict, see William B. Quandt (1977), *Decade of Decisions: American Foreign Policy Toward the Arab-Israeli Conflict, 1967–1976*, Berkeley: University of California Press, 4–15.

8   For an application of geopolitical analysis to the Middle East, see Geoffrey Kemp and Robert E. Harkavy (1997), *Strategic Geography and the Changing Middle East*, New York: Carnegie Endowment for International Peace. See also Zbigniew Brzezinski, Brent Scowcroft, and Richard W. Murpy (1997), *Differentiated Containment*, Washington, DC: Council on Foreign Relations Press, for a discussion of US enduring interests in the Middle East.

9   George Lenczowski (1980), *The Middle East in World Affairs*, Ithaca: Cornell University Press, is a classic sweeping history of international relations related to the Middle East.

10   Daniel Yergin (1991), *The Prize: The Epic Quest for Oil, Money and Power*, New York: Simon and Schuster, traces the rise of oil as a vital resource from the perspective of military advantage, as well as the role of this fact in the world wars of the twentieth century. See especially chapters 8–10 and 16–19.

11   D. Jason Berggren (2001), 'The New Kid on the Bloc: Muslims Responsible for Bush Win in 2000', *Middle East Affairs Journal*, 7/3–4, 155–77, at 167.

12   Mitchell Bard (1988), 'The Influence of Ethnic Interest Groups on American Middle East Policy', in Charles Kegley and Eugene Wittkopf, eds, *The Domestic Sources of American Foreign Policy*, New York: St Martin's Press, 61.

13   Ibid.

14   Ibid., 58–9.

15   Berggren, 165.

16   'Foreign Policy: It Works at Home', *The Economist* (20 April 2002), 27–8.

17   This land could be said to include Jordan and the Sinai, in addition to Israel, the West Bank and Gaza, Ahmad Faruqui; 'Bush Freezes Peace Process', 5 July 2002, online at http://www.counterpunch.org /faruqui0705.html.

18   'Christian Coalition of America Condemns Terror Attack in Tel Aviv', 6 January 2003, online at http://www. cc.org/becomeinformed/pressreleases010603.html.

19   The American Muslim Political Coordinating Council PAC (AMPCC) promoted a bloc vote in 2000, and endorsed Bush (see Berggren, 160). Bush encountered a difficult issue after 9/11, as at least one of his supporters, Florida professor Sami al-Arian, was linked to support for Palestinian Islamic Jihad (*USA Today*, 21 February 2003, A1).

20   Quandt, 15–24; see also Peter Grose (1983), *Israel in the Minds of America*, New York: Knopf.

21   Jeffrey Jones, 'Americans' Views of Israel More Positive than Last Year', *Gallup News Service*, 19 February 2003, online at http://www.gallup.com/poll/ releases/ pr030219 .asp. See also 'Foreign Policy: It Works at Home', which cites a Pew Poll citing similar sympathies and contrasts the numbers with other countries more sympathetic with the Palestinians.

22   On 'perspective', see Kristen Monroe (2001) 'Paradigm Shift: From Rational Choice to Perspective', *International Political Studies Review*, 22/2, 151–72. For an application of psychological decision-making theory to Israel, see Michael Brecher (1974), *Decisions in Israel's Foreign Policy*, London: Oxford University Press. For the 'Presidential Leadership perspective' related to US policy toward the Arab-Israeli conflict, see Quandt, 28–36.

23   Stephen Zunes (2002), 'The Swing to the Right in US Policy Toward Israel and Palestine', *Middle East Policy*, 9/3, 45–64.

24   Patrick J. Buchanan, 'Whose War?', *The American Conservative*, 24 March 2003, online at http://www.amconmag.com/03_24_03/cover.html.

25   Jim Lobe, 'Neoconservatives Consolidate Control over US Mideast Policy', *Foreign Policy in Focus*, 6 December 2002, online at http://www.bintjbeil.com/articles/en/021206 _lobe.html.

26   The Palestinian Authority was the designated representative body for Palestinians under an agreement with Israel in 1993, the Oslo Accords. Under the agreement, Arafat's Palestinian Authority would administer negotiated territories from Gaza and the West Bank. This provisional arrangement was intended to stay in effect while the two parties negotiated a 'final status' agreement on all outstanding issues. For historical reference, see Ian Bickerton and Carla Klausner (2002), *A Concise History of the Arab-Israeli Conflict*, 4th edn, Upper Saddle River, NJ: Prentice Hall.

27   At least 1920 Palestinians and 723 Israelis have been killed since the start of the revolt; see Mohammed Assadi, 'Palestinian Legislature Approves Premiership', *Reuters*, 10 March 2003, online at http://story.news.yahoo.com/news?tmpl=story&u=/nm/ 20030310/ wl_nm/ mideast_dc_52.

28   Ali Khani (2002), 'Sharon as Prime Minister of Israel', *Middle East Affairs Journal*, 7/1–2, 161–77, at 171–3.

29   Jonathan Broder, 'Bush Looks into Moving Embassy to Jerusalem', online at www.jrep.com/ Reporter/Article-38.html.

30   See 'AIPAC Praises US Leadership on UN Racism Conference; Regrets UN Decision', 28 August 2001, online at http://www.aipac.org/documents/AIPACrelease 0828.html.

31   See The Mitchell Plan, or Sharm el-Sheikh Fact-Finding Committee Final Report, online at http://usinfo.state.gov/regional/nea/mitchell.htm.

32   Ahron Bregman (2002), *Israel's Wars: A History Since 1947*, 2nd edn, London and New York: Routledge, 231.

33   See *The Tenet Plan: Israeli-Palestinian Ceasefire and Security Plan*, online at http: //www.yale.edu/lawweb/avalon/mideast/mid023.htm.

34   Yoav Appel, 'Palestinians Promise to Keep Peace', *Associated Press*, August 19 2002, online at http://story.news.yahoo.com/news?tmpl=story&u=/ap/20020819/ap_on_re_mi_ea/israel_palestinians_629.

35   Bregman, 231.

36   The fourth plane crashed in rural Pennsylvania after a struggle with passengers; its destination was unknown but suspected to be heading toward Washington, DC, for targets such as the White House or Capitol building.

37   Michael Hirsch (2002), 'Bush and the World', *Foreign Affairs*, 81/5, 18–19.

38   There were almost immediate calls for attacking Iraq right after 9/11 from some in the administration, particularly Defense Secretary Donald Rumsfeld and his Deputy, Paul Wolfowitz. There was no link to al-Qaeda nor evidence of Iraq's hand in the events of 9/11, but some suspected Saddam Hussein could be involved and, regardless, he was enough of a threat or nuisance that 9/11 could provide an impetus for support for regime change in Iraq. For the early discussions, see Bob Woodward (2002), *Bush at War*, New York: Simon and Schuster, 49; also 'Sept. 11 Attacks put US on Path to War', *Associated Press*, 19 March 2003, online at http://www.indystar.com/print/articles/8 /029946-5788-010.html.

39   Pillar lists the various instruments of counter-terrorism.

40   There is a substantial Christian Palestinian community as well.

41   See bin Laden interview transcript, reprinted as 'American Policies in the Middle East Justify Islamic Terrorism', in Laura Egendorf (ed.) (2000), *Terrorism: Opposing Viewpoints*, San Diego: Greenhaven Press, 123–30.

42   Robin Wright (2001), *Sacred Rage: The Wrath of Militant Islam*, New York: Touchstone, 268, emphasis mine.

43   Samuel Huntington's thesis that 'the West' and 'Islam' were culturally doomed to conflict is embraced by conservatives in each 'civilization'; thus Bush tried to deflate bin Laden's rhetoric pitting the world in terms of Islam versus infidel. Huntington (1996), *The Clash of Civilizations and the Remaking of World Order*, New York: Simon and Schuster.

44   Anton La Guardia (2002), *War Without End: Israelis, Palestinians, and the Struggle for a Promised Land*, New York: Thomas Dunne Books, 335. This refers to the British public proclamation backing the creation of a Jewish state in Palestine in 1917.

45   Randall Price (2001), *Unholy War: America, Israel and Radical Islam*, Eugene, OR: Harvest House Publishers, 40.

46   Previous administrations had varying opinions about the possibility of a Palestinian state, but none had made such a public commitment to such an outcome. Previous US involvement tended to follow a 'procedural bias' that left outcomes to the negotiating parties. Clinton made an open advocacy for a Palestinian state in the waning days of his term, but not in such a heralded and pronounced statement of intent (La Guardia, 335).

47   Jane Perlez and Patrick Tyler, 'Before Attacks, US Was Ready to Say It Backed Palestinian State', *New York Times*, 2 October 2001, A1.

48   Woodward, 197-8.

49   Speech reprinted in *Journal of Palestinian Studies* (Winter 2002), 164.

50   See http://www.un.org/News/Press/docs/2002/sc7326.doc.htm. Syria abstained, neither satisfied that the resolution went far enough for achieving a Palestinian state nor interested in voting against this symbolic statement.

51   Ewan MacAskill, *The Guardian*, 14 March 2002, online at www.guardian.co.uk/israel/story/0,2763,666909,00.html; see also UN Resolution 1397, online at http://ods-dds-ny.un.org/doc/UNDOC/GEN/N02/283/59/PDF/NO2289359.pdf.

52   Price, 10.

53   Letter reprinted in *Journal of Palestinian Studies* (Winter 2002), 164–5.

54   Quandt refers to 'procedural bias' as the US tendency to focus on the negotiation method rather than outcomes.

55 Camille Mansour (2002), 'The Impact of 11 September on the Israeli-Palestinian Conflict', *Journal of Palestinian Studies*, 31/2, 5–18, at 13.
56 Ron Fournier, 'Bush Urges Israel to End Incursion', Associated Press, 4 April 2002, online at http://story.news.yahoo.com/news?tmpl=story&u=/ap/20020405/ap_on_re_mi_ea/us _mideast_1029&printer=1.
57 Ibid; also Woodward, 324–5. Powell was criticized by some insiders for 'leaning too much' toward the Palestinians by suggesting an international conference, an idea he was ordered to retract.
58 Matt Spetalnick, 'Sharon Vows to Press on with Offensive, Defying US', *Reuters*, 8 April 2002, online at http://story.news.yahoo.com/news?tmpl=story&u=/nm/20020408/ts_nm /mideast_dc_1363&printer=1.
59 A pro-Palestinian rally held near the White House at the time did not receive US representation; see Steve Holland, 'Bush Steers Back to More Pro-Israeli Policy', *Reuters*, 20 April 2002.
60 Vicki Allen, 'Congress to Take up Pro-Israel Resolutions', *Reuters*, 2 May 2002, online at http://story.news.yahoo.com/news?tmpl=story&ncid=584&e=3&cid=584&u=/nm/ 20020502/pl_nm/mideast_congress_israel_dc_3.
61 Graham Fuller (2002), 'The Future of Political Islam', *Foreign Affairs*, 81/2, 48–60, at 28–9.
62 Steve Weizman, 'Likud Party Defies Sharon', *Associated Press*, 12 May 2002, online at http://story.news.yahoo.com/news?tmpl=story&cid=514&u=/ap/20020512/ap_on_re_mi_ ea/israel_palestinians_4087.
63 Nidal al-Mughrabi, 'Fatah Group Urges End to Suicide Attacks in Israel', *Reuters*, 29 May 2002, online at http://story.news.yahoo.com/news?tmpl=story&ncid=586&e=2&cid=586 &u=/nm/20020529/wl_nm/mideast_palestinian_fatah_dc_1.
64 'Suicide bomb kills 19 as Bush expected to announce peace plan', online at http://www. jordantimes.com/Wed/news/news1.htm.
65 Mohammed Assadi, 'Israeli Army Launches Reprisal Raid on Arafat HQ', *Reuters*, 6 June 2002, online at http://story.news.yahoo.com/news?tmpl=story&ncid=586 &e=2&cid=586 &u=/nm/20020606/wl_nm/mideast_dc_2484.
66 Woodward, 297, notes that Bush increasingly viewed Arafat as just 'evil'; see also Zunes, 54–5.
67 See Daniel Klaidman and Michael Hirsh, 'He Knows It, He Feels It', *Newsweek*, 8 April 2002, 28–9.
68 Randall Mikkelsen, 'Suicide Bombings Hardened Bush Rejection of Arafat', *Reuters*, 24 June 2002, online at http://story.news.yahoo.com/news?tmpl=story&cid=615&615&e=6 &u=/nm/20020624/pl_nm/mideast_usa_decision_dc_1.
69 Nathan Guttman, 'Solana: Palestinian People Must Choose Their Own Leader', *Ha'aretz Daily*, online at http://www.haaretzdaily.com/hasen/pages/ShArt.jhtml?itemNo=179734 &contrassID=1&subContrassID=0&sbSubContrassID=0.
70 Ahmad Faruqui, 'Bush Freezes Peace Process', 5 July 2002, online at http://www. counterpunch.org/faruqui0705.html.
71 Ibid.
72 Alistair Lyon, 'Bush Fails to Lift Arab Despair Over US Policy', *Reuters*, 25 June 2002, online at http://story.news.yahoo.com/news?tmpl=story&ncid=586&e=3&cid=586&u=/ nm/20020625/wl_nm/mideast_arabs_dc_1.
73 Khaled Amayreh, 'Assassins, bulldozers and human bombs', *Ahram*, online at http: //www.ahram.org.eg/weekly/2002/591/re1.htm.
74 Wafa Amr, 'Arafat Wins Cabinet Vote; Israel Coalition in Chaos', *Reuters*, 29 October 2002, http://story.news.yahoo.com/news?tmpl=story&ncid=586&e=3&cid=586&u=/nm/ 20021029/wl_nm/mideast_cabinet_dc.

75 See www.aipac.org/documents/stalwartner111802.html; http://usembassy.state.gov/posts/ ja1/wwwhse1246. html.

76 Tony Locy, 'FBI Charges Fla. Professor as Terror Fundraiser', *USA Today*, 21–23 February 2003, 1A.

77 Angela Brown, 'Feds Indict 7 in Texas Terror Probe', *Associated Press*, 18 December 2002, online at http://story.news.yahoo.com/news?tmpl=story2&cid=514&ncid=514&e=2&u=/ ap/20021218/ap_on_re_us/hamas_arrests_10.

78 Nidal al-Mughrabi, 'Israeli Forces Kill 10 Palestinians in Gaza', *Reuters*, 6 December 2002, online at http://story.news.yahoo.com/news?tmpl=story&cid=578&u=/nm/20021206/ ts_nm/ mideast_dc_32.

79 Amos Harel, 'Senior Officer: Qaida Chief in Region to Recruit Palestinians', *Ha'aretz*, 2 January 2003, online at http://www.haaretzdaily.com/hasen/pages/ShArt.jhtml?itemNo= 247563&contrassID=1&subContrassID=0&sbSubContrassID=0.

80 Noel Mwakughu, 'Suicide Bomb Kills Israelis, Kenyans; Qaeda Blamed', 28 November, 2002, online at http://dailynews.att.net/cgi-bin/news?e=pri&dt=021128&cat=news&st= newskenyaattacksdc.

81 Rawhi Abdeidoh, 'Al Qaeda Claims Kenya Attacks, Vows More', *Reuters*, 8 December 2002, online at http://dailynews.att.net/cgi-bin/news?e=pri&dt=021208&cat=internation al&st=internationalattackqaedajazeeradc.

82 Dan Williams, 'Arafat Tells Al Qaeda Not to Use Palestinian Cause', *Reuters*, 15 December 2002, online at http://story.news.yahoo.com/news?tmpl=story&ncid=586&e= 1&cid=586&u=/nm/20021215/wl_nm/mideast_dc.

83 Jeffrey Heller, 'Israel's Peres Reopens Dialogue with Palestinians', *Reuters*, 8 July 2002, online at http://story.news.yahoo.com/news?tmpl=story&ncid=586&e=1&cid=586&u=/ nm/20020709/wl_nm/mideast_dc_2915.

84 Cameron Barr, 'Intifada Fatigue Hits Palestinians', *Christian Science Monitor*, 5 July 2002, online at http://www.csmonitor.com/2002/0705/p01s03-wome.html.

85 Aluf Benn, 'Yehiyeh plan: PA forces to take over as IDF withdraws', *Ha'aretz*, 22 July 2002, online at http://www.haaretzdaily.com/hasen/pages/ShArt.jhtml?itemNo=189175& contrassID=2&subContrassID=1&sbSubContrassID=0.

86 Matt Spetalnick, 'Israeli Coalition Collapses, Elections Possible', *Reuters*, 30 October 2002, online at http://story.news.yahoo.com/news?tmpl=story&ncid=586&e=2&cid= 586&u=/nm/20021030/wl_nm/mideast_dc.

87 Akiva Eldar, 'American intervention in Israel's elections', *Ha'aretz*, online at http: //www.haaretzdaily.com/hasen/pages/ShArt.jhtml?itemNo=241378&contrassID=2&sub ContrassID=&sbSubContrassID=0&listSrc=Y.

88 Jeffrey Heller, 'Palestinian Suicide Blasts Draw Israeli Punishment', *Reuters*, 6 January, 2003, online at http://dailynews.att.net/cgi-bin/news?e=pri&dt= 030106&cat=internation al&st=internationalmideastexplosiondc.

89 Nidal al-Mughrabi, 'Violence Surges Days Before Israeli Election', *Reuters*, 24 January 2003.

90 Laura King and Megan Stack, 'Sharon Wins Easily in Israel', *Los Angeles Times*, 29 January 2003, online at http://latimes.infogate.com/content.php?page=AllArticleXml&f eed=latimes&type=xml&catkey=latimes_world&uniqueID=1043849790477158&bid=tr ib.la.lite&sid=48d63bac1eca45f2e6978c6e99136010&context=lite&liteuser=trib.la.lite: vps71. On Labor's refusal to join a coalition government with Likud, see Mark Heinrich, 'Israel's Mitzna Spurns Sharon Coalition Appeal', 3 February 2003, online at http:// story.news.yahoo.com/news?tmpl=story&ncid=586&e=3&cid=586&u=/nm/20030203/ wl_nm/israel_dc.

91 Jeffrey Heller, 'Sharon to Form Israel Govt, Oust Top Palestinians', 9 February 2003, online at http://dailynews.att.net/cgi-bin/news?e=pri&dt=030209&cat=international&st =internationalmideastdc.

92 Laura King, 'Arafat Welcomes Talks with Israelis', *Los Angeles Times*, 9 February 2003, online at http://latimes.infogate.com/content.php?page=AllArticleXml&feed=latimes&ty pe=xml&catkey=latimes_world&uniqueID=1044800180767012&bid=trib.la.lite&sid=48 d63bac1eca45f2e6978c6e99136010&context=lite&liteuser=trib.la.lite:vps71.

93 Megan Stack, 'Arafat Says He'll Appoint a Premier', *Los Angeles Times*, 15 February 2003.

94 Laura King, *Los Angeles Times*, online at http://latimes.infogate.com/content.php?page=a llarticlexml&feed=latimes&type=xml&catkey=latimes_world&uniqueID=10430721871 82105&bid=trib.la.lite&sid.

95 Steven Weisman, 'US Joins Partners on Plan for Mideast, but Not Timing', *The New York Times*, 21 December 2002, online at http://story.news.yahoo.com/news?Tmpl=story&ncid =68&e=1& cid=68&u=/nyt /20021221/ts_nyt/u_s__joins_partners_on_plan_for_mideast_ _but_not_timing.

96 'Report: Bush Decides to Oust Saddam Hussein', *Reuters*, 13 February 2002, http: //dailynews.yahoo.com/htx/nm/20020213/ts/attack_iraq_dc_4.html.

97 Woodward, 330–32, documents this debate.

98 On the ethical and legal aspects of the first Gulf War, see Michael Walzer (1992), *Just and Unjust Wars*, New York: Basic Books; also Martin Van Creveld (1992), 'The Persian Gulf Crisis of 1990-91 and the Future of Morally Constrained War', *Parameters*, 22/2, 21–40.

99 'King: Mideast Peace Conference Should be Based on UN Resolutions', *Jordan Times*, 7 May 2002, online at http://www.jordanembassyus.org/05072002001.htm.

100 Inal Ersan, 'Arabs Take to Streets to Protest War against Iraq', *Reuters*, 27 January 2003, online at http://dailynews.att.net/cgi-bin/news?e=pri&dt=030127&cat=international&st= internationaliraqprotestsdc.

101 Jonathan Broder, 'On Iraq, this time Israel is a player', *MSNBC*, 8 March 2003, online at http://www.msnbc.com/news/717008.asp#BODY.

102 Price, 37. Israel's intelligence gathering capabilities have been called 'vital' to overall US security, and there was some indication that Israel had forewarned 9/11 with its own intelligence information.

103 Amos Harel and Nathan Guttman, 'IDF quickens pace in its preparations for US war in Iraq', online at http://www.haaretzdaily.com/hasen/pages/ShArt.jhtml?itemNo=243490& contrassID=2&subContrassID=1&sbSubContrassID=0.

104 Neil MacFarquhar, 'Hezbollah Becomes Potent Anti-US Force', *The New York Times*, 24 December 2002, online at http://story.news.yahoo.com/news?tmpl=story&ncid=68&e=2 &cid=68&u=/nyt/20021224/ts_nyt/hezbollah_becomes_potent_anti_u_s__force.

105 'Sharon Says Iraq May Be Hiding Weapons in Syria', *Reuters*, 24 December 2002, online at http://story.news.yahoo.com/news?tmpl=story&ncid=586&e=1&cid =586&u =/ nm/ 20021224/wl_nm/iraq_israel_dc.

106 Rawhi Abdeidoh, 'Al Qaeda Claims Kenya Attacks, Vows More,' *Reuters*, 8 December 2002, online at http://dailynews.att .net/cgi-bin/news?e=pri&dt=021208&cat=international &st=internationalattackqaedajazeeradc.

107 Laura King, 'Ties to Iraq less Binding this Time', *Los Angeles Times*, 7 February 2003, online at http://latimes.infogate.com/content.php?page=AllArticleXml&feed=latimes&ty pe=xml&catkey=latimes_world&uniqueID=1044627415077190&bid=trib.la.lite&sid=48 d63bac1eca45f2e6978c6e99136010&context=lite&liteuser=trib.la.lite:vps71.

108 Israeli Ministry of Foreign Affairs, 'Iraq's Involvement in the Palestinian Terrorist Activity against Israel', January 2003, online at http://www.mfa.gov.il/mfa/go.asp?MFAH0n2h0.

109 'Hamas pledges support to Iraq', *USA Today*, 10 January 2003, online at http:// www.usatoday.com/news/world/2003-01-10-hamas-iraq_x.htm.

110 Jonathan Broder, 'On Iraq, this time Israel is a player'.

111 'President George W. Bush Speaks at AEI's Annual Dinner', 28 February 2003, online at http://www.aei.org/news/newsID.16197.filter/news_detail.asp.

112 Jonathan Broder, 'On Iraq, this time Israel is a player'.

113 'Mahathir Warns of Retaliation from More Muslims if US Attacks Iraq', 24 February 2003, online at http://english.peopledaily.com.cn/200302/24/eng20030224_112162.shtml; Abbas Salman, 'Protesters March Against War in Key US Gulf Ally', *Reuters*, 28 February 2003, online at http://dailynews.att.net/cgi-bin/news?e=pub&dt=030228&cat=news&st=newsir aqmarchesdc.

114 Daniel Sobelman, 'Arab League Members Oppose Iraq Attack', *Ha'aretz*, online at http://www.haaretzdaily.com/hasen/spages/267987.html.

115 Mohammed Assadi, 'Palestinian Legislature Approves Premiership', *Reuters*, 10 March 2003, online at http://story.news.yahoo.com/news?tmpl=story&u=/nm/200303 10/wl_nm/mideast_dc_52.

116 Jeffrey Heller, 'Israel Vows to Target More Hamas Leaders', *Reuters*, 9 March 2003, online at http://story.news.yahoo.com/news?tmpl=story&ncid=586&e=3&cid=586&u=/nm/20030309/wl_nm/mideast_dc.

117 'Bush Calls for New Diplomacy between Israel and Palestinians', *Associated Press*, 14 March 2003, online at http://www.nytimes.com/2003/03/14/international/middleeast/11WIRE-DIPLO.html.

118 Paisley Dodds, 'Palestinians OK Power-sharing Compromise', *Associated Press*, 19 March 2003.

119 Richard Curtiss (2001), 'The Cost of Israel to the American People', *Middle East Affairs Journal*, 7/3–4, 101–12, at 110.

120 Warren Hoge, 'A Sense of American Unfairness Erodes Support in Gulf States', *New York Times*, 2 October 2001, A6; Warren Richey, 'Muslim Opinion Sees Conspiracy', *Christian Science Monitor*, 6 November 2001, online at http://www.Csmonitor.com/2001/1106/p1s1-wogi.html; see also 'Poll: Muslims call US "ruthless, arrogant"', *Cnn.com*, 26 February 2002, online at http://www.cnn.com/2002/US/02/26/gallup.muslims.

121 The US has beefed up programs in public diplomacy in the battle for the 'hearts and minds' since 9/11. See Robert Kaiser, 'Making Sure the US Message Gets Heard', *Washington Post National Weekly*.

122 Interview of Tom Friedman on National Public Radio, online at http://www.npr.org/ramfiles/fa/20020529.fa.ram; or at http://freshair.npr.org/dayFA.cfm?display=day&todayDate=05%2F29%2F2002.

123 For an argument against a unilaterally declared Palestinian state, see Tal Becker, 'International Recognition of a Unilaterally Declared Palestinian State', *Jerusalem Center for Public Affairs*, online at http://www.jcpa.org/art/becker1.htm.

124 See 'Polling the Nation', online at http://poll.orspub.com.

Chapter 8

The War on Terrorism and the Just Use of Military Force

Patrick Hayden

Introduction

This chapter sketches a framework for thinking about the United States government's response to the terrorist attacks of 11 September 2001. In particular, it examines the moral and legal rules that apply to the US-led fight against terrorism, and articulates what I take to be the appropriate limits to waging the so-called 'war on terrorism'. Following the violent attacks of 11 September by al-Qaeda operatives one of the fundamental questions faced by the administration of George W. Bush, as well as by the broader international community, was how best to respond to the threat and reality of terrorism. The Bush Administration assumed that the answer is obvious and uncontroversial: resorting to war in order to strike back at terrorists, as well as those nations suspected of harboring them, was justified. Yet the Bush Administration has thus far failed to elaborate the normative judgments that led them to this answer, so that their justification for resorting to the use of armed force remains incomplete.

The complexity of the question concerning the just use of force – which brings together moral, legal, political and military issues – cannot be overstated, and its implications are profound with regard to the formulation of appropriate foreign policy. Debate surrounding the United States' response to the specter of international terrorism necessarily revolves around different conceptions of the national interest and how best to define and defend it. The willingness and the capacity of the United States, as well as other nations, to respond militarily to the form of 'warfare' embodied in international terrorism are therefore open to critical assessment so that we may begin to develop an understanding of how the war on terrorism, and its underlying policy are shaping our world.[1] Towards that end, I will set out the fundamental criteria of just war theory and the corresponding international laws of war, and apply these as the requirements that the United States and its allies must meet in order to be justified in resorting to military force.[2] The aim of this chapter is to analyze whether the war against terrorism is a justified use of military force or illegitimate aggression, and thus whether the war's pursuit is the result of good or bad foreign policy.

The Principles of Just War Theory

In traditional just war theory there are two basic categories of norms: *jus ad bellum*, the justice of the cause of resorting to war to begin with, and *jus in bello*, the justice of the means or conduct of war once it has begun.[3] Given these two categories, a comprehensive analysis of the just use of military force will consider whether warfare is justly begun as well as justly fought.

The structure of comprehensive just war theory also presupposes the priority of *jus ad bellum* to *jus in bello*. In other words, the two sets of norms are placed in serial order, with *jus ad bellum* lexically prior to *jus in bello*. This means that the just resort to military force must satisfy the norms of *jus ad bellum* before the norms of *jus in bello* come into play. The serial order thereby ensures consistency between, and coherency throughout, the two just war categories in order to prohibit the trading off of norms. While a war may be justly begun it is conceivable that it will be unjustly fought. The justness of any given war therefore must be determined in light of both sets of norms, and the failure to satisfy one set of norms will preclude judging the war as a whole to be just.

Before considering each of the just war categories it should also be noted that the normative conditions specified in the theory are not to be taken as merely subjective. In other words, individual states are disallowed from simply asserting that they have satisfied the norms of both categories, and the rest of the international community is neither obligated nor expected to accept their claims as self-evident. The norms of just war theory instead function as public and transparent universal moral principles against which state conduct ought to be assessed.[4] In this way, just war theory serves as the underlying normative foundation for corresponding rules and obligations embodied in international humanitarian law and the laws of war. Just war theory thus constitutes a reasonable guide to foreign policy questions concerning the use of military force, in particular those pertaining to the aims states are to have in mind when considering the use of force, and the means they may use or must avoid using in the conduct of war.

Jus ad Bellum

This section discusses the six major principles governing the justice of resorting to war. These principles can be stated as follows:

1 just cause: the war must be fought in a just cause;
2 right intention: states must have the right reason and proper motivation for going to war, which excludes war for personal or national gain, or for some other hidden purpose;
3 legitimate authority: the war must be declared publicly and waged exclusively by the competent authority having the right to do so;
4 last resort: recourse to war must be a last resort;
5 likelihood of success: those engaging in war must have a reasonable hope of success;
6 proportionality of the ends of war: the damage and harm that the war ultimately entails must be judged proportionate to the injustice which occasions it.

It should be kept in mind that no single principle by itself offers sufficient justification for the use of military force. Following the general trend in the just war tradition, the criteria here will be taken as individually necessary and jointly sufficient for a war to count as just. For instance, while a just cause is a necessary condition for the resort to war, it is not itself a sufficient condition. A state may go to war justly only when all the remaining *jus ad bellum* conditions are met as well. Thus, simple failure to meet any particular one of the criteria may warrant a judgment that the resort to war is unjust; conversely, satisfying all of the criteria may warrant a judgment that the resort to war is just. Nevertheless, even if sufficient justification exists, the criteria ought to be understood primarily as negative constraints on the decision (or conduct) of war. This proviso means the decision to go to war does not become mandatory simply because all *jus ad bellum* conditions are met; it means only that going to war is permissible. The purpose of the criteria is not to justify war in the sense of fostering or promoting it but only in the sense of defending morally what would otherwise be prohibited actions.

The first necessary *jus ad bellum* condition that must be satisfied, then, begins with the concept of 'just cause'. Traditionally, this has meant that a state considering going to war must identify an injury received, most notably aggression directed at its territorial integrity and political sovereignty. Injury might also arise when the human rights of innocent citizens are violated in some systematic and severe way, even in another state. Acceptable just causes therefore include self-defense from aggression, reclaiming people and territory wrongly seized or threatened by an aggressor, and defending or rescuing the innocent from gross violations of their human rights. A second, and closely related criterion that must be satisfied is that of 'right intention'. Most fundamentally, the principle of right intention means that a state must not only have the right cause to resort to armed force, it must also have the proper motivation, which is to achieve the just cause. A state may not use the concept of a just cause to prosecute a war for some secret end(s) incompatible with the cause, such as for purposes of material gain derived from the capture of territory and resources, or to exact revenge based upon religious or ethnic hatred. In addition right intention demands that a state must, prior to prosecuting war, commit itself to upholding all the other just war criteria.

The dual influence of just cause and right intention has led, since the end of the Second World War, to a general proscription of all first use of force or wars of aggression. Article 2(4) of the United Nations Charter, for instance, states that 'All members shall refrain ... from the threat or use of force against the territorial integrity or political independence of any state.' Thus, under the Charter the threat or use of force is illegal except in circumstances of self-defense and the collective use of force by the organization itself, for the purpose of securing a just cause. Offensive aggression thus constitutes an illegal, immoral and unjustified use of force, which provides an acceptable rationale for resorting to defensive war against the aggressor. Notably, the proscription of offensive aggression also provides a constraint on the possible abuse of the principle of just cause. In other words, the actual presence or imminent threat of overt aggression is a prerequisite to the just use of armed force; a mere suspicion about the possible occurrence of violence is insufficient justification.[5]

The principle of the 'proportionality of the ends of war' is intended to ensure that the good or end intended by war outweighs both the evil that induced the war and the evil that will result from the war itself. This principle clearly requires a consequentialist assessment of the foreseeable harm that likely will be caused by resorting to armed force, insofar as states must consider how their actions will affect their own citizens as well as the citizens of other states. If serious doubts exist as to whether the good that is generated by the use of force will be greater than the harm caused, then war should be avoided. Requiring a reasonable chance of success supports the 'principle of proportionality', insofar as the human costs of prosecuting a war should not be disproportional to the political objective being sought. A military campaign that has a high likelihood of failure will simply add additional misery to the harm caused by the initial aggression. The principle of 'last resort' adds further emphasis to the previous point. It stipulates that war may be undertaken only when all good-faith efforts to resolve the conflict through diplomacy, arbitration and other means that fall short of armed force have failed. Together, these three criteria aim to limit the suffering and destruction that inevitably accompany war.

The final *jus ad bellum* condition to be mentioned is that only a legitimate, competent authority – typically the political figure or institution in a national government holding sovereign power – is morally and legally entitled to declare war, and must express its intention to initiate war by means of a public declaration.

Jus in Bello

There are two just war principles regulating the way in which war is conducted once it has begun, thereby providing minimum standards for what is morally permissible in fighting. These are:

1 discrimination: combatants must distinguish between military targets and civilian populations, and non-combatants must be immune from attack;
2 proportionality of the means of war: all military actions taken in war must be reasonably expected to produce benefits that outweigh the expected harms or costs.

The significance of the *in bello* principles is that they require continual adherence to the norms of just war theory. While a state may be justified in initiating war by satisfying the *ad bellum* criteria, it is quite possible that the same state could violate the norms of *jus in bello* during the course of war. If a state were to conduct war in violation of the *in bello* criteria, its claim to be prosecuting a just war would be discredited.

Consequently, a war must be fought justly in order to be just in a complete sense. During the conduct of war, the principle of 'discrimination' (also known as the principle of noncombatant immunity) demands that no act of war may be intentionally directed at noncombatants. This condition clearly is intended to protect innocents from being targeted militarily either as direct ends or as indirect means to some further ends. The norm of noncombatant immunity was codified in Articles 22–28 of the Fourth Hague Convention of 1907, in the Fourth Geneva Convention of 1949 and in Articles 48–58 of the 1977 First Protocol to the Geneva Conventions.[6] The basis of the principle of discrimination is a moral distinction between combatants, whose activity purposefully contributes to aggression or the imminent threat of aggression, and noncombatants, who do not purposefully or actively contribute to aggression. Failure to draw this distinction implies that all persons, regardless of their guilt or innocence, are legitimate targets and, moreover, that there are no meaningful moral and legal constraints on the conduct of war. If this were the case, however, there would then be no basis for distinguishing between just and unjust, or legal and illegal wars. The resultant moral vacuum would undermine any claim to justice by both sides in a conflict.

Nevertheless given the nature of war it would be foolish to deny the possibility of noncombatant casualties. The doctrine of 'double effect' has been developed to address this problem, in light of the requirements of discrimination. What this doctrine recognizes is that there is a relevant distinction between intended and unintended consequences. In particular, certain actions may be performed for the purpose of causing a good end, yet which have bad unintended consequences or 'side effects'. The side effects may be wholly accidental or they may be foreseen, but as long as they are unintended with regard to the action taken to achieve the good effect, the action itself is permissible. For example, it may happen that a person kills an attacker while engaged in self-defense, even though the intention was not to kill the attacker but simply to fend off the attack and save the person's life. The act of self-defense here thus has two effects, one good and one bad. Extending the argument, it can be said that a military operation which aims at legitimate targets or objectives, but has accidental or some foreseeable bad consequences, is permissible provided it meets the following four conditions:[7]

1   the act is good in itself and its intended effect is morally acceptable;
2   the intention of the actor is good, that is, the actor aims narrowly at the acceptable effect, such that the bad effect is unintended, and not pursued as an end or as a means to the end;
3   actions are taken to minimize any foreseeable bad effects as much as possible;
4   the good effect is achieved and sufficiently outweighs the bad effect.

The doctrine of 'double effect' is defensible, then, only when the principle of discrimination is supplemented with the principle of 'proportionality'. Actors are responsible for reducing or minimizing the unintended effect as much as possible, and there exists a threshold to the acceptable limit of the possible bad effect; the good effect must be proportional to the foreseeable bad effect. If the foreseeable bad effect is disproportionate to the value of the intended action or objective, then the intended action is not justified. For this reason, certain weapons or methods, such as rape, torture, genocide and chemical and biological weapons, are prohibited in all cases and therefore are not subject to legitimization by the doctrine of double effect. Unintended civilian casualties are likely in war, yet combatants have an obligation to minimize the risks and harm they impose on civilians, even if that means that a particular military operation cannot be undertaken. Conversely, while it is impermissible to deliberately target noncombatants, some unintended civilian casualties are excusable.

Responding to Terrorism: Two Options

Terrorism is a notoriously difficult term to define, and one open to competing interpretive and normative conceptualizations.[8] It is fraught with ethical, political, legal and military dilemmas. Nevertheless, I think it possible to offer a workable definition that identifies the core meaning of the term, and it is necessary to do so in order that we might better understand what it is that is being responded to by the War on Terror. Terrorism can be defined as seemingly random and unpredictable acts or threatened acts of violence aiming at political, religious or cultural objectives, which target both direct and indirect victims – including innocent individuals, groups, institutions and governments – causing immediate harm and the inducement of fear.[9] A crucial distinction between terrorism and legal acts of warfare, then, is that perpetrators of terrorist acts intentionally target innocent third parties. This is done as a means to provoke the shock and fear designed to coerce the opposing party into some desired course of action or to focus attention on some particular cause. In this way, terrorism involves the deliberate transgression of international norms governing legitimate forms of violence, including the laws of war as they apply to innocent noncombatants. It should also be noted that terrorism is either domestic or international in scope. International terrorism consists of acts that transcend the national boundaries of the perpetrators or that are aimed at foreign nationals within the perpetrators' own country.

At present, the international law on terrorism consists of several disparate treaties concerning, for example, hijacking, kidnapping and hostage-taking, attacks against officials and diplomats as well as bombing.[10] While various terrorist acts are regarded as illegal, a comprehensive framework capable of guiding the actions of states confronted with, or supporting and perpetrating, international terrorism is only now beginning to emerge.[11] Consequently, the burden of responding to terrorist acts has fallen for the most part on individual states.[12] Given this situation, the efforts of the United States to respond to the acts of international terrorism directed against it from 11 September onwards have assumed two broad forms, namely, anti-terrorist and counter-terrorist measures and strategies.

Anti-terrorism refers to the employment by the government of administrative, police, judicial, penal, political and security resources, as well as tactics and equipment for the purpose of preventing terrorist attacks. Anti-terrorist measures taken by the government are also intended to apprehend and bring to justice suspected terrorists, and to punish convicted terrorists, thereby providing a deterrent effect. The creation of the new Department of Homeland Security is a prominent example of the US government's anti-terrorist measures.[13] In conjunction with government actions, security measures are also taken by the private sector at airports, train stations, industries and corporations in order to deter and prevent terrorism. Antiterrorist strategies can be characterized as nonviolent, since they operate through domestic and international regulative, legislative, juridical and security agencies rather than military forces.

In contrast, counter-terrorism involves the overt and covert use of military force by the government's regular military units and specialized state agencies, such as the CIA. Counter-terrorism focuses exclusively on the use of military resources, tactics and equipment for the purpose of targeting terrorists and eliminating their organizations. Counter-terrorism can include assassinating suspected terrorists, raiding and bombing the hideouts and headquarters of suspected or known terrorists, abducting suspected or known terrorists and declaring war on terrorist organizations, terrorist states or states that sponsor terrorist organizations. Thus, the US War on Terror can be properly understood as consisting of counter-terrorist measures and strategies designed to combat international terrorism and prevent harm to innocent citizens.

However, because counter-terrorism employs military force in pursuit of its objectives, it raises serious ethical, legal and political issues. Some of the covert activities that may be conducted by the government's special operations and intelligence forces in combating terrorism, such as kidnapping, assassination and torture, are not only immoral but potentially illegal as well.[14] Yet, the use of conventional military force in defense of the United States' territory and citizens may have justified claim to morality and legality. Thus, the counter-terrorist measures and strategies of the US War on Terror, as a form of potentially justifiable national self-defense must now be examined.

Applying Just War Principles to the US War on Terror

Counter-terrorism, as a critical foreign policy option, advocates the use of military operations against terrorists, states that harbor terrorists and terrorist-sponsoring states. The clearest example of US policy in this respect has been recourse to war in Afghanistan, commencing with Operation Enduring Freedom on 7 October 2001. However, the Bush Administration has made it clear that the War on Terror is open-ended, and may involve US military forces in numerous counter-terrorist operations in other countries over an indeterminate period of time. President Bush, in his 20 September 2001 address to a joint session of Congress, articulated the view which has become the basis of US policy for the expansive nature of the War on Terrorism: 'From this day forward, any nation that continues to harbor or support terrorism will be regarded as a hostile regime.'[15] His State of the Union Address on 29 January 2002 later reinforced the US position on war as a means to achieve security: 'Our War on Terror is well begun, but it is only begun ... . I will not wait on events, while dangers gather. I will not stand by, as peril draws closer and closer. The United States of America will not permit the world's most dangerous regimes to threaten us with the world's most destructive weapons.'[16] Given the broad and continuing operations of the War on Terror – including, as of the writing of this chapter, the commencement of the US invasion of Iraq – it will be impossible to offer a comprehensive analysis of its legitimacy as a whole. Thus, the focus of this section will be on the war in Afghanistan, followed by some concluding observations about the characteristics and aims of the war on terrorism as it has developed post-Operation Enduring Freedom.

Did the United States have just cause in resorting to war in Afghanistan? I believe the answer is yes. The attacks of 11 September involved the hijacking of civilian aircraft, kidnapping of their passengers, massive destruction of civilian and government property and killing of several thousand persons. The al-Qaeda attacks clearly amounted to serious, human rights-violating aggression that deprived innocent victims of their life and liberty. The attacks also struck at the territorial integrity and sovereignty of the United States. As we have seen, the principle of just cause can be vindicated in a most fundamental sense when military operations are undertaken for the purpose of national self-defense, as approved under Article 51 of the UN Charter.[17] Moreover, states are obligated to provide for the security of their citizens. Given that the Taliban regime had supported terrorism and harbored Osama bin Laden and large segments of the al-Qaeda network within Afghanistan, it seems reasonable to conclude that the United States was justified in invading Afghanistan in order to prevent future acts of violence against its citizens and national integrity.

Did the United States have the right intention in invading? The fact that the United States had very few national interests in Afghanistan indicates a lack of incentive to intervene for motives other than self-defense and security, and this was the United

States' avowed intent. Some critics have contended that the real motivation was to take focus off the possibility that the threat presented by the Taliban and al-Qaeda was merely the result of US policy in Afghanistan during the Cold War,[18] or perhaps to secure American control over strategic oil reserves in central Asia.[19] I doubt these latter claims are true, and in any event they seem much less plausible as manifestations of intent than the professed motivation of preventing future terrorist attacks. Nevertheless, one should acknowledge that purity of intention is probably illusory, and that there may be secondary motivations mixed with the primary, legitimate motivation which itself satisfies the condition of right intention.

The United States did publicly declare its resort to force, and did initiate conflict according to the principle of legitimate authority. On 12 September 2001, President Bush declared the previous day's attacks to be acts of war against the United States. That same day, NATO invoked Article Five of the Washington Treaty for the first time, which provides that an attack on one member of the Alliance will be regarded as an attack on every other member.[20] The Organization of American States triggered the Rio Treaty's provisions on collective self-defense in response to the attacks,[21] as did the Australian government, which invoked the collective defense clause in Article IV of the ANZUS Treaty.[22] In addition, the UN Security Council quickly enacted several resolutions that required all member states to pursue terrorists, dismantle financial support systems and prevent all forms of terrorism, and also created a Counter-terrorism Committee to monitor implementation of the resolutions.[23] On 14 September, the US Congress authorized the use of the armed forces against terrorists.[24] On 12 September, the Secretary of Defense directed the preparation of 'credible military options' to respond to international terrorism, under the guidance of General Tommy Franks. US Central Command recommended a military course of action that was approved by Secretary of Defense Donald Rumsfeld on 1 October. President Bush was briefed on the course of action on 2 October, and he directed that combat operations should begin on 7 October. US and British military operations against Afghanistan commenced on 7 October 2001 using aircraft and cruise missiles; Special Forces ground troops began operations in Afghanistan on 19 October. Both the United States and the United Kingdom notified the UN Security Council in writing that Operation Enduring Freedom was an exercise of individual and collective self-defense in compliance with Article 51 of the UN Charter.[25]

Was the United States' initiation of war the last resort? Questions arise concerning the satisfaction of this criterion. In particular, there is reasonable doubt as to whether serious attempts were made at a negotiated settlement. In his address to the joint session of Congress on 20 September 2001, President Bush identified al-Qaeda as the suspected perpetrators of the 11 September attacks, and emphasized the mutual interdependence of the Taliban government and al-Qaeda, with the former providing a safe haven for the latter and the latter helping to solidify the control of the former throughout much of Afghanistan. He also issued the following demands to the Taliban government:

> Deliver to United States authorities all the leaders of al-Qaida who hide in your land. Release all foreign nationals – including American citizens – you have unjustly imprisoned, and protect foreign journalists, diplomats, and aid workers in your country. Close immediately and permanently every terrorist training camp in Afghanistan and hand over every terrorist, and every person in their support structure, to appropriate authorities. Give the United States

full access to terrorist training camps, so we can make sure they are no longer operating. These demands are not open to negotiation or discussion. The Taliban must act and act immediately. They will hand over the terrorists, or they will share in their fate.[26]

Bush clearly indicated, then, that negotiation with the Taliban was not an option. Between 20 September and 7 October 2001, the launch date of the military campaign in Afghanistan, the US government declined to pursue bilateral discussions directly with the Taliban government, and opted instead to utilize the government of Pakistan as an intermediary. The Taliban did show signs of a willingness to make compromises, even suggesting that Osama bin Laden could be handed over to a third country for possible trial. Because the Bush Administration clearly had little interest in pursuing a diplomatic solution, it may be reasonable to conclude that the resort to force of war was too hasty and a good faith effort to satisfy the condition of last resort – preferably through multilateral and international diplomatic, economic, legal and other pressures – was not made.

Even so, the presence of some extenuating circumstances may mitigate the severity of this conclusion. Examples of such extenuating circumstances include the fact that the Taliban had close diplomatic relations with only a very few countries, including Pakistan. Thus, it might have made sense to use the Pakistani government as an intermediary rather than attempt to negotiate directly with the Taliban. In addition, the Taliban had demonstrated over time that they were not susceptible to the concerns of the international community, ignoring earlier pleas for changes to their regime, their treatment of women and their policy of destroying non-Islamic cultural artifacts. Furthermore, a condition of war already existed in Afghanistan, primarily between the Taliban and the Northern Alliance forces. Indeed, the UN Security Council had issued several declarations in the years between 1996 and 2001, addressing the ongoing conflict in Afghanistan and calling upon states to take action against the Taliban – including sanctions prohibiting the sale of arms and ammunition – for its support of terrorism and bin Laden.[27] All of this may lead to the alternative, plausible conclusion that any attempted negotiations with the Taliban were bound to fail in the end and thus would unduly delay critical defensive military operations.

Next are questions regarding the reasonable likelihood of success and proportionality. Applying the criterion of the likelihood of success requires assessment of the stated aims of the war in Afghanistan. In his 7 October Department of Defense news briefing, Secretary Rumsfeld explained that Operation Enduring Freedom had dual aims of carrying out both counter-terrorism and humanitarian relief operations.[28] Several specific objectives of the military operation were stated explicitly: to make clear to Taliban leaders that the harboring of terrorists was unacceptable; to acquire intelligence on al-Qaeda and Taliban resources; to develop relations with groups in Afghanistan opposed to the Taliban; to prevent the use of Afghanistan as a safe haven for terrorists; and to destroy the Taliban military allowing opposition forces to succeed in their struggle. Requiring a reasonable prospect of success before going into a war is obviously an imprecise criterion, and is certainly one open to controversy since it depends upon predicting the likelihood of both success and failure under complex and variable conditions. However, given the overwhelming advantage of US and coalition military forces over the Taliban and al-Qaeda forces there would have been little reason to doubt the success of Operation Enduring Freedom in achieving its objectives. Given the outcome to date of the war, subsequent events support the success of military operations in Afghanistan.

The principle of proportionality injects evident consequentialist concerns into the analysis of US policy on the war in Afghanistan. Assuming that the war in Afghanistan satisfied the requirements outlined above, in order to be just it must also be the case that the harm and damage it occasioned was proportional to the ends sought. The ends identified by the Bush Administration would seem justifiable insofar as they sought to eliminate al-Qaeda camps and hideouts, apprehend and extradite suspected terrorists and end the Taliban sponsorship of international terrorism. While armed force was employed to achieve these goals, the war's aim was to produce overall good consequences by eliminating the immediate threat of al-Qaeda and Taliban-sponsored terrorism at its source. The proportionality of the ends of war in this case are consistent with the intention to remedy injustice and produce a net gain for the cause of justice.

We must also consider proportionality of the means of war and discrimination, both applicable to the actual conduct of hostilities. In prosecuting Operation Enduring Freedom, US policy incorporated humanitarian and political objectives intended to avoid the infliction of unnecessary suffering and to consolidate a just and favorable resolution to the conflict that existed in Afghanistan under the oppressive Taliban regime. Humanitarian relief efforts constituted a central component of US policy, in recognition of such factors as the onset of winter, poor infrastructure conditions in Afghanistan and the deterioration of those conditions caused by the escalation of conflict. In his televised address to the nation announcing the start of military strikes in Afghanistan, President Bush stated: 'As we strike military targets, we will also drop food, medicine and supplies to the starving and suffering men and women and children of Afghanistan.'[29]

Questions were raised about the efficacy of air-dropping humanitarian supplies at the same time as conducting a bombing campaign, as this may have led to foreseeable harm to Afghan civilians and refugees.[30] The ability to deliver humanitarian supplies more effectively and safely increased with the collapse of the Taliban regime in early December 2001 and the subsequent access to secure land routes. In the first six months of the war, US military forces delivered more than 2.5 million humanitarian daily rations, 1,700 tons of wheat and 328,200 blankets.[31] US humanitarian assistance – totaling $588 million in the period between October 2001 and October 2002 – also has been supplemented by the extensive involvement of UN agencies, humanitarian NGOs and international financial contributions to Afghan relief and reconstruction.[32]

Criticisms and concerns also were raised about the ability to satisfy the criterion of discrimination over the course of a widespread bombing campaign.[33] General Richard B. Myers, the Chair of the Joint Chiefs of Staff, addressed this concern in an ABC TV interview on 21 October 2001. Myers stated:

> The last thing we want are any civilian casualties. So we plan every military target with great care. We try to match the weapon to the target and the goal is, one, to destroy the target, and two, is to prevent any what we call 'collateral damage' or damage to civilian structures or civilian population.[34]

Despite the stated intent to avoid as much as possible the infliction of civilian casualties and damages, such casualties and damages did occur. There were widespread reports of civilian injuries and deaths in Jalalabad, Kandahar, Kabul and elsewhere. It is difficult to ascertain the exact number of civilian casualties caused by the bombing campaign, as well as the ground operations conducted by US, coalition and Northern Alliance forces. The highest reported estimate was nearly 4,000 civilian deaths, although this estimate has been convincingly critiqued.[35] Other reports estimate the number of civilian deaths to be in the range of 1,000–2,500.[36] Obviously, high altitude bombing, despite the use of 'smart' bombs, is a far from accurate method of warfare. Still, the incidence of civilian deaths as a result of the bombing campaign must be weighed against the corollary doctrine of double effect. Civilian casualties and damage per se cannot be excused if the United States had acted indiscriminately. Yet, the evidence suggests that civilian deaths in Operation Enduring Freedom were, for the most part at least, unintended. This is not to deny the life-destructive nature of the war or the obvious tragedy of civilian deaths. However given the intensity of war the deaths of innocents are to be expected; this fact points to the necessity of adhering to the stringent observance of the proportionality rule. What is important here is that the civilian casualties were unintended and regrettable, resulting from various errors such as misdirected bombs, and that all reasonable and appropriate measures were taken to minimize damage and casualties. In addition, one can point to US and international efforts to remedy the human and material damage caused by the war through their immediate and ongoing relief and reconstruction efforts.

Extending the War Beyond Afghanistan: the New US Security Policy

The preceding discussion should make clear that I endorse the US war in Afghanistan as a morally and legally justifiable resort to force for purposes of self-defense and to combat the injustice of al-Qaeda's terrorism. US policy with respect to the war's justification and objectives was largely informed by and sensitive to the normative constraints of the just war tradition. Perhaps uncertainty surrounds the possibility that the United States ran afoul of the condition of last resort. As I discussed above, though, the answer to that question can be reasonably divided. My own judgment is that, owing to the previous unresponsiveness of the Taliban regime and the time-sensitive nature of attempting to apprehend al-Qaeda operatives and eliminate their camps, the United States at least had an excuse, and probably a justification, for launching the military campaign in Afghanistan when it did.

This assessment, however, in no way alleviates the grave concerns that I have about US policy as it has developed post-Operation Enduring Freedom. My key concern arises from consideration of what has come to be the foundation of US foreign policy in the war on terrorism. President Bush provided the first glimpse of the recently developed US position in a speech at West Point on 1 June 2002. There Bush cautioned that the United States faced 'a threat with no precedent' through the proliferation of weapons of mass destruction and the emergence of international terrorism. Given the nature of this new threat, Bush declared that the traditional strategies of deterrence and containment were no longer adequate and that 'if we wait for threats to fully materialize, we will have waited too long'.[37] The Office of the President then released, on 17 September 2002, a document titled 'The National Security Strategy of the United States', which clearly sets forth the distinctive new

statement of current US foreign policy. The document states that the US government
will defend:

> the United States, the American people, and our interests at home and abroad by identifying
> and destroying the threat before it reaches our borders. While the United States will constantly
> strive to enlist the support of the international community, we will not hesitate to act alone, if
> necessary, to exercise our right of self-defense by acting preemptively against such terrorists,
> to prevent them from doing harm against our people and our country.[38]

It also announces that, with regard to so-called 'rogue states and their terrorist
clients', the United States must be prepared to stop them 'before they are able to
threaten or use weapons of mass destruction against the United States and our allies
and friends'. Thus the United States 'must deter and defend against the threat before
it is unleashed'.[39] These words disclose a new policy of support for the presumed
right of the United States to wage preemptive war against both terrorists and so-called
rogue states engaged in the production of weapons of mass destruction. This policy
has come to be called the 'Bush Doctrine'.

Although the National Security Strategy document portrays the Bush Doctrine
as a logical extension of the Cold War strategy of deterrence to the new threats of
terrorism, it contains at least three significant and troubling developments. First, the
Bush Doctrine states an offensive rather than defensive policy. While the doctrine
expresses the US position as grounded in the legitimate right of national self-defense,
codified in Article 51 of the UN Charter, it declares rather causally that 'our best
defense is a good offense'.[40] As long as the perceived threat to national security is
deemed 'sufficient' by the Administration, then a 'compelling' case exists 'for taking
anticipatory action ... even if uncertainty remains as to the time and place of the
enemy's attack'.[41] Consequently, unilateral and preemptive war is now an officially
acknowledged element of US foreign policy. Second, the policy of preemptive war
is elevated to the position of a right of the United States, and indeed even a duty that
the United States is obligated to pursue. If the United States were to 'remain idle
while dangers gather', the doctrine holds, it would fail to satisfy its 'unparalleled
responsibility' to 'make the world not just safer but better'.[42]

Third, the far-reaching license to engage in preemptive strikes against perceived
threats asserted by the Bush Doctrine is granted almost exclusively to the United
States. This is because the doctrine articulates a further aim of US policy, namely,
to 'build and maintain' US military strength 'beyond challenge'.[43] In essence,
unassailable military strength is the foundation of the Bush Doctrine. The ability
to wage unilateral preemptive war – at any time and any place deemed necessary
– can be made operational only by maintaining permanent military superiority over
every other nation in the world. As the doctrine puts it: 'Our forces will be strong
enough to dissuade potential adversaries from pursuing a military build-up in hopes of
surpassing, or equaling, the power of the United States.'[44] Given the fluid dynamics
of global politics, the category of 'potential adversary' could refer to any country
whose military policies are considered by the Bush Administration to be at odds with
US national interests.

Finally, the doctrine reinforces the belief in American exceptionalism that it has
already expressed, by noting that the United States 'will take the actions necessary to

ensure that our efforts to meet our global security commitments and protect Americans are not impaired by the potential for investigations, inquiry or prosecution by the International Criminal Court (ICC), whose jurisdiction does not extend to Americans and which we do not accept'.[45] The Bush Administration's position with regard to the ICC is shortsighted in that many terrorist acts would be subject to prosecution under the ICC's Statute.[46] Choosing to prosecute suspected terrorists would be instrumental in supporting the international proscription of terrorist acts and strengthening collective security by minimizing the need for military action. In short, the doctrine declares that the United States will proceed to consolidate with relative impunity its position as the world's only military superpower, and reserve for itself the right to strike preemptively at any perceived threat with or without UN endorsement.

My concerns about the Bush Doctrine are reducible to the probability that it is inconsistent with the norms of just war theory and the codification of those norms in contemporary international law. I do not think the appeal to preemptive war, made possible by unmitigated military expansionism, is a correct and justifiable response to the threat of terrorism, and I think it fails for several reasons. First, the doctrine renders meaningless the notion of defensive and therefore legal war. A state's right to self-defense is not unqualified; in other words, any perceived threat does not itself constitute sufficient reason to resort to armed force. If defense is the basis for the morality and legality of war, there is no justification for intentionally harming those who have not yet harmed, or attempted to harm, one's own state. There is of course some merit to the claim that an actor is justified in employing defensive force in the face of an imminent threat.[47] What constitutes an 'imminent threat', however, is not entirely clear. Nevertheless, an imminent threat can be defined as an actual, immediate and identifiable danger to life and security. When such an imminent threat exists, that is, when it is clear that an attack is about to happen, the preemptive use of force is permissible. In such a situation, though, the burden of proof rests with the actor undertaking the preemptive action. A potential, hypothetical, distant or unidentifiable threat cannot count as imminent, and a state cannot properly be said to be defending itself against such generic threats.

Secondly, then, the Bush Doctrine collapses the distinction between preemptive strikes and preventive war.[48] Preventive war is the deliberate decision to resort to armed force simply because the actor perceives that it is to his advantage in maintaining his balance of power over potential adversaries. Here no imminent threat exists, rather the actor's perception is that 'striking first' will maintain a favorable balance of power before inevitable conflict occurs, and thus will also prevent the potential adversary from developing into an imminent threat.[49] Preventive war clearly is offensive rather than defensive and, as such, is illegal under international law. As mentioned above, the Bush Doctrine already employs the vague category of 'potential adversary' rather than actual adversary and also advocates the strategy that the 'best defense is a good offense'. Furthermore, the doctrine admits that the United States 'must adapt the concept of imminent threat to the capabilities and objectives of today's adversaries', in other words, revise the condition of imminent threat to that of 'sufficient threat'.[50] However, a legitimate act of self-defense is not a preventive attack against a potential adversary. A just actor cannot have the intention to initiate military violence simply because the actor assumes that some harmful event *could* happen when the event is not imminent. Unfortunately the Bush Doctrine seems to embrace this very possibility.[51]

Finally, the Bush Doctrine jeopardizes the criteria of last resort, proportionality and civilian immunity. It will be recalled that the condition of last resort requires that the actor not use military force against an imminent or actual threat if there is some other nonviolent way to avoid the threat. Although the doctrine does make mention of developing cooperative and multilateral agreements, these are spoken of almost entirely within the context of using such agreements to help strengthen America's military and intelligence capabilities. Little if any mention is made of developing cooperative mechanisms and institutions aimed at understanding the root causes of terrorism – such as accumulated anti-colonial grievances and anti-American sentiments, the failure to resolve the Israeli-Palestinian conflict and the ongoing sanctions against Iraq – and working towards political resolution of these precipitating factors. The Bush Doctrine conveys the impression that the Administration prefers to resort to war as the first rather than last resort.[52]

Moreover, the condition of proportionality requires that the actor use only the minimal (self-defensive) force necessary to terminate aggression or preempt a legitimately imminent attack. To be just, the force used to terminate or thwart an attack, if unavoidable, must be proportional to the actual or threatened violence used by the aggressors. Given the Bush Doctrine's emphasis on the deployment of an overwhelming US military presence across the globe,[53] the possibility is raised that any application of armed force against perceived adversaries will not be measured or restrained. The overall cost in lives and property that could result from the use of overwhelming military force in preventive war may exceed the value or gains sought by the war on terrorism's ultimate goal – achieving its just cause – and the probability is high that innocent persons would suffer foreseeable harm. All of these factors constitute a serious risk to the recognized norms of restraint on when and how states may use force.

There is no question that as we begin the twenty-first century terrorism is a major moral, political, legal and military problem of global scope. As the attacks of 11 September clearly demonstrated, terrorism seeks deliberately and violently to harm innocents and damage the security of states and the international community. Consequently, terrorism is both morally wrong and illegal. While the United States was justified in responding to the attacks perpetrated by al-Qaeda and supported by the Taliban, the permissibility and justness of the war in Afghanistan rests upon its having satisfied the interconnected principles of just war theory and international laws of war. However in pursuing its stated foreign policy goal of eradicating terrorism worldwide, on the basis of the classic realist aims and strategies outlined in the Bush Doctrine, the United States is now undermining the legitimacy of its war on terrorism.

Notes

1   For a discussion of how terrorism and modern forms of war differ see, for example, I. Detter (2000), *The Laws of War*, 2nd edn, Cambridge: Cambridge University Press; A. Guelke (1995), *The Age of Terrorism and the International Political System*, New York: St Martin's Press; and D. Lackey (1989), *The Ethics of War and Peace*, Englewood Cliffs, NJ: Prentice Hall. On the emergence of 'new wars' between states and non-governmental militants see M. Kaldor (1999), *New and Old Wars: Organized Violence in a Global Era*, Stanford: Stanford University Press.

2   The body of work on just war theory is vast, but the following works are of notable significance: J.B. Elshtain, ed. (1994), *Just War Theory*, New York: New York University Press; R.L. Holmes, (1989), *On War and Morality*, Princeton: Princeton University Press; P. Ramsey (1968), *The Just War: Force and Political Responsibility*, Lanham, Boulder, New York, Oxford: Rowman and Littlefield Publishers; R.J. Regan, (1996), *Just War: Principles and Cases*, Washington, DC: Catholic University of America Press; M. Walzer (1977), *Just and Unjust Wars*, New York: Basic Books.

3   Recent work in just war theory points to the need to consider a third category, *jus post bellum*, the justice of the cessation of hostilities and the subsequent transition from war to peace. See B. Orend (2002), 'Justice after War', *Ethics and International Affairs*, 16 (1): 43–56.

4   B. Orend (2000), 'Jus Post Bellum', *Journal of Social Philosophy*, 31(1), 117–37, at 119.

5   This point will be touched upon again in the final section of the chapter.

6   The texts of these documents can be found in A. Roberts and R. Guelff, eds (1999), *Documents on the Laws of War*, 3rd edn, Oxford: Oxford University Press.

7   These conditions are slightly modified versions of those found in Walzer, 153–5.

8   See the chapter by Mark Evans in this volume.

9   Based on Title 22 of the US Code, Section 2656f(d), the US State Department defines terrorism as 'premeditated, politically motivated violence perpetrated against noncombatant targets by subnational groups or clandestine agents, usually intended to influence an audience'. International terrorism is defined as 'terrorism involving citizens or the territory of more than one country'. See the State Department's annual report, 'Patterns of Global Terrorism: 2000', introduction, online at http://www.state.gov/s/ct/rls/pgtrpt/2000/2419.htm.

10   These include the 1963 Tokyo Convention (in-flight aviation safety), 1970 Hague Convention (aircraft hijackings), 1971 Montreal Convention (aviation sabotage), 1979 Hostages Convention, 1979 Convention on the Physical Protection of Nuclear Material (unlawful taking and using of nuclear material), 1988 Protocols to the Montreal Convention (extends the Convention to terrorist attacks on airports, ships, and fixed offshore platforms), 1997 Convention for the Suppression of Terrorist Bombings, and 1999 Convention for the Suppression of the Financing of Terrorism. Text of these and other related documents at the United Nations Treaty Collection, online at http://untreaty.un.org/English/Terrorism.asp.

11   The UN General Assembly approved the 'Declaration on Measures to Eliminate International Terrorism' (UN Doc. A/RES/49/60) on 9 December 1994, which was the first formal call to implement a comprehensive antiterrorist treaty framework.

12   This does not, of course, preclude multiple states developing collective mechanisms for responding to terrorism.

13   The Department was established officially on 25 November 2002, when President Bush signed the 'Homeland Security Act of 2002' into law. See http://www.whitehouse.gov/homeland/.

14   For example, the US government has stated that American citizens working abroad for al-Qaeda can be legally targeted and killed by the CIA. The Bush Administration claims that the authority to kill US citizens is granted under a secret directive signed by Bush after 11 September, which orders the CIA to covertly attack al-Qaeda anywhere in the world, making no exception for Americans. See J.J. Lumpkin (2002), 'American al-Qaida Operatives Can Be Targeted for Strikes', *Shreveport Times*, 4 December, A5. For an analysis of assassination as an instrument of foreign policy, its proscription, and its possible use as a counterterrorist measure, see W. Thomas (2001), *The Ethics of Destruction: Arms and Force in International Relations*, Ithaca and London: Cornell University Press, ch. 3.

15   'Address to a Joint Session of Congress and the American People', online at http://www.whitehouse.gov/news/releases/2001/09/20010920-8.html.

16 'The President's State of the Union Address', online at http://www.whitehouse.gov/news/releases/2002/01/20020129-11.html.

17 Article 51 states: 'Nothing in the present Charter shall impair the inherent right of individual or collective self-defence if an armed attack occurs against a Member of the United Nations, until the Security Council has taken measures necessary to maintain international peace and security. Measures taken by Members in the exercise of this right of self-defence shall be immediately reported to the Security Council and shall not in any way affect the authority and responsibility of the Security Council under the present Charter to take at any time such action as it deems necessary in order to maintain or restore international peace and security.'

18 P. Popham (2001), 'Taliban is a "Monster Hatched by the US"', *Independent*, 17 September, A4.

19 G. Monbiot (2001), 'America's Pipe Dream: The War Against Terrorism is also a Struggle for Oil and Regional Control', *Guardian*, 23 September.

20 For an analysis of this event see T. Lansford (2002), *All for One: Terrorism, NATO and the United States*, Aldershot, UK: Ashgate Publishing.

21 'OAS Resolution on Terrorist Threat to Americas' (21 September 2001), online at http://www.oas.org/OASpage/crisis/RC.24e.htm.

22 'Application of ANZUS Treaty to Terrorist Attacks on the United States' (14 September 2001), online at http://www.pm.gov.au/news/media_releases/2001/media_release1241.htm.

23 Resolution 1368 (12 September 2001), Resolution 1373 (28 September 2001), and Resolution 1377 (12 November 2001).

24 US Congress, S.J. Res. 23 ('Joint Resolution to Authorize the Use of United States Armed Forces against those Responsible for the Recent Attacks Launched Against the United States'), online at http://www.whitehouse.gov/news/releases/2002/10/20021002-2.html.

25 Letter dated 7 October 2001 from the Permanent Representative of the United States of America to the United Nations addressed to the President of the Security Council, UN SCOR, 56th Sess., UN Doc. S/2001/946; letter dated 7 October 2001 from the Chargé d'affaires a.i. of the Permanent Mission of the United Kingdom of Great Britain and Northern Ireland to the United Nations addressed to the President of the Security Council, U.N. Doc. S/2001/947.

26 'Address to a Joint Session of Congress and the American People', online at http://www.whitehouse.gov/news/releases/2001/09/20010920-8.html.

27 See, for instance, UN Security Council Resolutions 1193 (28 August 1998), 1214 (8 December 1998), 1267 (15 October 1999), 1333 (19 December 2000), and 1363 (30 July 2001).

28 'Statement of the Secretary of Defense', online at http://www.defenselink.mil/news/Oct2001/b10072001_bt491-01.html.

29 'Presidential Address to the Nation', online at http://www.whitehouse.gov/news/releases/2001/10/20011007-8.html.

30 E.A. Neuffer (2002), 'Food Drops Found to do Little Good', *Boston Globe*, 26 March, A1.

31 See the numerous transcripts published by the US State Department at online at http://usinfo.state.gov/topical/pol/terror/humanit.htm.

32 See the websites online at http://www.whitehouse.gov/news/releases/2002/10/20021011-1.html; http://www.usaid.gov/afghanistan/factsheet.html; http://www.icrc.org/Web/eng/siteeng0.nsf/iwpList78/5AD8FF827923A9C5C1256BC90059EF15; and http://www.unhcr.ch/cgi-bin/texis/vtx/afghan.

33 See N. de Torrenté (2002), 'Challenges to Humanitarian Action', *Ethics and International Affairs*, 16 (2), 2–8.

34 Richard Myers, interview with *This Week* on ABC TV (21 October 2001), online at http://www.defenselink.mil/news/Oct2001/briefings.html.

35 The high figure was given by Professor Marc H. Herold, online at http://www.cursor.org/stories/civilian_deaths.htm. The critique of Herold's report was made by Professor Jeffrey C. Isaac, online at http://www.indiana.edu/~iupolsci/docs/doc.htm.

36 See Carl Connetta, 'Operation Enduring Freedom: Why a Higher Rate of Civilian Bombing Casualties', Project on Defense Alternatives, online at http://www.comw.org/pda/0201oef.html; and Traynor (2002).

37 'Remarks by the President at 2002 Graduation Exercise of the United States Military Academy', online at http://www.whitehouse.gov/news/releases/2002/06/20020601-3.html.

38 'The National Security Strategy of the United States', http://www.whitehouse.gov/nsc/nss.html. See Part III, online at http://www.whitehouse.gov/nsc/nss3.html.

39 Ibid., see Part V, online at http://www.whitehouse.gov/nsc/nss5.html.

40 Ibid., Part III, online at http://www.whitehouse.gov/nsc/nss3.html.

41 Ibid., Part V, online at http://www.whitehouse.gov/nsc/nss5.html.

42 Ibid., Part V, online at http://www.whitehouse.gov/nsc/nss5.html, and Part I online at, http://www.whitehouse.gov/nsc/nss1.html.

43 Ibid., Part IX, online at http://www.whitehouse.gov/nsc/nss9.html.

44 Ibid.

45 Ibid. After coming to power the Bush Administration moved quickly to withdraw US support for the ICC, and formally retracted the US as a signatory to the Rome Treaty on 6 May 2002.

46 For instance, the Statue defines a crime against humanity as any of several listed acts 'when committed as part of a widespread or systematic attack directed against any civilian population, with knowledge of the attack'. The listed acts include murder and 'other inhumane acts of a similar character intentionally causing great suffering, or serious injury to body or to mental or physical health'.

47 For a useful analysis of the right of self-defense, with regard to individuals and political communities, see R. Norman (1995), *Ethics, Killing and War*, Cambridge: Cambridge University Press, esp. chs 4 and 5.

48 On preemptive strikes and preventive war see J. Baylis, J.J. Wirtz, E. Cohen, and C. Grey, eds (2002), *Strategy in the Contemporary World: An Introduction to Strategic Studies*, Oxford: Oxford University Press; J.S. Levy (1987), 'Declining Power and the Preventive Motivation for War', *World Politics*, 40 (1), October: 82–107; and Walzer.

49 Ibid., 76.

50 'The National Security Strategy of the United States', Part V, online at http://www.whitehouse.gov/nsc/nss5.html.

51 The claimed right to preventive war contained in the Bush Doctrine would, if acted upon, also set a dangerous precedent for numerous states (e.g. India, Pakistan, Russia, North Korea, Azerbaijan, etc.) to embark on their own 'first strike' campaigns.

52 Nelson Mandela has argued that 'the attitude of the United States of America is a threat to world peace ... [America] is saying ... that if you are afraid of a veto in the Security Council, you can go outside and take action and violate the sovereignty of other countries. That is the message they are sending to the world. That must be condemned in the strongest terms.' Interview published in *Newsweek* (10 September 2002), online at http://stacks.msnbc.com/news/806174.asp. Former President Jimmy Carter, in his lecture for receiving the 2002 Nobel Peace Prize, stated 'For powerful countries to adopt a principle of preventive war may well set an example that can have catastrophic consequences'. The Nobel Lecture given by The Nobel Peace Prize Laureate 2002, Jimmy Carter (Oslo, December 10, 2002), online at http://www.nobel.no/eng_lect_2002b.html.

53 'The National Security Strategy of the United States', Part IX, online at http://www.whitehouse.gov/nsc/nss9.html.

Chapter 9

Why Identify and Confront the 'Axis of Evil'?

Robert J. Pauly, Jr

Introduction

In his State of the Union address in January 2002, President George W. Bush characterized Iraq, Iran and North Korea as members of an 'axis of evil, arming to threaten the peace of the world' through the development and proliferation of nuclear, biological and chemical weapons of mass destruction (WMD) and the direct sponsorship of international and transnational terrorist organizations. More pointedly, he pledged that the United States would take the requisite action – ideally multilaterally but also unilaterally if necessary – to reduce if not eliminate the dangers those adversaries pose to its interests at home and abroad, emphasizing that 'all nations should know [that] America will do what is necessary to ensure our nation's security'.[1]

The overarching points Bush raised in promulgating his nascent 'axis of evil' approach – and the reiteration of those points over the subsequent weeks and months by the President and senior administration officials such as Vice President Richard Cheney, Secretary of State Colin Powell, National Security Advisor Condoleezza Rice and Secretary of Defense Donald Rumsfeld – beg two related questions.[2] First, how accurate is it to identify Iraq, Iran and North Korea as the principal focal points of a collective 'axis of evil'? Second, what foreign policy implications does that connection carry for the United States and its allies, particularly those situated in Europe, the Middle East and Asia? This chapter addresses each of these critical questions generally before providing deeper analyses of the Iraqi, Iranian and North Korean cases in particular.

The Axis of Evil

As to the first question, there are both strengths and weaknesses in Bush's identification of Iraq, Iran and North Korea as members of an 'axis of evil', with the proverbial balance falling in favor of the former rather than the latter. Positively, regarding the veracity of the 'axis of evil' classification, Iran, Iraq and North Korea exhibit three fundamental similarities. First, all three are governed by autocratic regimes: an Islamic theocracy with a multi-party but largely powerless parliament in Iran, and one-man military dictatorships administered by Saddam Hussein[3] and Kim Jong Il in Iraq and North Korea, respectively. As Rumsfeld has argued, the 'one thing that is common is the viciousness of those regimes, the way they are repressing their people'.[4] Second, militarily, they have long pursued the acquisition and proliferation of WMD and

– especially in the case of North Korea – missile systems to deliver those munitions, and are each listed by the US Department of State as sponsors of international terrorism. Third, they possess the military and political capacity to undermine regional and global stability generally and threaten the national interests of the United States and its allies specifically.[5]

However, all three states also exhibit many distinctive characteristics, most notably so in the economic and cultural/religious contexts. Economically, for instance, Iran is the wealthiest member of the trio by a considerable margin, possessing a per capita gross domestic product (GDP) of $6,300 as opposed to $2,500 in Iraq and $1,000 in North Korea. Additionally, its military expenditures are markedly lower as a proportion of GDP than is true of the regimes in Baghdad and Pyongyang, both of which continue to pour billions of dollars into their armed forces annually. Furthermore, with respect to religion, Shia Islam is central to the theocratic governance of the Iranian society, whereas Saddam Hussein's Baath Party-dominated state is secular in orientation and North Korea is an atheistic dictatorship.[6]

Given their similarities, especially with respect to the threats posed by the volatile combination of autocratic – and thus domestically unaccountable political systems – and largely unchecked WMD and missile developmental programs, Bush's 'axis of evil' characterization is prudent but also challenging in terms of its foreign policy implications. Three such implications are positive. First, Bush placed emphases on the long-term nature and global scope of the war on terror broadly while linking that conflict explicitly to the dangers presented by states that have signed but consistently violated the provisions of the Nuclear Non-Proliferation Treaty (NPT). Second, he left room for diplomatic engagement with Iraq, Iran and North Korea but stressed that absent progress on that front, the United States would not hesitate to take military action against any of the three. Third, in putting Baghdad, Tehran and Pyongyang on notice explicitly, he also implied an openness to take similar measures against other suspected state sponsors of terrorism such as Cuba, Libya, Sudan and Syria – and thus encouraged those actors to alter their behavior voluntarily or suffer whatever consequences Washington deems appropriate.[7]

Conversely, Bush's warnings also carry three potentially negative implications. First, the threat, let alone the conduct, of a second Persian Gulf War is likely to alienate American allies across the Middle East and thus complicate the logistics of any military operations the United States undertakes. Second, strident action against either Iraq or Iran could undermine Washington's relations with its European allies, many of which – most significantly France, Germany and the United Kingdom – maintain diplomatic relations with Tehran and have also expressed reservations about launching a new war against Iraq. The same is true in the Far East context, where Japan and South Korea are understandably reluctant to further exacerbate relations with North Korea.[8] Third, by raising these issues, Bush has created the expectation that the United States will act forcefully in the near term. As a result, if it does not do so, his threats will likely to be viewed either as lacking practical legitimacy or as mere rhetorical tools designed to bolster support for the development of effective regional or national missile defense systems.

Notwithstanding the relevance of these general observations, deeper analyses of the implications of Bush's 'axis of evil' approach vis-à-vis Iraq, Iran and North Korea in particular are indispensable in the context of this essay. In order to achieve that end, incisive sections focusing on 1) Iraq, 2) Iran and 3) North Korea are presented below. Each section addresses the following three questions. First, why single out and threaten to confront the members of the 'axis of evil' now? Second, what options should the United States consider in order to make good on the President's pledge? Third, what economic, military and political costs and benefits will such measures entail?

Iraq

There are four interconnected reasons why the United States has rightly chosen to confront Baghdad now rather than later. First, and most significantly, Iraq has demonstrated both the technical and logistical capacity to acquire, and the political will to utilize, WMD. Saddam's regime spent $10 billion on its nuclear program in the 1980s and was within months of constructing a fission bomb prior to the start of the 1991 Persian Gulf War.[9] Additionally, United Nations (UN) weapons inspectors uncovered evidence of vast Iraqi chemical and biological weapons programs prior to their expulsion in December 1998, some of the elements of which were deployed against both Iranian soldiers and Iraqi dissidents during the 1980s.[10] Second, if allowed to maintain its pursuit of WMD procurement unhindered, Iraq's potential to threaten the stability of the Persian Gulf region and American access to the oil supplies therein will only increase. As Cheney asserted in making the case for the use of force against Saddam in an August 2002 speech, the 'Iraqi regime has in fact been very busy enhancing its [WMD] capabilities ... These are not weapons for the purpose of defending Iraq; these are offensive weapons for the purpose of inflicting death on a massive scale, developed so Saddam can hold the threat over the head of anyone he chooses, in his own region or beyond'.[11] Third, according to one recent Central Intelligence Agency (CIA) estimate, Baghdad also may develop missiles with the range to strike targets in the continental United States by 2015 if not forced to abandon its current path. Fourth, Iraq remains on Washington's list of state sponsors of terrorism, which only adds to the range of potential threats it poses to American security interests at home and abroad.[12]

Taking each of these points into account, it is critical for the United States to eliminate Iraq's WMD development programs before it acquires the capacity for effective nuclear blackmail. Time is necessarily of the essence. However, notwithstanding the convenience of confronting Saddam as part of the ongoing war against terror, the Bush Administration would be wise to plan and pursue its action against Baghdad pragmatically. The Administration should do so in the context of a three-stage approach. Bush opened the first stage with his verbal warning to Iraq. In addition, the United States must demonstrate a consistent willingness to try to cultivate a measure of political support among its allies in the Greater Middle East and Europe – North Atlantic Treaty Organization partners Britain, France, Germany and Turkey, and Persian Gulf power brokers Saudi Arabia and Egypt in particular – for military action against Baghdad, assuming Saddam continues to ignore, if not openly violate, UN sanctions. To that end, Cheney traveled to the Middle East in March 2002 for consultations with regional leaders in order to determine the extent of support Washington is likely to receive and thus the logistical hurdles it will have to clear – bases of operations for air and ground forces, for instance – if forced to act unilaterally.[13]

It is also critical that the second stage of the above approach includes diplomatic as well as military measures. Initially, the United States should set a deadline for compliance on Iraq's behalf that, if not met, will trigger military action. The time allotted prior to that deadline, in turn, has to be sufficient to allow for the buildup of a substantial American military presence in the region, whether massed at bases on allied soil, on US naval ships in the Persian Gulf or in combination. If carried out properly – ideally over two to four months, but contingent on the support (if any) forthcoming from Saudi Arabia, Kuwait, Turkey, Syria, Jordan, Egypt, Oman, the United Arab Emirates, Bahrain and Qatar – the buildup itself will help both to pressure Iraq to readmit UN weapons inspectors (including but not limited to Americans) and mute international criticism that Washington is acting rashly. If required, US military action must prove uncompromising and continue until Saddam's regime has been removed from power, a point the Bush administration has to make clear from the outset. The means to achieve that end should include air and land strikes coordinated to whatever extent feasible with the support of domestic Iraqi opposition forces. Additionally, the United States must maintain a long-term civil-military presence in Iraq to ensure that its neighbors, especially Iran, do not threaten a nascent democratic regime in Baghdad. Powell, for one, has emphasized the significance of this final point, explaining that 'we would like to see a regime come in that represents all the people of Iraq, that would be democratically based. It will be a tough thing to do because there is not that tradition in Iraq, but the people of Iraq are as deserving of that new opportunity as were the people of Afghanistan'.[14]

Any action the Bush Administration takes against Iraq will entail both costs and benefits. There are three relevant costs. First, American threats – let alone military action – designed to remove Saddam from power will complicate Washington's relations with its allies in Europe and the Middle East. The evolving Russo-Iraqi relationship is one potential stumbling block. Notwithstanding the personal rapport evident between Bush and Russian President Vladimir Putin in their diplomatic engagements since the events of 11 September 2001, Moscow has announced its intentions to strike a new multi-billion-dollar trade agreement with Iraq, a pact that will almost certainly exclude overt Russian political support for American military operations in Iraq.[15] Many Arab states, most notably Saudi Arabia and Egypt, have also discouraged US strikes on Baghdad, which Egyptian President Hosni Muburak has warned would trigger 'chaos ... in the region'.[16] And, although US plans for Iraq have drawn somewhat grudging support from the United Kingdom, the French, and even the usually dependable Germans, have refused to endorse Bush's call to arms.[17]

Second, an operation of the scope necessary to topple Saddam's regime is likely to result in casualties that dwarf those sustained in toppling the Taliban in Afghanistan. Powell, who served as Chairman of the Joint Chiefs of Staff during the 1990–1991 Persian Gulf War, has assumed a cautionary stance relative to administration hawks such as Cheney and Rumsfeld regarding the potential military costs of a large-scale war against Iraq. In a February 2002 interview, for example, he noted that there 'are lots of options, [but] I don't want to single out specific ones such as a full-scale Desert Storm type attack ... I think I will let the United States military leadership determine what kind of an operation it would be and let them, rather than journalists and pundits determine what will be a cakewalk or not a cakewalk'.[18] Third, the increased US force presence in the Middle East may trigger destabilizing domestic unrest in those states that align themselves with – much less offer direct assistance to – Washington. While the potential for such reactions to cause governments to fall is minimal, it is significant enough to erode if not eliminate outright any diplomatic support in and beyond the Middle East for an American-led Gulf War II.

The probable benefits are also threefold. First, by harnessing (through diplomacy) if not eliminating (via military force) Iraq's WMD programs, Washington can reduce the threats Baghdad poses to regional stability and ensure maintenance of the indispensable access to Persian Gulf oil that the United States and its European and Asian allies now enjoy. Second, the liquidation of Saddam's regime, provided it is followed by the development of a legitimate democratic government, will ameliorate the living conditions of ordinary Iraqis substantially and perhaps improve the standing of the United States in the eyes of other repressed lower-class Muslims across the region. Third, if achieved, these outcomes will bolster US credibility and render any opposition expressed by its transatlantic allies (or, for that matter, the Russians or Chinese) insignificant over the long term. Ultimately, so long as the United States carries out the rhetorical threats Bush has promulgated in a robust but pragmatic manner – emphasizing diplomacy first, followed by substantial and sustained military action and a long-term commitment to democracy in Iraq – the potential benefits clearly exceed the costs Washington will have to bear along the way.

Iran

There are four compelling reasons why the Bush Administration has chosen to confront Iran at this juncture. First, Tehran is in the process of acquiring and refining WMD and the means to use them to strike targets within and beyond the Greater Middle East. Notwithstanding its status as a signatory to the NPT, Iran is currently developing a series of nominal civilian reactors (with Russian help) that could provide the fissile materials necessary to construct atomic weaponry. In addition, Washington suspects Iran has broken its obligations under the provisions of the Chemical Weapons Convention (CWC) and Biological Weapons Convention (BWC) and may have the capacity (again thanks to Moscow's collusion) to deliver missiles armed with WMD to the continental United States by 2015.[19] Second, while Iran has not been linked directly to the events of 11 September 2001, it remains on the Department of State's list of sponsors of terrorism and is under suspicion for complicity in the June 1996 bombing of the Khobar Towers US military housing complex in Saudi Arabia.[20] Third, and relatedly, Tehran continues to undermine what little is left of the fleeting Israeli-Palestinian peace process by providing economic, military and political support to terrorist organizations such as Hamas, Hezbollah and Islamic Jihad.[21] Fourth, and most significantly, in each of these ways Iran presents a clear and present danger to American interests. As Rice has concluded, 'Iranian behavior puts it squarely in the "axis of evil" – whether it is weapons of mass destruction or terrorism or any of those things. It's a complicated situation, but I think the behavior speaks for itself'.[22]

In light of these observations, it is indeed prudent for the United States to confront Iran now rather than later. And, conveniently, the ongoing war against terrorism serves as a useful vehicle to employ in challenging an autocratic Iranian regime that (fortuitously for Washington's purposes) is struggling to repress the democratic ambitions of political reformers who gained a parliamentary majority – albeit in a largely powerless body (the *Majlis*) – in February 2000.[23] Rumsfeld, for one, has argued that the 'thought that [reform-minded members of the *Majlis*] should be under the thumb of the extremists that govern [Iran,] is just a crime, it's a shame for those people ... I'm not going to be naïve and hold my breath, but I think that is not beyond the possibility that the Iranian people could throw off that regime'.[24] Ultimately, in order to help foster that type of governmental change from within, the Bush Administration must act pragmatically rather than rashly through political, economic, and as a last resort, limited military means.

Politically, Bush's warning was designed to put the Iranians and American allies in and beyond the Middle East alike on notice as to the seriousness of his concerns over Tehran's development of WMD and sponsorship of regional and transnational terrorist organizations. Next, the United States should focus on the reduction of transatlantic differences vis-à-vis relations with Iran. One useful way Washington could proceed on this front, for example, would be by linking a de-emphasis of the 1996 Iran-Libya Sanctions Act with concrete improvements in the mullahs' treatment of advocates for domestic political reform as judged directly by Western European diplomats in Tehran. Those diplomats, in turn, would act as middlemen to enable the Bush Administration to better express its support – rhetorical as well as financial – for parliamentary representatives struggling to increase their influence relative to that of the all-powerful clerical Iranian executive branch.

Economically, sanctions emanating from Washington must reflect Iranian behavior (both positively and negatively), particularly with respect to WMD threats and the prosecution of the war on terror. Instead of concentrating exclusively on punitive measures, the United States should also impress upon Tehran the fact that American investment is possible if the mullahs alter their present train of thought regarding the development of WMD and sponsorship of terrorist groups. One way the mullahs could demonstrate that kind of a shift would be by allowing the reformers more influence in domestic and foreign affairs. This type of change, albeit unlikely to occur in the short term, could help to clear the path for cooperative ventures (the piping of Caspian Sea oil and gas reserves through Iran to the West, for instance) over the long term.

Militarily, the United States should remain circumspect regarding the use of force against Tehran, at least until it has first dealt effectively with both Saddam and enigmatic North Korean despot Kim Jong Il. The potential for democratic change from within is greater in Iran – as evidenced by the reformers' aforementioned electoral gains – than is the case for either Iraq or North Korea. In addition, Iran's considerably larger relative geographic size and population would be sure to present more daunting logistical challenges for US forces in the case that they are eventually deployed there. Thus, for now, the Bush Administration should not consider military action any more robust than launching air strikes against WMD developmental threats, if clearly identified, and conducting special operations to liquidate terrorist groups supported by the mullahs.

As is true of the Iraqi case, each of these recommended courses of action also has potential costs and benefits, of which the latter exceed the former. The costs are threefold. First, Bush's rhetoric could strengthen the mullahs' resolve, rendering any easing of economic sanctions less probable and thus reducing the potential for US firms to profit from future investment in Iran. Second, European willingness to overlook Tehran's WMD transgressions and sponsorship of those terrorist groups that claim their fight is a just one for Palestinian sovereignty as opposed to an illegitimate and indiscriminate war against the West at large, could create a transatlantic rift that proves difficult to defuse, particularly given the emphasis Washington has placed on confronting the 'axis of evil'. Third, if the United States does eventually resort to military action, an attack on Iran is likely to result in substantially more casualties than was the case in either Afghanistan or the 1991 Persian Gulf War.

By contrast, there are also four potential benefits to the above policy prescriptions. First, Bush's warning itself has the potential to change Iranian behavior for the better as evidenced by Tehran's February 2002 roundup of al-Qaeda suspects who fled west from Afghanistan.[25] Second, intransigence by the mullahs may eventually mitigate their own influence, especially among members of Iran's growing middle class, and perhaps to a greater extent if bolstered by overt and covert American and Western European political and economic assistance. Third, and more significantly in terms of national security, any reductions in Iran's capacity to develop and deliver WMD over increasingly greater distances and its willingness to support terrorism, no matter how small, will reduce threats to the United States itself and its forces stationed abroad. Fourth, any progress Washington achieves in moderating Tehran's behavior is likely to increase the Bush Administration's own credibility – among allies, adversaries and neutral observers alike – to back its rhetoric with concrete and effective action.

North Korea

The Bush Administration's choice to confront Pyongyang at this juncture is both just and sensible for the following four reasons. First, North Korea has demonstrated the technical capability and political will to develop WMD, and also to acquire and profit from the sale of missiles capable of delivering those munitions over progressively longer and longer distances. Most notably, Pyongyang was caught producing more plutonium than allowed under the auspices of the NPT, prompting the negotiation of a 1994 Framework Agreement with the United States, South Korea and Japan to install less proliferation-friendly reactors in North Korea, the implementation of which has since stalled. Additionally, Kim's regime has not signed the CWC and is suspected of possessing stockpiles of sarin and VX gases and experimenting with anthrax, plague, cholera and smallpox despite signing the BWC in 1987. And, perhaps most significantly, North Korea has assisted pariah states such as Syria, Libya and Iran with their missile development programs, alarmed Tokyo by test-firing a three-stage Taepodong-1 rocket that skirted the Japanese coast in August 1998 and may, according to CIA estimates, be able to strike targets in the continental United States by 2015.[26]

Second, Kim runs a de facto one-man dictatorship that has watched hundreds of thousands of his state's citizens struggle to feed themselves, while he spends nearly one-quarter of its GDP maintaining a one-million-man army – one necessarily countered by the stationing of a robust American military presence along the border of the demilitarized zone (DMZ) established as a result of the 1950–53 Korean War.[27] Even Powell, the most dovish of Bush's senior advisors, has stated explicitly that Kim's dictatorship 'is evil. Not the people of North Korea, but the regime itself and the way it has conducted its business for the last 50 years'.[28] Third, Kim's intransigence and his actions – the 1998 and 2003 rocket tests and reluctance to reciprocate vis-à-vis South Korean President Kim Dae Jung's 'sunshine' policy, for example – present threats to Far East regional stability generally and the security of American allies in particular.[29] And fourth, North Korea is on the Department of State's list of sponsors of terrorism, which – conveniently for Washington's purposes, albeit justly in light of the proliferation dangers its WMD programs present – leaves it as an adversary in the context of the war on terror.

Given these points, it is essential that the United States impress upon Kim Jong Il that it will not stand by nearly so idly as did the Clinton Administration while North Korea threatens American interests. However, the Bush Administration should take care to do so pragmatically through political, economic, and as a last resort, limited military means. Politically, two interconnected measures are necessary to achieve this end. The first was Bush's rhetorical warning, which intentionally served notice to American allies and adversaries within and beyond the Far East that he will not tolerate unmitigated North Korean development and proliferation of WMD and missile systems. Second, the United States must follow up on Bush's February 2002 diplomatic mission to the Far East by continually striving to convince the Japanese and South Korean governments of the indispensability of the cultivation and maintenance of a united front in relations with Pyongyang. It should do so by emphasizing that Washington will support Seoul's 'sunshine' policy but only if it demands reciprocity from the North on issues such as the reconstruction of rail lines linking the two states.[30]

Economically, the United States must stress to both Kims that North Korea's requests for financial inducements – most notably $1 billion from Washington to end its missile export program and an even more outrageous $1 billion from Hyundai to finance South Korean tourist trips to the North – will not be answered positively without the prior creation of credible behavioral verification mechanisms.[31] The Bush Administration should also consider conditioning trade relations with the Chinese on the extent to which Beijing nudges North Korea toward compliance with American demands. Militarily, the Administration must act circumspectly, perhaps bolstering its presence on the DMZ, but ruling out the use of force against Pyongyang unless Washington acquires unequivocal evidence that Kim Jong Il is close to acquiring missiles with the capacity to deliver WMD to targets in Hawaii, Alaska or the continental United States.

There are potential costs and benefits associated with each of these courses of action, of which the latter clearly exceed the former definitively. The costs are twofold. First, maintaining a robust, albeit essential, deployment of forces on the DMZ while concurrently prosecuting the war against terrorism may strain the American military, especially when the latter undertaking includes large-scale operations against Iraq. Second, pressuring North Korea could undermine Washington's alliance with South Korea and exacerbate further already tenuous Sino-American relations. On the other hand, these suggested courses of action are also likely to generate four significant benefits. First, if pursued unequivocally, the prescribed political and economic measures may very well induce Kim Jong Il to negotiate before the use of force becomes unavoidable. Second, singling out North Korea provides balance in the context of the war on terror, demonstrating that Bush's focus on the elimination of WMD threats to American security is truly global and not directed universally toward any distinctive ethnic, national or religious group. Third, Washington's willingness to act decisively to mitigate if not eliminate these threats is, in turn, sure to bolster its international credibility. Fourth, the development and implementation of initiatives to identify and confront the 'axis of evil' generally and North Korea in particular will sharpen the strategic clarity of US foreign policy while enhancing the security of American citizens at home and abroad.

Conclusions

In order to determine the extent to which Bush's initiative will prove helpful or detrimental to the conduct of the war against terrorism over both the short and long terms, an incisive cost-benefit analysis is instructive, one best handled contextually in terms of economic, military and political concerns. Economically, the United States is, and will almost certainly remain, dependent on Middle Eastern oil, the flow of which could eventually be stanched by Iranian and Iraqi regimes left unchecked to develop WMD and the means to deliver them at a regional if not intercontinental range. Militarily, engaging in a war against Iran, Iraq or North Korea singly and on a small scale – let alone collectively and concurrently – is likely to entail casualties on a scale substantially larger than has been the case to date in Afghanistan or the previous Persian Gulf War. Politically, in order to justify the physical consequences and ensure that American credibility remains intact among allies as well as adversaries, any such action must be taken decisively. Furthermore, the United States must demonstrate a long-term commitment to cultivate friendly, democratic governments in those formerly despotic states it defeats, one manifested in the deployment of peacekeeping troops and provision of economic assistance commensurate to its GDP relative to that of its regional allies.

In contrast to the Clinton Administration's political poll-based equivocation, the Bush Administration's unambiguous challenge to pariah states and transnational terrorist groups comes adroitly packaged in an interest-based blueprint comparable to President Ronald Reagan's masterful rollback of the Soviet empire in the final act of the Cold War. If carried out prudentially – with diplomacy as the first option, followed by military action only in cases where Washington's demands are not met – President Bush's initiative is likely to greatly reduce the threats posed by terrorism and its state sponsors. Ultimately, the potential benefits of Bush 'axis of evil' approach clearly outweigh the costs but only if pursued in a comprehensive manner over the long term rather than treated as a short-term response to the events of 11 September 2001 or strictly as a means to promote indiscriminate increases in defense spending.

Notes

1   George W. Bush (2002), 'State of the Union Address', *White House Office of the Press Secretary* (29 January).
2   For examples, see Richard Cheney (2002), 'Speech to Veterans of the Korean War', *White House Office of the Press Secretary* (29 August); Richard Cheney (2002), 'Speech to Veterans of Foreign Wars 103rd National Convention', *White House Office of the Press*

Secretary (26 August); 'Secretary Rumsfeld Interview with Newt Gingrich', *US Department of Defense* (13 July 2002); Condoleezza Rice (2002), 'Remarks on Terrorism and Foreign Policy at Paul H. Nitze School of Advanced International Relations', *White House Office of the Press Secretary* (29 April); 'Colin Powell, Interview on NBC's "Meet the Press"', *US Department of State* (17 February 2002); 'Colin Powell, Interview on CNN's "Late Edition"', *US Department of State* (17 February 2002).

3   Saddam Hussein will be referred to as Saddam in all subsequent references in this essay, as has been the norm in scholarly publications since the 1990–1991 Persian Gulf War.

4   'Secretary Rumsfeld Interview with Newt Gingrich'.

5   'Iran'; 'Iran'; and 'Korea, North', *CIA World Factbook*, online at http://www.cia.com, 2002; 'Know Thine Enemy', *Economist* (31 January 2002).

6   Ibid.

7   Bush, 'State of the Union Address'.

8   'Colin Powell, Interview on CNN's "Late Edition"'. In an interview with CNN's Wolf Blitzer, Powell acknowledged that: 'there is a bit of a stir in Europe [over President Bush's "axis of evil" approach,] but it's a stir I think we will be able to manage with consultations, with contacts of the kind I have almost everyday with my European colleagues. And we will find a way to move forward that will gather the support we need.'

9   'Secretary Rumsfeld Interview with Newt Gingrich'; 'Know Thine Enemy'.

10   'Phoney War', *Economist* (3 August 2002); Cheney, 'Speech to Veterans of Foreign Wars'.

11   Cheney, 'Speech to Veterans of Foreign Wars'.

12   'Phoney War'; 'Know Thine Enemy'.

13   'America and the Arabs', *Economist* (23 March 2002); 'Unwilling Allies Against Saddam', *Economist* (16 March 2002). At the time of this writing, the basically unilateralist military scenario is beginning to unfold.

14   'Colin Powell, Interview on NBC's "Meet the Press"'.

15   'Blowing your Chances', *Economist* (22 August 2002).

16   Quoted in 'Putting your Cards on the Table', *Economist* (29 August 2002).

17   'Putting his Cards on the Table'; 'Phoney War'.

18   'Colin Powell, Interview on CNN's "Late Edition"'.

19   'Blowing your Chances'; 'Know Thine Enemy'.

20   'Background Note: Iran', *US Department of State* (December 2001).

21   'The Spectre of being Next in Line', *Economist* (11 April 2002).

22   'Remarks on Terrorism and Foreign Policy'.

23   'Background Note: Iran'.

24   'Secretary Rumsfeld Interview with Newt Gingrich'.

25   'Locking them up', *Economist* (23 February 2002).

26   'Know Thine Enemy'.

27   'Korea, North'.

28   'Colin Powell, Interview on CNN's "Late Edition"'.

29   'Sunshine and Ice', *Economist* (7 February 2002); 'Dollars, Please', *Economist* (1 November 2001).

30   'Sunshine and Ice'; 'Eyeballing Kim Jong-Il', *Economist* (21 February 2002); 'With Due Respect, Mr. President', *Economist* (21 February 2002).

31   'Dollars, Please'.

CONCLUSION
REFRAMING THE WAR ON TERROR

Chapter 10

'Terrorism' in the Moral Discourse of Humanity

Mark Evans

Terrorism and Moral Conviction

It has often been said by commentators of many ideological hues that we are living in an age of moral 'uncertainty'. If (fittingly enough) it is hardly certain that they are all talking about exactly the same phenomenon, we can nevertheless formulate one very influential version of their proposition thus: a significant and perhaps growing number of us have experienced an erosion of belief relating to the sources of the objective authority which moral judgments claim for themselves (for example, 'murder is wrong' is a fact and those who disagree with it are objectively in error). This has actually stripped away much of our confidence that even our deepest moral convictions are anything more than subjective 'matters of opinion', personal feelings or predilections, and these have no more objective authority over other views than the statement '*I like* banana ice cream' has over the statement '*you like* chocolate ice cream' (statements which are not venturing claims about any supposed objective superiority of either flavor).

Put another way: without a belief in, say, God or some equivalent basis to account for the possibility of objective validity in judgments about good and evil, and right and wrong, we have subjectivized our beliefs about morality's wellspring.[1] Further, this has had the consequence of *relativizing* our moral convictions, radically transforming our moral outlooks. This loss of confidence in *moral judgmentalism* – the practice of passing moral judgment on the beliefs and acts of others in terms of objective right and wrong – has, so the claim runs, prompted a reconfiguration of our moral convictions to suppress any suggestion of objective superiority over opposing views. The whole practice, indeed, of *moral convictionism* – very simply, the practice of having certain convictions about what is right and wrong – is thereby rendered deeply problematic.

For some experiencing it, this loss has generated an exaggeratedly heightened sensitivity to others' opinions, an attitude of tolerance that makes it almost a matter of principle that one has no *right* to challenge the validity of any opposing judgments. The banal truisms that people trust their belief in 'X is wrong' to be valid or justified, and that people with different beliefs hold *their* beliefs as justifiable, slide (perhaps almost imperceptibly) into the very different (and much more controversial) claim that 'the status of X *itself* is only a matter of my personal opinion and I therefore have no objective grounds to claim that X is valid and holds for anyone who does not share it (I have no grounds other than my own opinion on which to say they are wrong and I therefore cannot say so)'.[2] This move is tantamount to an abstention from moral judgmentalism and it is unclear that it would make sense to talk of one having moral 'convictions' at all. We can call this the 'abstentionist' position. For others, relativism is pushed to yield an altogether new conviction: each moral view can only be thought of as being 'as good as any other' and no claims which state or imply the contrary can therefore be regarded as acceptable or valid. We can call this the 'equal validity' position.[3]

From my experiences both as a teacher and through informal debate on such matters, I am disposed to accept the contention that some such view does indeed have widespread currency in the West today, particularly but not exclusively among younger generations. What makes 'uncertainty' such an appropriate term to characterize its mindset is not so much the philosophical confusions with which it is evidently beset (and which I shall briefly review shortly) but the fact that, when put under pressure, it so often rapidly collapses into untenability as a form of moral response, a way of actually living moral life. The events of 11 September 2001, though tragically not unique in this regard, have helped to force a brutal realization of this fact. How can anyone think, one might ask, that no objective matters of good and evil – no matters of moral *truth* – were at stake in the calculated sacrifice of thousands of lives by the hijackers, in the horror and the bravery of their hostages and those in the buildings they attacked? No matter what one thinks about 11 September, and its causes and aftermath, can one really characterize to oneself the reactions to the moral *enormity* of it all as *just* my opinion, unwilling to impugn and indeed incapable of impugning their polar opposites? How could anyone confront 11 September with such moral spinelessness?

And yet, if events of such magnitude in our lives jolt us into appreciating that perhaps we have not so readily abandoned all the objective moral convictions of yore, some may still fear that they become manifest in our thinking despite ourselves. We may still be at a loss to account for the grounds upon which we judge the motives and consequences of the hijackings, and consequently we may still feel the grip of the relativist view that we have no right to pretend that our morality is superior to our opponents (that, for example, those appalled by the attacks should not think their views to be superior to the hijackers who evidently felt that *they* were morally justified in their actions).

Now it might be thought that these musings of the moral philosopher and the cultural critic are somewhat tangential to an empirically-driven assessment of the post-11 September 'War on Terror' conducted by the United States and its allies. In fact, they are absolutely germane for numerous reasons. For a start, 'terrorism' and hence the 'War on Terror' are morally loaded terms and their very application implies the making of moral judgments. (By calling the events of 11 September 'terrorism' to distinguish them from the violence subsequently unleashed on Afghanistan, for example, is to pass moral judgment on them.) Obviously, any analysis constructed around these terms will founder if we are afflicted by moral uncertainty. Such uncertainty may well have provided one of the motivations for a type of 'realist' analysis which has been employed with regards to 11 September and its aftermath and which sets out deliberately to eschew the adoption or assumption of definite moral convictions and judgments on the events. This sets up a debate between what can be called the 'moral-judgmentalist' versus the 'historical-political understanding' approaches to studies of, and formulations of practical responses to, 11 September. As such, one of the challenges is the resolution of this debate in order to determine which methodology we ought to employ. Hence, the concerns of the moral/political philosophers are far more central to this project in ways it is easy to overlook or dismiss, and any gulf currently separating them from it needs to be bridged.

The first task of this chapter is to propose that the reasons for moral uncertainty do not necessitate the abandonment of moral judgmentalism and should be resisted. Uncertainty's philosophical grounds, such as they are, are not enough by themselves to settle the debate between 'moral judgment' and 'historical-political understanding' and one should feel no embarrassment at approaching this whole issue with certain moral convictions, whatever they may be, to the fore. The chapter then turns to the debate itself and argues that 'historical-political understanding's' attempted avoidance of moral judgmentalism fails on numerous scores. Finally, the basic elements of an appropriately attuned mindset for the analytical-prescriptive task at hand are outlined.

One thing this chapter will not do is to proclaim at length and with great and putatively decisive authority what is right and wrong about 11 September and its aftermath. Its aim is only to vindicate the practice of entertaining and employing definite moral convictions, *whatever they may be*, in the analysis of it.[4] Nevertheless, this part of the argument might look decidedly hollow if no attempt was made to sketch how such convictions might be constructed. Accordingly, the chapter offers a conception of 'terrorism' as an evaluative epithet – and herein lies an important future challenge for this line of inquiry. For I contend that the internationalization of the 'War on Terror' prompts us to incorporate important cosmopolitan elements into our thinking about terrorism and morality. In the same way that it is no longer a matter for individual states alone to deal with as matters of domestic politics, we should explore the ways in which we can posit terrorism as a concern for humanity such that we give this international concern a sound moral basis. In some ways the theory of the new, more morally sound international order promised in the wake of the Cold War remains almost as primordial as its evidently hesitant and fragmentary empirical realization. Much needs to be done even to theorise this particular utopia before it can hope to act as an inspiration in the reconfiguration of world politics.

Defending Moral Judgmentalism

The vastness and complexity of the issues surrounding what has here been sweepingly characterized as 'the' problem of moral uncertainty must be acknowledged. Such philosophical puzzles can only be addressed in a highly simplified and attenuated form in a chapter of this length.

In the last section, the characterization of moral uncertainty was set forth in terms of an initial doubt over morality's source and the consequent authority that it claims for itself. In a persuasive interpretation of Western moral culture, the West's basic moral principles are seen as having theistic origins: people initially treated them as God's commands and their objective authority, their *truth*, was guaranteed because His existence and His right to create moral rules were taken as objective facts. One can therefore see how moral uncertainty might arise once the existence of God is doubted, denied altogether or otherwise sidelined from the business of grounding moral conviction. If, for example, one says that God does not exist, on what grounds might one still claim objective authority for the moral principles that religion has left behind?[5]

It would be wrong to dismiss altogether as obviously wrong-headed the metaphysical and epistemological worries which accompany reflections on the nature of morality (for example, and respectively, 'does God exist?' and 'how can we be sure that what we think we know He has willed is indeed what He has willed?': such questions in general are often called matters of 'metaethics'). As the late John Rawls persuasively argued, one should expect the exercise of free thinking by rational and reasonable people in a democratic society to generate a conflicting diversity of views on this question.[6] There is 'reasonable disagreement' over such matters because of their essential indeterminacy (it is not unreasonable to believe in God or in atheism or to be agnostic). In these conditions it cannot therefore be regarded as unreasonable for people, when they survey the conflicting range of metaethical views, to manifest uncertainty over the basis on which moral judgments can be made.

But it *is* unreasonable to think that metaethical uncertainty necessarily mandates a subjectivization/relativization of one's views because this leads into obviously self-contradictory, or self-refuting, positions. If A believes in the objective existence of God and B is an unswerving atheist, then the truth of one of the views necessarily entails the falsehood of the other. The reasonable-disagreement thesis may mean it is reasonable for both views to be entertained by different people and that can be safely regarded as a strong reason for socially and politically tolerating both. But that thesis does not – indeed, cannot – mean that it is reasonable for a single person to think both are equally valid in the sense of being true. So we can acknowledge the metaethical reasons why moral uncertainty arises, but we ought not to think that this must necessarily uncouple us as individuals from any determinate, objectivized (i.e. presented as objective truth) view of our own.

Consequently, if we do not have to relativize the validity of our views about the source of morality, then we do not have to relativize its content either. It is pertinent here to bear in mind that moral arguments – the point of debating the rightness of something and the language we use in such debates – are generally structured in a way that assumes there is objective right and wrong. We do not engage in a moral debate *merely* to state opinions and hear others' opinions, the kind of dialogue we might have if we all came together to learn about each other's favorite flavor of ice cream. There is no argument, no contestation, in such a process at all yet this is what the relativists would have us believe moral debate is about. The facts that this is 1) at odds with the general practice of moral debate and that 2) the latter is something in which we, perhaps rather frequently, engage (particularly when events such as 11 September jolt our consciences) once again show that relativism is an attitude which – despite the hold it may have over many – begins to flounder on inspection.

The relativist might respond by urging that one should consciously give up the practice of moral argument as a search for right, or at least better, answers to moral questions. But the equal-validity and abstinence positions they recommend as far as moral judgmentalism is concerned are too deeply flawed to provide satisfactory alternative stances. Similarly to the flaw identified in metaethical realism above, from the mere fact that different people with different beliefs *think* they are justified in their beliefs (that they *think* their beliefs are right, or at least right for them) it does not logically follow that we should say that they *are* justified in believing them (that they *are* right, or at least right for them). Who would really want to say that, because Hitler believed that the extermination of the Jews was morally justified, it was no more or less justifiable for him to believe this than it is for us to believe that he was horrendously wrong? The equal-validity position is also simple-mindedly self-refuting. It ascribes equal validity on the basis that there is no objective yardstick external to people's opinions by which they can be objectively ranked for validity (defined as the accuracy by which they track what is actually morally true). But the very idea that each opinion must therefore be regarded to be as valid as every other has to rely upon precisely some such 'external' yardstick itself, for how else is the comparative judgment of equal worth to be obtained? The equal-validity hypothesis is not one, after all, that you find *inside* very many of the moral outlooks under comparison. So it paradoxically passes a judgment *against* the claims of views it says cannot be objectively impugned and cannot therefore be considered as any more respectful of rival views than the kind of judgmentalism it attacks.

The abstinence position may be a more coherent response to moral uncertainty. Nevertheless, I have already questioned whether it is really existentially tenable: the events of 11 September are among those which have such moral import and magnitude that it is really difficult to think that it is inappropriate to take a moral stand on them. Or, if one happens to be very morally ambivalent about them, is there no limit to non-judgmentalism? Can, say, the Holocaust be contemplated without immediate moral judgment coming to the fore? Who would *want* to abstain from objectivizing judgmentalism on the paedophiliac pornographer who films the rape of babies for his sexual gratification?

The claim about the ultimate indispensability of moral conviction and judgment in human experience dovetails with a claim that some definite moral convictions are actually indispensable in the business of justifying morality. To explain: we might say that our metaethical doubt has left us lacking a *justifying* theory, producing the uncertainty in our moral convictions. Such a theory would be able to tell us what the principles of morality are and why we should follow them. Our civilization's thinkers have expended considerable effort to furnish us with just such a theory to try to dispel such uncertainty. But how do such justifications actually proceed?

Consider one such justificatory theory: utilitarianism, which purports to show that the right act is the one which can reasonably be expected to maximize the greatest happiness of the greatest number of people (that this is an unfairly antiquated formulation of the theory is not germane to the argument). Now when we ask ourselves whether this is the right justificatory theory, by what criterion do we typically seek to answer the question? I suggest that we do so by determining whether the theory generates the kind of principles we would be prepared to accept. So, for example, utilitarianism may be thought to justify the enslavement of a small minority of people to serve the majority, making their lives happier – and hence maximizing total happiness more than would any other social arrangement. But if we grant that this is not something we believe an adequate account of morality would sanction (on the grounds that nothing, not even 'total happiness', could justify slavery), we actually use this conviction to conclude that utilitarianism fails as a justificatory theory.

It may be immediately objected that this renders justification an entirely circular process: we are evaluating an account of how to generate principles of morality by testing whether it generates the principles we want it to. The tail is wagging the justificatory dog and, indeed, the whole business of justification looks entirely otiose: if we already have the principles we want to justify at hand and are giving them such decisive authority in determining the validity of a justificatory theory, why do we need anything else to 'justify' them at all? Must we not be implicitly assuming that they are already justified if we employ them to test the adequacy of a justificatory theory? What else could we want?

Now for reasons that need not detain us here I do not think that justificatory dog-wagging makes the justificatory enterprise wholly redundant.[7] But it does show us that we probably ought to expect a lot less from justificatory theory than might be demanded, or that we assumed that it set out to deliver. Or, perhaps better, we need not expect much from it in that we do not have to *suspend* all of our moral convictions prior to the acceptance of such a theory. In other words, metaethical uncertainty should not lead to the abandonment of all moral convictions. To be sure, some such convictions might reasonably falter under uncertainty. If one accepted a moral principle *simply* because one was told that this is what was specified by the moral authority accepted (if, say, you believed that sex before marriage was sinful simply because that was what your religion specified), and one then doubted the existence and/or veracity of that authority (if, say, you lost your faith), then it may be reasonable to reject the principle. The point, however, is that for most of us there are certain principles whose strength – the basis on which we hold them as our moral convictions – is greater, or deeper, than any account of the authority from which it springs. We believe that murder is wrong not simply because our religion says so; justificatory dog-wagging here would suggest that if we found our religion did not actually support this belief, it would be the religious faith and not our conviction about the rightness of the principle that would be impugned.[8]

To conclude this passage of argument, it should be stressed that nothing in what has been said implies the misguided idea that the businesses of moral conviction and judgment are always simple, straightforward, unreflectively dogmatic applications of principles that should be obvious to all. Of course, people are typically faced with many very difficult moral questions and some sort of at least initial uncertainty here is not only unavoidable but quite desirable as we grapple with their complexity. Rawls's 'reasonable-disagreement' thesis, after all, applies as much to substantive questions of right and wrong, and the like, as it does to metaethical beliefs. All that the present argument seeks to establish is that we should not think such difficulties warrant a complete suspension or relativization of all our convictions. At heart, or so I have proposed, and sometimes despite ourselves, we do entertain some basic convictions in answer to what we think are very *simple* moral questions: that ethnic cleansing, child abuse, rape, torture and so on are just plain wrong, for example. For many of us, 11 September and its consequences posed some very simple as well as difficult moral questions – and the considerations which give rise to moral uncertainty should not lead us to suppress what plain moral convictions we might have in analyzing them.

Moral Judgment versus Historical-political Understanding?

Vindicating the practices of moral conviction and judgment demonstrates that there is a real debate between the moral-judgmentalist and historical-political-understanding approaches to the kind of project undertaken in this book. The latter approach often informs the claim, frequently heard in the wake of 11 September, that the United States and its allies 'needed to understand' the grievances that brought al-Qaeda into being: the implication at least sometimes being that they would come to see that they bore a significant degree of responsibility themselves for the attacks due to their past and present behaviour on the world stage. Such 'understanding' has often been *counterposed* to moral judgmentalism over the justice of the attacks and the military response to them, despite the fact that the inquiries of those developing this supposedly non-moral-judgmental methodology typically amount to critiques (particularly of the West).[9] Indeed, the kind of moral judgmentalism that, for example, proceeds from the conviction that, say, the hijackings were absolutely wrong is sometimes held to be inimical to 'understanding' and consequently to be a dangerously unthinking stimulant of (unwarranted) violence in response (in this instance, the war in Afghanistan).

A representative example of this viewpoint is a piece by Andrew Chitty attacking an argument which proposed to evaluate the nature of the US-led response to 11 September according to certain moral criteria.[10] Chitty claims that such 'moralism' has a devastating tendency to neglect historical context: 'for the more we know about the historical antecedents of any act, the less easy it is to be satisfied with passing a moral judgment on it, and moralism demands such judgment'.[11] Far from taking the attacks seriously, moral judgmentalism neglects their full political and historical significance. 'The language of extreme moral condemnation is the standard precursor to violence'[12] yet it is not, so Chitty claims, central to the decision-making concepts and processes of the American foreign policy establishment. Thus, 'in the sphere of international relations, public moral discourse in the West is little more than a means of selling decisions that have already been arrived at by other means to the domestic population in a language they can understand'.[13] As a representative of the anti-war movement, he claims that this cynical 'instrumentalization' of moral discourse helps to explain why the movement 'has been quite right to be wary of adding its voice to an already deafening public roar of moral condemnation of September 11'.[14] But another reason for the rejection of moral judgmentalism is hinted at in his concluding remark that the anti-war movement should develop its intellectual response to the 'War on Terror' not by 'a fruitless counterposition of moral judgments' but what he describes as 'a patient collective effort to understand the basic roots of the war'.[15]

By nature a polemical essay, it is perhaps unfair to subject this particular text to much conceptual scrutiny, but it is a usefully bald statement of the critique of moral judgmentalism. The critique can be broken up into the following claims:

1. moral judgmentalism encourages overly rapid and ill-informed analysis and decision-making;
2. the more that historical and political contextual factors are taken into account, the less easy it is to pass moral judgment (the implication being, it seems, that sensible moral judgment becomes impossible at a certain point);
3. that the language of moral condemnation is cynically employed to justify decisions, such as the war in Afghanistan, which have not been reached via moral considerations;
4. that moral judgmentalism in general tends to encourage violence;
5. that arguing about moral judgments is 'fruitless'.

If one or more of these claims are justified, then it seems clear that a serious analysis of 11 September and its aftermath ought to eschew moral judgmentalism which, among other things, would involve either developing a value-neutral concept of 'terrorism' or (if I am right that it can only be coherently understood as itself a morally judgmental concept) abandoning it altogether in our analysis. Fortunately, we not eschew nor abandon it, for this assault on moral judgmentalism ultimately fails to convince.

Perhaps the central mistake in Chitty's argument is the unwarranted generalizations about moral judgmentalism it draws from problems associated only with specific instances of it. Reviewing the claims in order:

1 I have no particular quarrel with the claim that 11 September elicited some instantaneous moralizing responses which lacked the sensitivity to historical and political context that would have improved them. But not only would I oppose the idea that the immediate elicitation of such responses was wrong (as moral beings, this was a very human phenomenon), I also see no reason why moral judgmentalism cannot insist upon the acquisition of this sensitivity in a particular instance before a *settled* conviction is obtained as a necessary prerequisite for justified decision-making;

2 acquiring contextual understanding may well make the business of passing moral judgment more complex in some cases, but this is not a necessary general truth and hence there is no reason to propose that an adequate understanding will always preclude sensible moral judgment. The two do not necessarily exhibit this inverse connection: it is perfectly possible to understand fully the grievances behind al-Qaeda's actions whilst still coherently condemning the murderous destruction of the Twin Towers;

3 I do not deny the propensity of moral judgmentalism to be used cynically in the official justification of policy decisions which have not been taken on moral considerations alone. I would reject, but lack the space to substantiate, the sweeping assumption that moral considerations are *entirely* absent in the calculations and consultations which lead to all such decisions. But the fact that moral concepts and the practice of judgmentalism can be abused is absolutely no reason to jettison them. Rather, it should be a call to defend morality against such abuse. It is highly significant that politicians feel constrained to employ moral reasons in public justifications for their policies. We should accept their assumption that it is morality that legitimizes beliefs and actions here and, if we wish to oppose our political leaders, we should do so on the moral ground they are attempting to occupy for themselves;

4 if a disposition to violence is often whipped up by moral condemnation and exhortation, it is again obvious that this is not a necessary consequence: pacifism, after all, can be as deep a moral conviction as any. (In the next section we will also see how even a moral justification for violence, far from being 'knee-jerk' and indiscriminate, can in fact be a highly sensitive and nuanced affair);

5 it is unclear in what sense Chitty thinks the exchange of moral viewpoints would be 'fruitless', although moral-uncertainty considerations may well be at work here. If he has indeed been led to this claim by some version of the 'reasonable disagreement' hypothesis, it is pertinent to challenge the assumption that a non-moral-judgmentalising contextual understanding will be any less susceptible to reasonable contestation.[16] Furthermore, most importantly and perhaps obviously, one might very well wonder how a critical posture is possible (in this case, an anti-war-on-terror position) without it being in some sense morally judgmentalist.

The facts we garner as we deepen our contextual understanding do not 'speak for themselves' in this regard – or at least not with one voice. Evaluative judgments are made both in the selection and interpretation of these facts, and the same broad events can consequently be rendered in very different ways (hence the possibility that historical-political understanding is also prone to reasonable disagreement). Having had to make evaluative judgments from the very start, why must we necessarily think that we should thereafter cease to make them – particularly when, in Chitty's case, the whole point of the exercise is to defend a specific evaluative standpoint?

It seems fair to say that Chitty's critique of moral judgmentalism is in fact an opposition to a specific set of moral judgments which conflicts with his own (the latter seemingly to be that the attacks were not unambiguously unjustified morally and that the war in Afghanistan was definitely unjust). If I am right that moral judgmentalism cannot be dispensed with and need not be suppressed, his critique can nevertheless help us to stress that responsible judgmentalism should be sensitive to context and to the possibility that rival views may incorporate considerations that ought to be taken seriously and which may prompt desirable revisions to current convictions. An excellent example of this stipulation is the application of the concept of terrorism: a normative concept which requires considerable analysis before it can be justifiably attached to an act of political violence.

Conceptualizing Terrorism

Human beings are political animals because they are social animals whose groupings diverge from each other in interests and outlooks within a world whose finitude makes it impossible for them all to fulfil those interests and live according to those outlooks to their complete satisfaction. The resulting conflicts between them must be managed somehow: people must confront each other, deal with one another as a result – and politics is the process by which they do so, whether it be peacefully or violently (or, most likely, some combination of the two), or under just or unjust social arrangements and rules of engagement.

This quick and highly partial characterization of politics helps to introduce the concept of terrorism. For one claim which is generally accepted is that terrorism is one type of coercive political engagement: the use of violence to pursue a political end. And if we accept the claim that 'terrorism' is a morally loaded term, we can see that we apply it to an immoral use of violence for a political end. It is not the way in which political interests should be advanced among the community of fellow human beings.

The relevance of introducing 'terrorism' in this way will shortly become apparent. But let us recognize, before we proceed, that the term has been thought particularly vulnerable to moral uncertainty and relativism as encapsulated in the well-worn saying 'one person's terrorist is another person's freedom-fighter'. Now if this utterance is simply a way of making the claim that 'because one person calls just what another person calls unjust we cannot/should not say who is right and wrong in this regard', we have already dismissed that conclusion. I think we can and should use 'terrorism' as an objectively, morally judgmental epithet using the considerations set out below (which, by the way, make it possible that one can be *both* a terrorist and a freedom-fighter).

Its evaluative character has unfortunately allowed it to be used overly promiscuously and polemically to cover just about any act of violence one wishes to condemn. If we wish to render the concept intelligible and useful, we should not expect it to be able to account for all of these various usages. In particular, we should not pretend that all acts of illegitimate political violence must be fitted into it.

As a preliminary, I think it is helpful to distinguish a terrorist campaign from war in the sense that the latter is conducted on a certain magnitude, with a relatively high degree of organization among the conflicting military forces and employing certain types of tactic that are not found in terrorism. (Admittedly the boundaries may be blurred between the two concepts in some circumstances but we would not, I take it, want to call the Nazi conquests, though clearly immoral, 'terrorist acts'.) But I think that an act of violence can be judged as terrorist and hence immoral on the basis of at least some of the criteria which are familiarly used to identify just and unjust wars. The criteria in full are as follows:[17]

1 *jus ad bellum*: to believe one has the right to inflict violence upon others, one must be able to show that:
   a the cause is just (traditionally this has meant self-defence against unjust aggression, but recent instances of humanitarian intervention indicate that sometimes large-scale protection of other human beings' fundamental interests against murderous aggression may also count);
   b the justice of the cause is sufficiently great as to warrant violence (that the use of violence does not negate countervailing values of greater weight);
   c that even if the cause is just, the use of violence is actually motivated by that cause and not some other hidden reason;
   d that the use of violence is genuinely a last resort: all peaceful alternatives which may also secure justice to a reasonable degree have been exhausted;
   e the powers using such violence can be acknowledged to be legitimate: in some sense they have the right to use it;
   f on the basis of available knowledge and reasonable understanding of the situation, the powers must be as confident as they reasonably can be of achieving their just objective without yielding longer-term consequences that are worse than the status quo;
2 *jus in bello*: to fight a war justly, one must employ:
   g discrimination in the selection of targets: avoiding the direct targeting of noncombatants and taking all reasonable measures possible to avoid the deaths of innocents;
   h proportionality in the use of force required to secure the just objectives;
3 *jus post bellum*: to secure the justice which was sought in conflict, one must ultimately be prepared to:
   i take full responsibility for one's fair share of the costs of the conflict's aftermath in constructing a just and stable peace;
   j take full and proactive part in the processes of forgiveness and reconciliation that are central to the construction of a just and stable peace.

One should, of course, expect difficulties in applying these criteria, which are a mixture of the evaluative and the empirical, accurately and fairly. But if we remain emboldened to retain certain convictions about the nature of justice, we can remain committed in principle to the idea that we can objectively discriminate between just and unjust uses of political violence. For anyone thinking, along with Chitty, that this kind of theory makes us overly disposed to violence in explicitly setting out the conditions under which it may be justified, it should be noted that the nature of the criteria strongly suggests that any moral justification for violence is to be regarded as the lesser of two evils. And as the lesser of two evils is still an evil, a just conflict must still be considered as one fought in a morally tragic situation (that is, one in which it is impossible to avoid doing something that comes at great moral cost, that in some sense is still wrong). The deep humility this ought to prompt should motivate one to a sincere and rigorous contemplation of the criteria, far removed from the wilfully blind rush-to-arms Chitty fears.

If we fear that the analytical distinction between acts of war and acts of terrorism may be too exculpatory of the former, we may reasonably gather from the stringency of the criteria that many wars have failed to qualify as just, and therefore as justified.[18] Indeed, it strikes me as a significant advantage of this approach that it brings wars and other acts of political violence under the same moral standard.[19] So in the same way that there could be a just war there could be a morally justified use of violence on a sub-war scale (a necessary revolutionary insurgency against an unjust regime, for example). The point about terrorist violence, however, is that it will by definition fail to be justified on one or more of the just-war counts. Very often (though this is a contingent and not a necessary feature), a terrorist act will fail on many of them. I certainly believe this applies to 11 September. Even if one grants the claim that al-Qaeda emerged from some deep-seated grievance against the West and its impact upon the Islamic world and that the attackers were sincere in their devotion to their cause (criteria (a) and (c)) it seems extraordinarily difficult to think that the attacks could qualify as justified on other criteria (such as (b) and (d) to (j)).

Certain criteria are obviously more decisive than others. Without meeting (a), for example, an act of violence can never hope to pass as justified. Satisfying (a) alone, however, is clearly not enough: one might indeed be fighting for the freedom of one's community from oppression and yet be employing such indiscriminate and disproportionate violence for the cause that one deserves the terrorist label (hence the possibility of being both a freedom-fighter and a terrorist). Conversely, (e) does not appear to be as decisive a consideration as (a) in some circumstances. Legitimacy (as being anything other than 'having right on one's side', which would seemingly be already established under (a)) can be a decidedly murky affair in certain situations. Moreover, a properly constituted authority such as a legitimate state (thereby meeting criterion (e)) may nevertheless use sub-war violence in ways which fail to be justified on other counts: hence, I do think it makes sense to talk of 'state terrorism'.

One could doubtless go on along these lines with the rest of the criteria, well beyond the remaining space available here. What is in general clear is that any presentation of just-war theory which insists that each and every criterion must be met is overly stringent. A certain leeway in the combination of criteria which suffice to label an act as terrorist may be unavoidable given the variety of acts which might fall into the category. But we now have a framework which allows us to use 'terrorism' as an objective evaluative concept.

Terrorism as a Crime Against Global Civil Society

To prepare for the final part of the present argument, let us return to the thumbnail sketch of the nature of politics offered at the start of the previous section. Terrorism, we can say, is an immoral, illegitimate means of pursuing a political end among other human beings. In order to claim this, we must have a conception of how politics *ought* to be done. My proposal is that we develop such a conception out of the fundamental notion that each human being is the bearer of a certain set of basic rights simply by virtue of being human. Here is where my argument expresses its own deepest moral convictions and displays the basis upon which its own judgmentalism rests: regardless of any difficulties we may face in trying to justify this ascription of human rights (and the philosophical controversies surrounding this issue indicate that it may be no easy task), we may nevertheless remain committed to the idea that humans do have human rights. (Any adequate justificatory argument for them would therefore exhibit the 'dog-wagging' characteristic.) Those who disagree with this proposition will doubtless decline to follow the rest of the argument. If they do so on moral uncertainty grounds, then we have already rejected the justification for such hesitancy. If their disagreement arises because they entertain alternative moral convictions, then we should consider whether any position that conflicts with the idea of human rights is one to which we would be prepared to grant any credence. I suspect few of us would.

People are not said to possess human rights by virtue of belonging to a specific political community such as a state even though the institutions of such a community may have primary responsibility for protecting the rights of its members. This claim is made when we condemn certain states who fail to respect the rights of their citizens: the idea of a rights-violation presumes possession of a right which cannot be enjoyed or exercised. When we learn of rights-violations by states we feel connected in our concern to the other human beings in question: 'this is not how human beings, like us, should be treated'. I think this allows us to propose the idea of a human moral community: a *global civil society*.[20] It is an *idea* in the sense that we do not pretend it has been fully realized in practice, but it is what is implicit in our human-rights-based moral thinking and in the principles that key artefacts of the existing international order embody (such as the Universal Declaration of Human Rights).

Global civil society has no specific ends of its own to pursue beyond the facilitation of its members' variegated ways of life in a manner which allows people to exercise their rights. But now recall the point that humans are political animals who are thereby compelled to make claims for their interests in the midst of other people making claims of their own. The moral logic of global civil society demands that the political process be conducted within its norms, by ways which – as far as is possible – respect the rights of the people who participate in it (which is *ipso facto* everybody). I believe that this implies a peaceful and democratic form of politics, with recourse to violence only as a last resort to strengthen, not undermine, global civil society (the ultimate just cause). And on this basis, terrorism as a means of pursuing a political objective is one which fundamentally violates its norms: using force in violation of the rights of fellow human beings to achieve an objective by means that, if extended and generalized, would destroy global civil society and lead to a chaos in which social life (and hence, given our mutual interdependence, life itself) would ultimately become impossible.[21]

A lot more needs to be said if we are to complete the theory of global civil society. There are a few important features in support of the contention that this theory offers a fruitful way of thinking about, and conceptualizing how we tackle, terrorism in the future. First of all, it decenters the state in our moral viewpoint, and hence, in what practical measures may seem to follow from it. I do not wish to deny that membership of a state may have intrinsic value (it is intrinsically valuable for some that they are Americans or British, or whatever), but – as the evolving norm of humanitarian intervention has powerfully suggested[22] – the right of a state to exist and to exercise sovereign power over its citizens, is not absolute. These institutional rights are conditional on the state doing as much as it reasonably can to facilitate the rights that its citizens have as members of global civil society, and on its ability to coexist on rights-respecting terms with other political communities. Put slightly differently, states – as the means by which politics is conducted within particular subsets of the human community – exist on the sufferance of that community.

We should not leap from this to the conclusion that intervention by some states in the affairs of other states on human-rights grounds is always and everywhere justified or obligatory. Many complex moral and practical considerations come into play in such circumstances.[23] However, the same moral theory that condemns terrorism as a violation of the norms of global civil society can also condemn states. A state-centric view of the world naturally privileges the state as a 'way of doing politics' and might resist the possibility of moral equivalence between certain states and terrorist organizations. In such circumstances, the danger of hypocrisy is heightened: the state wantonly employs violence for its own ends and tries to occupy a moral high ground by condemning its opponents as terrorist, for example. Just because an institution is a state, however, is insufficient to permit it any presumption of such superiority.

Thinking about terrorism in the context of crimes against global civil society also chimes with the greater internationalization of the fight against terrorism that has emerged since 11 September. Previously terrorism had, by and large, been treated as a domestic policy matter. While I do not wish to deny that many terrorist campaigns should probably remain such on grounds of relevance and practicality, it is clear that the nature of many others demands international concern: take, for example, the globally fragmented nature of al-Qaeda and its multinational targets and the internationally destabilizing consequences of the Israeli-Palestinian conflict. We need, and are beginning to develop, multinational policies and organizations to tackle these problems. Unilateral military action by states against others even on terrorism/aggression grounds is increasingly seen as illegitimate, as became evident in the pressure placed on the Bush Administration to seek UN approval for its campaign against Iraq. A cosmopolitan political morality such as that conceptualized in the theory of global civil society can provide the moral basis for these developments.

One might immediately object that the course of events initiated by 11 September is far removed from this tale of 'global cooperation against an evil scourge in the name of a universal human morality'. Many critics of the administration of George W. Bush hold, for example, that the veneer of multilateralism thinly disguises an aggressive new unilateralism fuelled by an imperialistic arrogance borne of the United States' status as the sole remaining superpower and shorn of any genuine consistent moral concern. Yet one need not disagree with some such analysis to embrace the concepts of human rights and the global civil society as ideals which inform our aspirations for the world, which even the most cynical of political leaders feels constrained publicly to acknowledge and which can form the basis – should one wish to support it – of this critical viewpoint. As we saw in the discussion of historical-political understanding, it is highly mysterious as to how a critique can be mounted without entertaining moral ideals – and if the critique is meant to imply that things could and should be done differently, that surely indicates that the ideals are ones that can be realistically harboured.

Some who have ready recourse to political violence might argue that the world is too far removed from such ideals to believe there is any point in entertaining them. They see no point in thinking and acting politically in any terms other than those of raw power unadorned by moral constraints. In response we have to say that, if it is going to be possible objectively to identify which acts of violence are just and unjust, and therefore when an act counts as a terrorist act, it is necessary to believe that the world is not so far away from realizing the ideals of justice that there is no point making such judgments. We do not live in an utterly amoral or immoral world, in which moral ends are utterly futile and naïve. It may be stretching matters to say that we are in a 'nearly just' world (not least because it might seriously mislead us into underestimating just what needs to be done to secure justice as best as we can). It may well be the nature of moral ideals, as aspirations of humanity, that they can never be fully realised: there will always be moral shortfalls. This has never been a good reason not to hold them, however, as regulative guides to present-day conduct. And it may not be unreasonable to think that there are few injustices remaining in the world whose rectification legitimately warrants the use of violence as the last reasonable means.

The need for continued and concerted interrogation of the concept of terrorism is also evident in the vigilance we must maintain over how governments have responded to the perceived increased threat from terrorists. Many critics have argued that drastically illiberal legislation has been passed which significantly damages citizens' civil liberties out of proportion to the menace with which they seek to oppose.[24] If at least part of the opposition to terrorism is based upon the claim that the latter seeks fundamentally to disrupt liberal democracy, then governments are in grave danger of paradoxically undermining liberal democracy in their attempts to protect it. Only clear thinking about our moral principles can explain how this paradox might be avoided.[25]

Notes

1   Bafflingly, this does not always entail an official commitment to secularism. Sometimes, the nature of belief in God changes in ways which lead to peculiarly incoherent assertions, such as: 'God's existence itself is only a matter of my belief and I have no warrant to believe that those who deny it are wrong.' Since when have true religious believers been able consistently to believe that their God was simply a creation of their own minds? See the discussion in the chapter's second section.

2   In other words, on moral questions our opinions are no longer conceptualized as tracking the *facts* of the matter. There are no criteria external to them which could validate or falsify them; it is in that sense that they are 'just' opinions.

3   Two authors of strikingly different political persuasion who have interpreted significant trends of modern culture in such terms are A. Bloom (1987), *The Closing of the American*

Mind, New York: Basic Books, and C. Taylor (1991), *The Ethics of Authenticity*, Cambridge MA: Harvard University Press.

4   To demonstrate the good faith in which the argument is offered, I will nevertheless venture my view that though some legitimate grievances might have motivated the attacks (though as the precise motivations of those concerned are hardly transparent, the relevance of these to any justification for the attacks must remain obscure), the attacks themselves were completely immoral. There is much, though, in the West's subsequent War on Terror, both in international affairs and domestic politics, that also crosses the threshold of immorality. The arguments that may be given in favor of these propositions may be constructed from the considerations adduced in this chapter's section on the concept of terrorism.

5   See G.E.N. Anscombe (1958), 'Modern Moral Philosophy', *Philosophy*, 33, 1–19.

6   J. Rawls (1996), *Political Liberalism*, 2nd edn, New York: Columbia University Press.

7   Given that our overall moral outlooks may well be a rather ragbag collection of incomplete, inconsistent and/or *ad hoc* principles and judgements, a justificatory theory may have a genuinely reformative and creative function in helping to order them. Nevertheless, I think the account of dog-wagging is largely accurate with respect to the kind of very basic moral conviction which is at play in the present argument.

8   Apart from the task suggested in n. 7, it might be thought that justificatory dog-wagging leaves moral and political philosophers with precious little to do. In fact, there is much that they can achieve by attempting to deduce and/or infer *further* moral conclusions from the basic, 'settled' convictions we assume as starting-points.

9   Hence 'critical realism' may be an appropriate alternative formal title for the approach.

10 See A. Chitty (2002) 'Moralism, Terrorism and War – Reply to Shaw', *Radical Philosophy* 111 (January/February), 16–19; the article is a response to M. Shaw (2002), 'Ten Challenges for "Anti-War" Politics', *Radical Philosophy*, 111 (January/February), 11–16.

11 Chitty, 17.

12 Ibid.

13 Ibid., 18.

14 Ibid.

15 Ibid., 19.

16 It seems highly probable that Chitty shares the Marxist assumption that an objective social-scientific (and critical) theory is possible, and can be qualitatively contrasted with the 'obsolete verbal rubbish' (Marx's words) of morality as being nothing other than a mystified presentation of ruling-class self-interest.

17 Just war criteria can be formulated in various ways and my inclusion of *jus post bellum* remains somewhat unconventional. Nevertheless, they invariably share the basic form presented here. For further discussion of these criteria and their application see the chapter by Patrick Hayden in this volume.

18 Indeed, such is their stringency that it would be consistent and not implausible to argue that to all intents and purposes they lead to a virtual pacifism. Although I would not go this far, the moral reservations over the War on Terror I expressed earlier arise from what I judge to be certain shortfalls with respect to these criteria.

19 This might suggest that the theory should be renamed, perhaps as 'just violence theory'. Its familiarity will, however, lead me to retain the traditional nomenclature for the time being.

20 The following argument in part follows M. Frost (2002), 'Global Civil Society: An Ethical Profile' in Hovden, Eivind and Keene, Edward, eds, *The Globalization of Liberalism*, Basingstoke: Palgrave, 152–72.

21 For those familiar with Hobbes's *Leviathan*, we can put this proposition in terms of those who attempt to advance their ends by means which are ultimately destructive of global civil society are plunging us closer to an impossibly violent anarchic 'state of nature'.

22 For an argument that such a norm has emerged as a substantive, politically acknowledged principle in international relations, see N. Wheeler (2000), *Saving Strangers*, Oxford: Oxford University Press.

23 I discuss some of these in M. Evans (2002), 'Selectivity, Imperfect Obligations and the Character of Humanitarian Morality', in Alexander Moseley and Richard Norman, eds, *Human Rights and Military Intervention*, Aldershot: Ashgate, 132–49.

24 I venture that the need for genuine cosmopolitanization of our thinking and practice is also evident in the continued detention of al-Qaeda and Taliban suspects by the USA at Guantanamo Bay, the legal status of whom as far as their captors are concerned remains, at the time of writing, disturbingly uncertain (more than a year after most were captured).

25 I was prompted to develop this defense of a moral approach in the analysis of 11 September and its consequences by stimulating discussions with colleagues in the Department of Politics and International Relations, University of Wales Swansea and with the members of its political theory workshop: for these, I am very grateful. I also thank Anne Evans for her customary help in removing errors from the typescript.

APPENDICES

Appendix A

List of Foreign Terrorist Organizations

Abu Nidal Organization (ANO)
Abu Sayyaf Group
al-Aqsa Martyrs Brigade
Armed Islamic Group (GIA)
Asbat al-Ansar
Aum Shinrikyo
Basque Fatherland and Liberty (ETA)
Communist Party of the Philippines
Gama'a al-Islamiyya (Islamic Group)
Hamas (Islamic Resistance Movement)
Harakat ul-Mujahidin (HUM)
Hizballah (Party of God)
Islamic Movement of Uzbekistan (IMU)
Jaish-e-Mohammed (Army of Mohammed)
Jemaah Islamiyya
al-Jihad (Egyptian Islamic Jihad)
Kahane Chai (Kach)
Kurdistan Workers' Party (PKK)
Lashkar-e Tayyiba
Lashkar i Jhangui
Liberation Tigers of Tamil Eelam (LTTE)
Mujahedin-e Khalq Organization (MEK)
National Liberation Army (ELN)
Palestinian Islamic Jihad (PIJ)
Palestine Liberation Front (PLF)
Popular Front for the Liberation of Palestine (PFLP)
PFLP-General Command
al-Qaeda
Real IRA
Revolutionary Armed Forces of Columbia (FARC)
Revolutionary Nuclei
Revolutionary Organization 17 November
Revolutionary People's Liberation Army (DHKP)
Salafist Group for Call and Command
Shining Path (Sendero Luminoso)
United Self-Defense Forces of Colomia (AUC)

Source: 'Report on Foreign Terrorist Organizations', Office of the Coordinator for Counterterrorism, US Department of State (5 October 2001) [updated October 2002].

Appendix B

Significant Terrorist Incidents (up to 11 September 2001)

15 January 1990
The Tupac Amaru Revolutionary Movement bombed the US Embassy in Lima.

13 May 1990
The New People's Army killed two US Air Force personnel near Clark Air Base in the Philippines.

18–19 January 1991
Iraqi agents planted bombs at the home of the US Ambassador to Indonesia and at the USIS library in Manila.

17–21 January 1992
The Red Scorpion Group kidnapped a US businessman in Manila, Philippines and the National Liberation Army and the Revolutionary Armed Forces of Colombia (FARC) kidnapped two US businessmen in Colombia.

17 March 1992
Hizballah bombed the Israeli Embassy in Buenos Aires.

31 January 1993
The Revolutionary Armed Forces of Colombia (FARC) kidnapped three US missionaries.

26 February 1993
Islamic terrorists associated with Umar Abd al-Rahman and Osama bin Ladin bombed the World Trade Center in New York City.

14 April 1993
Iraqi intelligence agents attempted to assassinate former US President George Bush in Kuwait.

25 February 1994
Jewish right-wing extremist machine-gunned Muslim worshippers in Hebron.

23 September 1994
The Armed Forces of Colombia (FARC) kidnapped a US citizen in Colombia.

24 December 1994
The Armed Islamic Group hijacked an Air France flight to Algeria.

8 March 1995
Terrorists killed two US diplomats and wound another in Karachi.

20 March 1995
The Aum Shinri-kyu cult attacked a crowded subway station with Sarin nerve gas in Tokyo.

19 April 1995
Right-wing extremists bombed the federal building in Oklahoma City.

4 July 1995
The al-Faran Kashmiri separatist group kidnapped and killed US citizens and others in India.

21 August 1995
Hamas bombed a bus in Jerusalem.

13 September 1995
Terrorists bombed the window of the US Embassy in Moscow in response to US strikes against Serbs in Bosnia.

13 November 1995
The Islamic Movement of Change bombed a military compound in Riyadh.

19 November 1995
An Islamic terrorist bombed the Egyptian Embassy in Islamabad.

8 January 1996
Guerrillas from the Free Papau Movement kidnapped 26 people in Indonesia.

19 January 1996
The Revolutionary Armed Forces of Colombia (FARC) kidnapped a US citizen in Colombia.

31 January 1996
The Liberation Tigers of Tamil Eelam bombed a bank in Sri Lanka.

9 February 1996
The Irish Republican Army detonated a bomb in London.

15 February 1996
Terrorists fired rockets at the US Embassy in Athens.

16 February 1996
Guerrillas of the National Liberation Army kidnapped a US citizen in Colombia.

26 February 1996
A suicide bomber blew up a bus in Jerusalem.

4 March 1996
Hamas and the Palestinian Islamic Jihad bombed a shopping mall in Tel Aviv.

13 May 1996
Arab gunmen opened fire on a bus carrying students in Bet El, Israel.

31 May 1996
Former Contra guerrillas kidnapped a USAID relief worker in Nicaragua.

9 June 1996
Terrorists killed a US citizen in Zekharya, Israel.

15 June 1996
The IRA detonated a bomb at a shopping center in Manchester, England.

25 June 1996
Radical Islamic terrorists bombed the US military's Khobar Towers housing facility in Dhahran.

20 July 1996
The Basque Fatherland and Liberty organization detonated a bomb at the Tarragona International Airport in Spain.

1 August 1996
The Algerian Armed Islamic Group exploded a bomb at the home of the French Archbishop of Oran.

17 August 1996
The Sudanese People's Liberation Army kidnapped missionaries in Mapourdit.

13 September 1996
The Patriotic Union of Kurdistan kidnapped French and Canadian relief workers in Iraq.

1 October 1996
Assassins killed the South Korean Counsul near his home in Vladivostok, Russia.

1 November 1996
The Sudanese People's Liberation Army kidnapped International Red Cross workers in Sudan.

3 December 1996
Algerian terrorists bombed a Paris subway train.

11 December 1996
The Revolutionary Armed Forces of Colombia (FARC) kidnapped a US citizen.

17 December 1996
The Tupac Amaru Revolutionary Movement took hundreds of people hostage at the Japanese Ambassador's residence in Lima.

2–13 January 1997
Apparent Egyptian terrorists mailed letter bombs worldwide.

4–17 February 1997
Paramilitary terrorists abducted UN staff in Tajikistan.

14 February 1997
Armed guerrillas kidnapped a US oil engineer and Venezuelan pilot in Colombia.

23 February 1997
A Palestinian gunman opened fire on tourists at the Empire State Building in New York City.

24 February 1997
The National Liberation Army kidnapped a US citizen in Colombia.

7 March 1997
FARC guerrillas kidnapped a US mining employee in Colombia.

12 July 1997
The Military Liberation Union bombed a hotel in Havana.

4 September 1997
Hamas suicide bombers denoted bombs in a shopping mall in Jerusalem.

23 October 1997
ELN rebels kidnapped employees of the Organization of American States in Colombia.

30 October 1997
al-Sha'if rebels kidnapped a US businessman near Sanaa in Yemin.

12 November 1997
The Islamic Inqilabi Council (Islamic Revolutionary Council) shot US businessmen at their hotel in Karachi.

17 November 1997
al-Bama'at al-Islamiyya terrorists killed tourists at a temple near Luxor in Egypt.

19 February 1998
Georgian rebels abducted UN military observers.

21–23 March 1998
FARC rebels kidnapped a US citizen and killed others near Bogata.

15 April 1998
Somali militiamen abducted Red Cross and other international relief workers in Mogadishu.

1 August 1998
IRA terrorists detonated a bomb in Banbridge, Ireland.

7 August 1998
Osama bin Ladin's terrorist network bombed the US Embassy in Nairobi, Kenya and the US Embassy in Dar es Salaam, Tanzania.

15 August 1998
IRA terrorists detonated a bomb outside a courthouse in Omagh, Ireland.

18 October 1998
The National Liberation Army bombed the Ocensa pipeline in Colombia.

15 November 1998
Terrorists robbed and kidnapped members of the family of a US businessman in Colombia.

2 January 1999
National Union for the Total Independence of Angola (UNITA) rebels shot down an Angolan aircraft.

14 February 1999
The Allied Democratic Forces exploded a pipe bomb in a bar in Uganda.

16 February 1999
The Kurdistan Workers' Party stormed and occupied the Greek Embassy in Vienna, taking the Greek Ambassador and other hostage, and storming other diplomatic posts in France, Holland, Switzerland, Britain and Germany.

25 February 1999
FARC rebels kidnapped and killed US citizens working for an international conservation organization in Colombia and Venezuela.

1 March 1999
Hutu rebels attacked, abducted and killed tourists in Uganda.

23 March 1999
The National Liberation Army (ELN) kidnapped a US citizen in Colombia.

30 May 1999
ELN terrorists attacked a church congregation and kidnapped US citizens and others in Colombia.

27 June 1999
A terror group known as Enough is Enough in the Niger River attacked and kidnapped a team of international employees of Shell Oil in Nigeria.

4 August 1999
The Armed Forces Revolutionary Council kidnapped UN representatives in Sierra Leone.

1 October 1999
Burmese dissidents seized the Burmese Embassy in Bangkok, holding people hostage.

23 December 1999
The People's Liberation Army kidnapped a US citizen in Colombia.

24 December 1999
Terrorists hijacked an Indian Airlines plane from Kathmandu to New Delhi.

27 January 2000
The Basque Fatherland and Liberty organization set fire to a car dealership in Spain.

1 May 2000
The Revolutionary United Front attacked a UN facility, killed UN peacekeepers, and kidnapped members of UN relief mission in Sierra Leonne.

8 June 2000
Terrorists killed the British Defense Attache in Athens.

27 June 2000
ELN militants kidnapped a woman and her infant son, a US citizen in Colombia.

12 August 2000
The Islamic Movement of Uzbekistan took US citizens hostage in Kyrgyzstan.

1 October 2000
Terrorists bombed a church in Dushanbe, Tajikistan.

12 October 2000
The Popular Liberation Army kidnapped Spanish oil workers in Ecuador.

12 October 2000
Terrorists associated with Osama bin Ladin bombed the *USS Cole* in Aden Harbor, Yemen.

30 December 2000
The Moro Islamic Front detonated a bomb near the US Embassy in Manila.

17 January 2001
Lashkar-e Tayybe militants attempted to seize an airport in India.

4 March 2001
Terrorists exploded a bomb outside the British Broadcasting Corporation's studio in London.

9 March 2001
ETA terrorists killed policemen with a bomb in Hernani, Spain.

22 April 2001
Hamas detonated a bomb at a bus stop in Kfar Siva, Israel.

1 June 2001
Hamas bombed a nightclub in Tel Aviv.

9 August 2001
Hamas bombed a restaurant in Jeruselum.

11 September 2001
al-Qaeda terrorists hijacked four commercial airliners and crashed two into the twin towers of the World Trade Center, one into the Pentagon, and one crashed in a field in western Pennsylvania.

Source:　Office of the Historian, US Department of State.

Select Bibliography

Ackerman, B. (1998), *We the People: Transformations*, Cambridge, MA: Belknap Press.

Ackerman, B. (1991), *We the People: Foundations*, Cambridge, MA: Belknap Press.

Ackerman, B. and Golove, D. (1995), *Is NAFTA Constitutional?*, Cambridge, MA: Harvard University Press.

Allison, G. and Zelikow, P. (1999), *Essence of Decision: Explaining the Cuban Missile Crisis*, 2nd edn, New York: Longman.

Arnold, A. (1983), *Afghanistan's Two-Party Communism: Pparcham and Khalq*, Stanford, CA: Hoover Institution Press.

Baker, J.A. III (1995), *The Politics of Diplomacy: Revolution, War and Peace, 1989–1992*, New York: Putnam's.

Baylis, J., Wirtz, J.J., Cohen, E. and Grey, C., eds (2002), *Strategy in the Contemporary World: An Introduction to Strategic Studies*, Oxford: Oxford University Press.

Bloom, A. (1987), *The Closing of the American Mind*, New York: Basic Books.

Burnham, W.D. (1970), *Critical Elections and the Mainspring of American Politics*, New York: W.W. Norton.

Carruthers, P. and Smith, P.K., eds (1996), *Theories of Theories of the Mind*, Cambridge: Cambridge University Press.

Chubb, J. and Peterson, P., eds (1985), *The New Direction in American Politics*, Washington, DC: Brookings Institution Press.

Cordovez, D. and Harrison, S.S. (1995), *Out of Afghanistan: The Inside Story of the Soviet Withdrawal*, New York: Oxford University Press.

Daalder, I.H. et al. (2002), *Protecting the American Homeland: One Year On*, Washington, DC: Brookings Institution Press.

Davies, M. and Stone, T., eds (1995), *Folk Psychology*, Oxford: Blackwell Publishers.

Dekmajian, R.H. (1995), *Islam in Revolution: Fundamentalism in the Arab World*, 2nd edn, New York: Syracuse University Press.

Dennett, D. (1987), *The Intentional Stance*, Cambridge, MA: MIT Press.

Detter, I. (2000), *The Laws of War*, 2nd edn, Cambridge: Cambridge University Press.

Elshtain, J.B., ed. (1994), *Just War Theory*, New York: New York University Press.

Falkowski, L.S., ed. (1979), *Psychological Models in International Politics*, Boulder: Westview Press.

Farnham, B.R. (1997), *Roosevelt and the Munich Crisis: A Study of Political Decision-Making*, Princeton, NJ: Princeton University Press.

Fulbright, J. (1972), *The Crippled Giant*, New York: Random House.

Fuller, G.E. and Lesser, I.O. (1995), *A Sense of Siege: The Geopolitics of Islam and the West*, Boulder: Westview Press.

Gaddis, J.L. (1982), *Strategies of Containment: A Critical Appraisal of Postwar American National Security*, New York: Oxford University Press.

Garthoff, R. (1984), *Détente and Confrontation: American-Soviet Relations From Nixon to Reagan*, Washington, DC: Brooking Institution.

Gates, R. (1996), *The Ultimate Insider's Story of Five Presidents and How They Won the Cold War*, New York: Simon and Schuster.

Gohari, M.J. (2000), *The Taliban: Ascent to Power*, London: Oxford University Press.

Graubard, S.R. (1992), *Mr. Bush's War: Adventures in the Politics of Illusion*, New York: Hill and Wang.

Guelke, A. (1995), *The Age of Terrorism and the International Political System*, New York: St Martin's Press.

Hammond, T.T. (1984), *Red Flag Over Afghanistan: The Communist Coup, the Soviet Invasion and the Consequences*, Boulder: Westview Press.

Hermann, M.G., ed. (1977), *A Psychological Examination of Political Leaders*, New York: The Free Press.

Hess, S. (2002), *Organizing the Presidency*, 3rd edn, Washington, DC: Brookings Institution Press.

Holmes, R.L. (1989), *On War and Morality*, Princeton, NJ: Princeton University Press.

Kaldor, M. (1999), *New and Old Wars: Organized Violence in a Global Era*, Stanford, CA: Stanford University Press.

Khan, R.M. (1991), *Untying the Afghan Knot: Negotiating Soviet Withdrawal*, Durham, NC: Duke University Press.

Kunda, Z. (2002), *Social Cognition: Making Sense of People*, Cambridge, MA: MIT Press.

Lackey, D. (1989), *The Ethics of War and Peace*, Englewood Cliffs, NJ: Prentice Hall.

LaFeber, W. (1995), *The American Age: US Foreign Policy At Home and Abroad*, 2nd edn, New York: W.W. Norton.

Lansford, T. (2002), *All for One: Terrorism, NATO and the United States*, Aldershot: Ashgate Publishing.

Ledeen, M.A. (2002), *The War Against the Terror Masters: Why It Happened, Where We Are Now, How We Will Win*, New York: St Martin's Press.

Logevall, F., ed. (2002), *Terrorism and 9/11: A Reader*, Boston: Houghton Mifflin.

Martin, J.L. and Neal, A.D. (2002), *Defending Civilization: How Our Universities Are Failing America and What Can Be Done About It*, Cambridge, MA: MIT Press.

McMichael, S.R. (1990), *Stumbling Bear: Soviet Military Performance in Afghanistan*, London: Brassey's.

Menges, C.C. (1988), *Inside the National Security Council: The True Story of the Making and Unmaking of Reagan's Foreign Policy*, New York: Touchstone Books.

Munson, H., Jr (1988), *Islam and Revolution in the Middle East*, New Haven: Yale University Press.

Nelson, M., ed. (2000), *The Presidency and the Political System*, Washington, DC: CQ Press.

Norman, R. (1995), *Ethics, Killing and War*, Cambridge: Cambridge University Press.

Patterson, B.H., Jr (2000), *The White House Staff: Inside the West Wing and Beyond*, Washington, DC: Brookings Institution Press.

Pollack, K.M. (2002), *The Threatening Storm: The Case to Invade Iraq*, New York: Random House.

Ramsey, P. (1968), *The Just War: Force and Political Responsibility*, Oxford: Rowman & Littlefield.

Rawls, J. (1996), *Political Liberalism*, 2nd edn, New York: Columbia University Press.

Regan, R.J. (1996), *Just War: Principles and Cases*, Washington, DC: Catholic University of America Press.

Roberts, A. and Guelff, R., eds (1999), *Documents on the Laws of War*, 3rd edn, Oxford: Oxford University Press.

Rosenberg, E.S. (1982), *Spreading the American Dream: American Economic and Cultural Expansion*, New York: Hill and Wang.

Sivan, E. (1985), *Radical Islam*, New Haven: Yale University Press.

Skowronek, S. (1997), *The Politics Presidents Make: Leadership from John Adams to Bill Clinton*, Cambridge, MA: Belknap Press.

Smith, C.A. and Smith, K.B. (1994), *The White House Speaks: Presidential Leadership as Persuasion*, Westport, CT: Praeger.

Sprout, H. and Sprout, M. (1956), *Man-Milieu Relationship Hypothesis in the Context of International Politics*, Princeton, NJ: Princeton University Press.

Stich, S., ed. (1996), *Deconstructing the Mind*, Oxford: Oxford University Press.

Taylor, C. (1991), *The Ethics of Authenticity*, Cambridge, MA: Harvard University Press.

Thomas, W. (2001), *The Ethics of Destruction: Arms and Force in International Relations*, London: Cornell University Press.

Tucker, R.W. and Hendrickson, D. (1992), *The Imperial Temptation: The New World Order and America's Promise*, New York: Council on Foreign Relations Press.

Walch, T., ed. (1997), *At the President's Side: The Vice Presidency in the Twentieth Century*, Columbia, MO: University of Missouri Press.

Waltz, K.N. (1957), *Man, the State, and War*, New York: W.W. Norton.

Walzer, M. (1977), *Just and Unjust Wars*, New York: Basic Books.

Wheeler, N. (2000), *Saving Strangers*, Oxford: Oxford University Press.

Whicker, M.L., Pfiffner, J.P., and Moore, R.A., eds (1993), *The Presidency and the Persian Gulf War*, Westport, CT: Praeger.

Wildavsky, A., ed. (1975), *Perspectives on the Presidency*, Boston: Little, Brown.

Woodward, B. (2002), *Bush at War*, New York: Simon & Schuster.

Zakaria, F. (1998), *From Wealth to Power*, Princeton, NJ: Princeton University Press.

Index